TEACHER'S E

CLOSE READING of COMPLEX TEXTS

Diane Lapp
Barbara Moss
Maria Grant
Kelly Johnson

Sadlier School

Cover: *Series Design:* Silver Lining Studios. **Photo Credits:** age fotostock/Wavebreak Media: T4. Dreamstime.com/Bronwyn8: T5. Getty Images/Tetra Images: T14. iStockphoto.com/AVAVA: T16; kali9: T15; monkeybusinessimages: T6. SuperStock/Stockbroker: T7. age fotostock/R. Guenter: 184; Alaska Stock Images/Mark Kelley: 68. Alamy Stock Photo/Mary Evans Picture Library: 70; Scott Camazine: 123; Andrei Orlov: 39; Alamy LIve News/ZUMA Wire/David Bro: 158; Art Directors & TRIP: 111; Cal Sport Media/Steve Dalmado: 44; Fairbanks Daily News-Miner/ZUMAPRESS.COM/John Wagner: T20 *top,*103, 115; Keystone Pictures USAKeystone Pictures USA: 160; Military Images: 58; Mint Images Limited: 50; Pulsar Imagens: T20 *bottom center,* 157, 165; Science History Images: 178, 188; US Marines Photo: 59; VStock: 62. Associated Press/J. Scott Applewhite: 116; Sue Ogrocki: 26. Courtesy of The Bancroft Library, University of California, Berkeley/Andrew Lawson Portrait, Lawson, Andrew--POR 6: 21. Dreamstime.com/Kira Kaplinski: 122; Ivaylo Sarayski: 140; Brad Thompson: T19 *bottom center,* 67, 76; Monkey Business Images: 98. Fotolia.com/f11photo: 152; vanden: 75. Getty Images/skodonnell: 14; David Greedy: 113; David Hanson: 176; Fred W. McDarrah: T19 *top center,* 31, 41; National Geographic/Carsten Peter: T20 *top center,* 121, 131; QAI Publishing/UIG: 130; Stock Montage: 35; The Denver Post/Andy Cross: 5, 12. Glacier National Park/T.J. Hileman: 133 left. iStockphoto.com/Steve Debenport: 40; jamesbenet: 23; artisticco: 86. Library of Congress: 57; Prints & Photographs Division/LC-D4-10727: T19 *bottom,* 85, 94; LC-DIG-det-4a11109: 95; LC-DIG-ds-07750: T19 *top,* 13, 16; LC-DIG-ggbain-08316: 93; LC-USZ62-21222: T20 *center,* 139, 141; LC-USZ62-26279: 17. The Metropolitan Museum of Art, New York/Gift of Mr. and Mrs. Wan-go H. C. Weng, 1989: 79, 80. NASA/Goddard Space Flight Center Scientific Visualization Studio The Blue Marble Next Generation data is courtesy of Reto Stockli (NASA/GSFC) and NASA's Earth Observatory: 134. Shutterstock.com/aurielaki: 170; VladisChern: 104; Oleg Golovnev: 88; Monkey Business Images: 32. Superstock/Ragnar Th. Sigurdsson: 129. Reuters/Brendan McDermid: 112. U.S. Geological Survey/Greg Pederson: 133 right. Wikimedia Commons/Dixie Highway Association: 148; Library of Congress Prints and Photographs Division, Records of the National Child Labor Committee: T19 *center,* 49, 52; The Packer Lab - Bee Tribes of the World: T20 *bottom,* 175, 183. **Text Credits:** U.S. Geological Survey: 21; Bureau of Labor Statistics: 25, 61, 97; U.S. Department of Education: 39; Library of Congress: 75; John F. Kennedy Presidential Library and Museum: 105; Corporation for National and Community Service: 111, 115; NOAA Climate.gov: 129; NASA: 133; National Park Service: 151; **Illustration Credits:** Joe LeMonnier: 166.

William H. Sadlier, Inc.
9 Pine Street
New York, NY 10005-4700

Printed in the United States of America.
ISBN: 978-1-4217-1428-8
1 2 3 4 5 6 7 8 9 10 WEBC 21 20 19 18 17

CONTENTS

Teaching Students to Read Closely and Critically

Close reading is a powerful instructional strategy designed to help students develop the reading, writing, speaking, listening, and viewing skills crucial to success in college and the workplace. During close reading, students have a close, deep encounter with a complex text, whether a traditional written text or a visual text. Close reading engages students in the analysis of the language of texts, moving them beyond superficial understanding. They read and reread challenging texts, digging more deeply into the text with each subsequent reading.

Students participate in a broad range of scaffolded literacy activities during close reading. They annotate the text as they look for key information. They answer text-dependent questions at increasingly challenging levels of difficulty. They talk about the text, working collaboratively with their peers to grapple with the deeper meanings within it. They write in response to the text by articulating opinions, arguments, and explanations based on the text itself. Through these and other scaffolded experiences, students develop the critical analytic reading skills they need to succeed in every content area, whether science, social studies, mathematics, or English language arts.

Close Reading of Complex Texts addresses multiple aspects of content-area literacy in a single program. With the support of their teachers, students develop improved comprehension of all text types in a variety of disciplines, through deliberate, ongoing, and scaffolded literacy instruction.

Research into essential aspects of close reading confirms its efficacy.

- Reading complex texts, when coupled with teacher scaffolding, can accelerate reading achievement (Shanahan, 2014).
- The multiple readings required during close reading contribute to improved fluency, which has a strong link to reading comprehension (Paige, 2011).
- Close reading provides deliberate practice with complex texts over time, which contributes to reading performance (Ericcson, Krampe, & Tesch-Romer, 1993).
- The careful attention to vocabulary and syntax required by close reading is strongly correlated to improved reading comprehension (Goff, Pratt & Ong, 2005).

The ability to negotiate challenging texts in science, social studies, mathematics, and English language arts is essential to student success throughout the grades as well as in a college or career setting. Think, for example, of your content-based textbooks during your freshman year of college and the challenges they posed even for good readers. Think, too, about your local mechanic reading from an auto repair manual as he fixes your car's air conditioning. Both of these disciplinary texts contain challenging content-specific vocabulary terms, heavy concept loads, and visual features, including maps, graphs, charts, and timelines. They pose unique challenges for readers, regardless of topic.

Students who have learned to read successfully in the primary grades often struggle in the middle grades when faced with the demands of reading rigorous texts in multiple subject areas. In some cases, these students have not been exposed to the informational texts that are central to learning in these disciplines. ***Close Reading of Complex Texts*** provides students with many opportunities to read texts from a variety of genres, including informational texts, thereby broadening their knowledge about how these texts work, and what they mean.

Developing Students' Critical Comprehension

Each of the book's ten units contains four thematically related texts, including a Visual Text, that students closely read and analyze. Each engaging text set represents a range of genres. Text sets encourage students to dig deeply into a specific content-related theme by building rich connections across texts.

Research indicates that using a range of genres can improve students' reading comprehension and conceptual understanding of a topic (Hoffman, Sailors, Duffy, & Berettas, 2004; Corvette, Wright, & Hwang, 2016). In addition, reading a range of texts about a topic helps to build students' background knowledge. When students increase their knowledge base through encounters with multiple text genres, they are better prepared to learn from texts they will experience in the future (Duke, Pearson, Strachan, & Billman, 2011). Exposure to a broad range of text types also prepares students for the multiplicity of text genres they will encounter on high-stakes assessment.

A key feature of ***Close Reading of Complex Texts*** is the inclusion of Visual Texts, which are gaining increasing importance in the lives of students. Their engagement potential and their prominence in recent state standards make them important inclusions in close reading. According to Stone (2007), we can "no longer treat reading as being solely about print or about the understanding of individual texts. Rather, we need to address a full range of modalities being used by young people" (p. 60).

A Focus Question unifies the text sets. Students accumulate evidence to support their answers to the Focus Question as they work through the unit. At the end of the unit, students synthesize their learnings from the different texts and write an extended response to the Focus Question. In this way, each unit builds students' knowledge of the authors' purposes, the characteristics of different genres, and the similarities and differences between the presentation of information.

Engaging in Multiple Readings of Complex Texts

First, Second, and Third Reads, focused by independent annotation and collaborative conversations about Text-Dependent Questions from the Teacher's Edition, invite analysis of what the text means at deeper levels.

During each First Read, students gain general understanding of the text, or what the text says. They annotate, make notes, and respond to broad Text-Dependent Questions, such as, *What is this text about?*

During the Second Read, students deepen their understanding of how the text works. These Text-Dependent Questions require them to analyze language and the organizational structures used to convey information and describe experiences.

Students synthesize the insights uncovered in earlier readings during their Third Read. They make inferences about author's positioning, or what the text means. Students also make connections across topically related texts.

It is not necessary that students reread the entire text during each Read. The goal of a reread is to deepen understanding, and sometimes an additional Text-Dependent Question that pushes students to consider just one sentence is all that is needed for students to accomplish this understanding. Teachers may choose to use particular questions based on their ongoing in-class assessment of student understanding. In this way, the close reading task is personalized to meet the needs of a particular classroom of students. The goal, however, is always for the teacher to guide students to access complex, high-level content in meaningful ways.

Students should accomplish all three Reads of a text in one day so that their developing understanding of the information is uninterrupted. The text can always be revisited the next day, especially if it is being compared to another topically related text.

Features of the Student Worktext

Together with the instruction and questions in this Teacher's Edition, the Student Worktext of ***Close Reading of Complex Texts*** provides the framework that students need to gain a deeper understanding of the complex texts they read. The **Getting Started** unit takes students through the elements that they will apply during close readings of the program texts. Units 1–10 reinforce the application of each of those elements.

In addition to Focus Questions and the visual and traditional texts themselves, Units 1–10 of the Student Worktext include the following recurring features:

Self-Monitoring Strategies
The Self-Monitoring Strategies chart that appears before Text 1 in each unit engages students in metacognitive thinking and reminds them of the strategies that will help them better understand each of the unit texts.

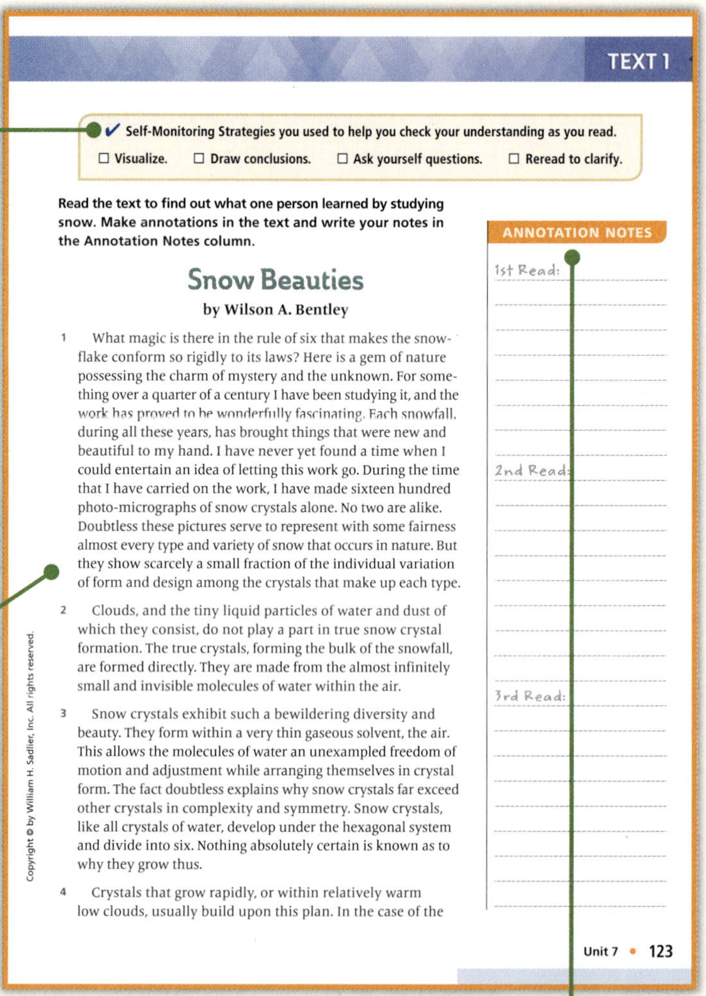

TEXT 1

✔ Self-Monitoring Strategies you used to help you check your understanding as you read.

☐ Visualize. ☐ Draw conclusions. ☐ Ask yourself questions. ☐ Reread to clarify.

Read the text to find out what one person learned by studying snow. Make annotations in the text and write your notes in the Annotation Notes column.

Snow Beauties

by Wilson A. Bentley

1 What magic is there in the rule of six that makes the snowflake conform so rigidly to its laws? Here is a gem of nature possessing the charm of mystery and the unknown. For something over a quarter of a century I have been studying it, and the work has proved to be wonderfully fascinating. Each snowfall, during all these years, has brought things that were new and beautiful to my hand. I have never yet found a time when I could entertain an idea of letting this work go. During the time that I have carried on the work, I have made sixteen hundred photo-micrographs of snow crystals alone. No two are alike. Doubtless these pictures serve to represent with some fairness almost every type and variety of snow that occurs in nature. But they show scarcely a small fraction of the individual variation of form and design among the crystals that make up each type.

2 Clouds, and the tiny liquid particles of water and dust of which they consist, do not play a part in true snow crystal formation. The true crystals, forming the bulk of the snowfall, are formed directly. They are made from the almost infinitely small and invisible molecules of water within the air.

3 Snow crystals exhibit such a bewildering diversity and beauty. They form within a very thin gaseous solvent, the air. This allows the molecules of water an unexampled freedom of motion and adjustment while arranging themselves in crystal form. The fact doubtless explains why snow crystals far exceed other crystals in complexity and symmetry. Snow crystals, like all crystals of water, develop under the hexagonal system and divide into six. Nothing absolutely certain is known as to why they grow thus.

4 Crystals that grow rapidly, or within relatively warm low clouds, usually build upon this plan. In the case of the

ANNOTATION NOTES

1st Read:

2nd Read:

3rd Read:

Unit 7 • 123

Multiple Reads
First, Second, and Third Reads help students gain the deepest insights about the text they are reading. Students read and reread a text or part of a text, developing greater understanding with each Read.

Annotations and Annotation Notes
By using specific annotation symbols to mark directly on the text, students identify questions, confusing language or sections, and important ideas or words that support their deepened understanding. The Annotation Notes column allows them to expand on or clarify their thinking.

Return to the Text

Respond to Reading, which appears after Text 1, asks students to demonstrate their understanding of the text with a graphic organizer, summary, and other text-related questions. Comprehension Check after Texts 1, 2, and 3 gives teachers the opportunity to assess students' inferential understanding.

Return to the TEXT

Respond to Reading: Snow Beauties

Review your annotations and notes.
Think about how they can help you summarize the text.

1. Use this chart to help you summarize the text.

Summary Chart		
	Informational Text	
Who?	the people or subjects	
What?	the topic or problem	
Where?	the location or region events occur	
When?	the era, year, or time	
How?	the events, steps, or processes	

2. Write a 2–3 sentence summary of the article "Snow Beauties."

Analyze and Synthesize Across Texts

After students have read all the texts in a unit, they use the Focus Question to synthesize their learning and draw conclusions across the texts. A graphic organizer helps students organize text evidence and their Annotation Notes.

ANALYZE and SYNTHESIZE ACROSS TEXTS

Return to the Focus Question: What can we learn from close study of ice and snow?

Review your answers to questions about the texts as well as your annotations and Annotation Notes, and think about the discussions you've had about the texts. How does that information help you answer the Focus Question?

Use the graphic organizer to organize information about the texts.

1. In the appropriate box, record the details that help you answer the Focus Question.
2. Make connections between those details to answer the Focus Question. Write your answer in the box provided.

Summer in Antarctica (Visual Text)

Climate at the Core

Snow Beauties

Sizing Up the Earth's Glaciers

What can we learn from close study of ice and snow?

REFLECT How did making connections between the four texts enable you to answer the Focus Question?

WRITE

Writing About the Focus Question

Now that you have answered the Focus Question using all four texts, expand on your thinking and communicate your ideas through your writing.

USE EVIDENCE

- Explain what people learn from the close study of ice and snow. Use at least one piece of evidence from the Visual Text and at least two pieces of evidence from Texts 1, 2, and 3 to support your answer.
- If you need more room, use additional paper.

MONITOR

- Use the Writing Checklist as you write to make sure your writing meets all the necessary criteria.
- Use the rubric on page 138 when you have completed a first draft of your writing to help you evaluate, revise, and edit your work.

WRITING CHECKLIST ✓

Does my writing . . .

- ☐ answer the Focus Question?
- ☐ have a clear organizational structure?
- ☐ cite the correct amount of text evidence?
- ☐ correctly use language, spelling, and conventions?

Write

The unit culminates in a writing activity that requires students to demonstrate critical thinking, cite textual evidence, and engage in intertextual analysis in their responses.

Reflect

These metacognitive elements ask students to explain their thinking.

Features of the Teacher's Edition

The Teacher's Edition supports busy teachers as they implement ***Close Reading of Complex Texts***. Scaffolded supports streamline the instructional process, providing Text-Dependent Questions, modeling of strategic thinking, discussion prompts, writing prompts, and more.

UNIT 7

Focus Question What can we learn from close study of ice and snow?

Texts for Close Reading

Unit 7 • 121

GENRE STUDY

Discuss with students the genres of "Snow Beauties," "Climate at the Core," and "Sizing Up the Earth's Glaciers."

Remind students that *genre* refers to the format and features of a text and typically falls into one of two categories—literature or informational text. Literature is a creative work that doesn't necessarily rely on facts, and informational text includes factual information.

Each text in this unit is informational. With the class, list the features of articles, such as bylines, subheads, and graphics that support the text. Discuss ways in which the publishing medium can affect the written and visual content, such as the difference in space available online and in print.

INTRODUCE THE UNIT

Focus Question

Have students read the Focus Question on Worktext page 121. Tell students that the texts they will read will help them answer the question.

Texts for Close Reading

Have students read to themselves the summaries about the texts in this unit.

There is no need to explain what students should expect to find in their close readings or to do any pre-teaching about the subject matter.

TEXT COMPLEXITY

Summer in Antarctica
- Style: documentary
- Knowledge demands: medium
- Levels of meaning: literal

Snow Beauties
Quantitative: 1060L
Qualitative
- Structure: conventional
- Language: academic
- Knowledge demands: high
- Levels of meaning: literal/inferential

Climate at the Core
Quantitative: 1100L
Qualitative
- Structure: conventional
- Language: academic
- Knowledge de
- Levels of mea

Sizing Up the Ear
Quantitative: 11
Qualitative
- Structure: con
- Language: aca
- Knowledge de
- Levels of mea

Text Complexity

Text Complexity information for each unit text includes quantitative information in the form of Lexile levels and qualitative areas of focus. In all instances, the third consideration of text complexity, task and reader, is the same since all students are reading the same complex text.

Genre Study

This feature supports teachers as students explore aspects of the unit texts' genres.

Set a Purpose

Each text includes a purpose for reading that text as well as a separate purpose for each different Read. In addition, the purposes relate to the Focus Question and support students' analyses across multiple texts.

TEXT 1

✔ Self-Monitoring Strategies you used to help you check your understanding as you read.
☐ Visualize. ☐ Draw conclusions. ☐ Ask yourself questions. ☐ Reread to clarify.

Read the text to find out what one person learned by studying snow. Make annotations in the text and write your notes in the Annotation Notes column.
Sample annotations and notes appear throughout the text.

Snow Beauties

by Wilson A. Bentley

1 What magic is there in the rule of six that makes the snowflake conform so rigidly to its laws? Here is a gem of nature possessing the charm of mystery and the unknown. For something over a quarter of a century I have been studying it, and the work has proved to be wonderfully fascinating. Each snowfall, during all these years, has brought things that were new and beautiful to my hand. I have never yet found a time when I could entertain an idea of letting this work go. During the time that I have carried on the work, I have made sixteen hundred photo-micrographs of snow crystals alone. No two are alike. Doubtless these pictures serve to represent with some fairness almost every type and variety of snow that occurs in nature. But they show scarcely a small fraction of the individual variation of form and design among the crystals that make up each type.

2 Clouds, and the tiny liquid particles of water and dust of which they consist, do not play a part in true snow crystal formation. The true crystals, forming the bulk of the snowfall, are formed directly. They are made from the almost infinitely small and invisible molecules of water within the air.

3 Snow crystals exhibit such a bewildering diversity and beauty. They form within a very thin gaseous solvent, the air. This allows the molecules of water an unexampled freedom of motion and adjustment while arranging themselves in crystal form. The fact doubtless explains why snow crystals far exceed other crystals in complexity and symmetry. Snow crystals, like all crystals of water, develop under the hexagonal system and divide into six. Nothing absolutely certain is known as to why they grow thus.

4 Crystals that grow rapidly, or within relatively warm low clouds, usually build upon this plan. In the case of the

ANNOTATION NOTES

1st Read:
Bentley photographed snowflakes for years, and found that no two were alike.

2nd Read:
language is very formal

What does he mean by "formed directly"? —reread paragraph 2

3rd Read:
Bentley is making a scientific study, but he is also captured by the beauty of his subject.

Unit 7 • 123

English learners as they provide guided opportunities and support in expressing ideas about the text. They also provide students with rich, structured conversation opportunities and time to develop collaborative conversation behaviors (for example, listening and responding to or building on the responses of others).

How Do I Use It? Instead of responding in generic ways to student responses during discussions ("Great," "That's right," "And what else?"), use students' answers as opportunities to develop language and deepen comprehension by selecting one or two accountable talk moves to focus on during each discussion (e.g., "Can anyone add to what ______ said?").

TEXT 1

Snow Beauties

Tell students that they will read to find out what one person learned by studying snow.

1st READ

Set a Purpose

Tell students they will be reading to find out about William Bentley's work.

Have students read "Snow Beauties" independently, annotating as they read. Circulate and make notes of students' markings, questions, and confusions. Your notes can be used to inform instruction and as data for informal assessment.

Text-Dependent Questions

1. What is this text about? (A man who studied snow crystals and how they form.)

2. What did Bentley learn through his study? (He learned about the conditions in which snowflakes form.)

Think Aloud *I had trouble understanding the language in paragraph, 2, so I'll reread and use a graphic organizer to clarify. Bentley contrasts two ideas, which I can put in a T chart. The first idea is that liquid particles do not form snowflakes. Instead, Bentley says, crystals form directly from molecules of water in the air. Now I think I understand. The water goes from a gas straight to ice crystals without ever being liquid.*

Partner Talk Have students discuss the gist of this text.

Unit 7 • 123

TEXT 2

Read the text to find out what climate information scientists learn from ice. If you need to read any sections more than once, note the reason in the Annotation Notes column.
Sample annotations and notes appear throughout the text.

Climate at the Core

by Amy Dusto

This article was published by the National Oceanic and Atmospheric Administration (NOAA). The NOAA studies Earth's weather, climate, and atmosphere.

1 Like a prehistoric fly trapped in amber, airborne relics of Earth's earlier climate can end up trapped in glacial ice for eons. These relics include dust, air bubbles, sea salts, volcanic ash, and soot from forest fires. To climate scientists, these relics tell a story about how our planet's climate and atmosphere have changed over thousands of years.

2 What they find out could have an impact on worldwide civilization within a few generations. This is especially true in coastal regions. Ice cores may reveal whether Antarctica's western ice sheet melted fully the last time Earth's climate warmed to the temperatures the planet is predicted to reach in the next two centuries. If it did, it's likely to again. That would raise sea levels enough to threaten many seaside cities.

Like the concentric circles of tree rings, the layers of an ice core represent one year of the ice sheet's growth via snowfall.

ANNOTATION NOTES

1st Read: Information about Earth's past is trapped in glaciers.

2nd Read: The first paragraphs describe the importance of the research.

3rd Read: How can scientists know whether an ice sheet melted just from studying cores?

TEXT 2

Climate at the Core

Tell students that they will read to find out what information scientists learn from ice.

1st READ

Set a Purpose

Tell students they will be reading to find out what can be found in ice.

Have students read "Climate at the Core" independently, annotating the text as they read. Circulate and note students' markings, especially questions and confusions.

Text-Dependent Questions

1. What is this text about? (Sample answer: It is about the study of ice cores, which are tubes of ice that scientists drill out from within ice sheets or glaciers.)

2. What are scientists studying in the ice cores? (Sample answer: Scientists study sea salt, pollution, and air trapped in the cores.)

3. Vocabulary: Figurative Language Discuss the use of figurative language in a scientific text.

Paragraphs 1 and 4: What is the effect of the author's use of figurative language such as "Like a prehistoric fly trapped in amber" and "coffee-can-wide"? (Sample answer: The figurative language helps readers visualize and understand an unfamiliar topic or object by comparing it to something familiar.)

Partner Talk Have students discuss what scientists learn by studying ice cores.

into smaller, easier-to-manage chunks. This process strengthens independent thinking and literacy confidence.

How Do I Use It? When you note students are unable to answer a question about the text, ask several layered questions related to the question. Begin with a question that calls for a recall of information provided explicitly in the text. For example, when constructing scaffolding for question 2 on page 128, ask, *What parts of the snowflake did Bentley look at? What were the conclusions he drew?* Each subsequent question should dig a little deeper. Now ask, *What other information would Bentley need to construct a story about how a snowflake forms?* Continue until the student arrives at an answer for the original text-dependent question.

Text-Dependent Questions

Teachers guide student understanding during each Read by asking Text-Dependent Questions, or TDQ's. TDQ's are derived from the information presented in the text and require students to return to the text for the answers.

Vocabulary

Carefully crafted TDQ's help students unlock word meaning through context, connections, and evidence from the text in ways that are most effective in supporting academic language development.

TEXT 2

9 The ratio of "light" oxygen to "heavy" oxygen in a sample, for instance, reveals a great deal. It tells scientists the global temperature when the ice formed. It takes colder temperatures for water vapor containing the lighter oxygen to turn into precipitation. Examining the gasses trapped in ice cores is how scientists first learned something extraordinary. They discovered that the amount of carbon dioxide and the global temperature have been linked for at least the last million years of Earth's history.

10 Osterberg even thinks ice cores will help figure out whether Antarctica's western ice sheet melted 125,000 years ago. That's the last time Earth's climate warmed to the temperatures the planet is predicted to reach in the next two centuries.

11 Scientists hope to collect a new ice core from the eastern side of the Trans-Antarctic Mountains. Today, they separate the East and West Antarctic Ice Sheets. Much of the land under the West Antarctic Ice Sheet is below sea level. If the ice sheet did disintegrate, then the proposed ice core drilling location would have been coastal real estate 125,000 years ago.

12 "We would see much warmer temperatures and higher levels of sea salt reflected in the ice core chemistry if this location was hundreds of miles closer to the ocean in the past," Osterberg said.

13 Before the climate fossils can tell their stories, however, they must be retrieved. Rugged researchers may spend multiple summers scoping never-before-explored areas on glaciers before trekking out to collect a core.

Scientists drill out ice cores using hand or power tools, depending on the depth and hardness of the ice.

ANNOTATION NOTES

1st Read: Scientists can tell the temperature and location of oceans from ice cores.

Scientists might be able to tell if the ice sheet melted.

2nd Read: Third section explains exactly what helps scientists learn more about the climate.

Trans-Antarctic Mountains—check map

3rd Read: Reread pararaphs 11–12: what info do researchers connect to tell if land was closer to the ocean?

Think Aloud

Optional Think Alouds throughout the unit support teachers in modeling their strategic reading processes as they demonstrate Self-Monitoring Strategies. Think Alouds offer students opportunities to look inside the mind of an expert reader and then apply these strategies as they read challenging texts independently.

How Do I Use It? Students may experience two common problems with analyzing versus summarizing. Some students may be able to retell or recall without being able to make connections or inferences in order to more deeply analyze the text. Scaffolded questions can lead to greater understanding. *What do these two things have in common? Why do you think the author wrote this?* More sophisticated students may make inferences without realizing it, and draw conclusions that are not supported by text evidence. For these students, asking them to cite evidence and explain thinking is essential. *I understand what you're thinking. Can you show me where it says that in the text?*

TEXT 2

Climate at the Core

3rd READ

Set a Purpose

Tell students they will read to make connections in the text.

Text-Dependent Questions

1. How will scientists' work with ice cores affect their understanding of today's climate? (Sample answer: Cores provide a record of climate patterns that can be used to compare to and make predictions about today's climate.)

Scaffolded Support Use the following scaffolded question and sentence frame as necessary to build comprehension.

What information do ice cores provide a record of?

Scientists use the information from ice cores to ________.

2. What would evidence that the ice sheet melted indicate? (Sample answer: It would indicate the temperature and atmospheric conditions that would cause the sheet to melt again.)

Think Aloud *The text says the scientists will be looking for higher levels of sea-salt ice in the core from the Trans-Antarctic Mountains. I can conclude that the presence of sea salt would prove that what is now dry land was once under or close to the ocean.*

Partner Talk Have students discuss how making connections helped them understand the text.

TEXT 2

Climate at the Core

2nd READ

Set a Purpose
Tell students they will read to examine the text's structure.

Text-Dependent Questions

1. How does the author organize information about the process scientists use to study ice cores? (Sample answer: The author follows the ice cores from the glacier to the lab, step by step.)

Scaffolded Support Use the following sentence frame as necessary to build comprehension.

The event that is described first is ______.

Think Aloud *I'll reread for transition words to figure out how the author presents information. The words "first" and "then" in paragraph 8 tell me the text is describing a procedure.*

2. What is the effect of the description of the melting ice sheet at the beginning of the article? (The author builds tension by describing the dramatic melting of the ice sheet before explaining what the research scientists are doing.)

3. **Vocabulary: Multiple-Meaning Words** Discuss a word with multiple definitions.

Paragraph 8: What is the meaning of *composition* in this context? (Here it refers to the make-up of something, in this case the atmosphere.)

Partner Talk Have students discuss how the structure of the article helps reveal the author's purpose.

TEXT 2

ANNOTATION NOTES

1st Read:
Scientists take apart the ice cores and study their contents in the lab.

2nd Read:
Second section describes how scientists get info from cores.

"Look for patterns" suggests they have to check many samples before they understand it.

3rd Read:
Scientists put a lot of effort into ice cores—the information must be important.

Formation of Ice

Under pressure, the weight of accumulated snowflakes squeezes out the air, and the flakes become denser. Lower temperatures cause melted crystals on the surface to refreeze and stick together, and they are transformed into ice. This metamorphosis takes place over many years (up to 3,500 in Antarctica).

3 "We have some evidence that may have happened, but we aren't sure," says Erich Osterberg, who studies ice cores in the Department of Earth Science at Dartmouth College.

4 To unlock the information inside an ice core, researchers in the lab may melt or crush the sample bit by bit. Each deeper layer represents a slightly earlier time in the Earth's climate history. The ice arrives in small strips, about 1-by-1 inch apiece. These are smaller slices of the roughly three-foot-long, coffee-can-wide pieces a drill pulls out of a glacier.

5 Sometimes researchers are studying actual bubbles of the early atmosphere, trapped in the ice as it formed. To collect them, they crush the sample under a vacuum hood. This keeps other air out while they pull the newly released air into vials.

6 Scientists run melted samples through various instruments. They are looking for tiny pieces of pollution, like sulfates, traces of metals, or radioactive fallout, or natural aerosols like dust or volcanic ash.

7 Because every clue in the ice is miniscule, measurements must be incredibly precise. This holds true whether it's a grain of sea salt or an air bubble. Any analysis must be done in a "clean room" setting. The researchers wear body suits and multiple layers of gloves. The room must have ultraclean filters and vents to keep the air pure. "Even a fingerprint from a ! scientist holding the core can ruin the sample," Osterberg says.

8 Researchers first analyze many ice core slices. These may each represent anywhere from a week to a year of time. Then they look for patterns to track changes in the atmosphere's composition and temperature, and what activity on Earth shaped it.

PROFESSIONAL DEVELOPMENT

Intertextual Analysis: Analyzing vs. Summarizing

What Is It? Analysis involves making inferences and drawing conclusions in order to understand the most important meanings, themes, and messages of a text. Analysis draws from what the text says but goes beyond what is directly stated.

Why Is It Important? Text analysis represents a higher-order thinking skill that is essential to school, citizenship, and work. Additionally, the ability to be metacognitively aware of one's own inferences and conclusions and the evidence that does or does not support those thoughts is important to build students' judgment.

Partner Talk and Collaborate

The Teacher's Edition identifies strategic points at which students collaborate with their peers to answer TDQ's, respond to the text, and pose new questions. The questions and prompts engage students in using the language of the text as teachers assess peer performance.

Return to the TEXT

Stop and Assess
Use the following to assess your students' understanding of the text.

Item 1 answers indicate:	
2	author's purpose of informing and persuading about the value of snowflakes, with at least two pieces of text evidence.
1	author's purpose of either informing or persuading, with insufficient text evidence.
0	no understanding of author's purpose, and no supporting evidence.

Item 2 answers indicate:	
2	the inference that Bentley studied atmospheric conditions as well as snowflakes, with two examples of text evidence.
1	the description of Bentley studying snowflakes, with insufficient text support.
0	no understanding of Bentley's methods, and no text evidence.

Item 3 answers indicate:	
2	snowflakes are important in the arts and science, with specific text examples.
1	snowflakes are important in either arts or science, with some text evidence.
0	no understanding of snowflakes' importance, and no supporting evidence.

Option: If you choose not to work with Texts 2 and 3 and to conclude the unit here, use the Visual Text and "Snow Beauties" to answer the Focus Question: What can we learn from close study of ice and snow?

Return to the TEXT

Comprehension Check: Snow Beauties

Answer the questions to demonstrate an understanding of what the text means.

1. Why did Bentley write this text?
Cite evidence from the text to support your answer.
Sample answer: Bentley wrote this text to explain what he had learned about snowflakes and to encourage others to study them. Bentley first describes how much effort he has put into his work by stating that he's made "sixteen hundred photo-micrographs" over "a quarter of a century." He tries to explain the "marvelous and mysterious" way that all snowflakes grow differently. In paragraphs 7 and 8, he lists the industries and institutions that value snowflakes, and says that he hopes "these wonderful bits of pure beauty will soon come into their own."

2. What inferences can you make about how Bentley studied snowflakes and their formation? Provide the text you used as a basis for your inferences.
Sample answer: Bentley's main method was to look very carefully at the tiny structures of snowflakes, and try to link them to the conditions in the clouds where they formed. Bentley notes that every snowflake has six sides, but that they differ "in the shape, size or thickness of their primary rays" and "[t]hese rays in turn, vary in the number, size or shape, of the secondary branches." Bentley also observed the conditions from which the flakes fell, noting that some flakes form "within relatively warm low clouds," while others fall during "snow flurries." I can infer that Bentley must have noted the clouds and conditions of the snowfall before photographing the flakes.

3. Summarize Bentley's perspective on the importance of snowflakes.
Cite text evidence to support your ideas.
Sample answer: Bentley believes that snowflakes are or will become important to the arts, industry, and science. He notes that many types of decorative artists, including "wall paper manufacturers" and "silk manufacturers" have begun using snowflake patterns. Scientists are also studying snowflakes to understand "the forms and habits of growth of crystals."

PROFESSIONAL DEVELOPMENT

Layered Questions: Scaffolding

What Is It? Layered questions are a series of text-dependent questions related to the same topic that are designed to guide a student into a deeper level of comprehension. The first layered question requires a surface understanding. Each subsequent layered question tunnels deeper into a text's meaning, guiding the student step-by-step to a more complete understanding.

Why Is It Important? Text-dependent layered questions provide a scaffold for students to answer questions about the text that they can't answer on their own. Layered questions model how to think through a difficult question by breaking up a complex idea

Stop and Assess

In conjunction with the Student Worktext's Comprehension Check, rubrics support teachers' assessment of students' understanding of the text purpose for Texts 1, 2, and 3.

Professional Development

Select spreads of the Teacher's Edition feature Professional Development boxes that include point-of-use application to provide context for instruction.

Building Vocabulary

Designed to help students develop independence in strategically identifying and unlocking new terms, ***Close Reading of Complex Texts*** provides students with rich vocabulary experiences. In addition, it builds on students' existing language abilities by emphasizing focused collaborative conversations designed to increase students' metacognitive awareness and discussion skills.

For example, Text-Dependent Questions in which students are directed to determine word meanings through context clues are provided for each lesson in the Teacher's Edition. In addition, the Teacher's Edition's Collaborate activities provide discussion prompts designed to develop student's oral language abilities.

The Teacher's Edition focuses students on key terms central to the text's meaning by exploring topics including: multiple-meaning words, denotation and connotation, idioms, foreign words, and figurative language. Teachers may choose to create additional Text-Dependent Questions that require students to explore text meaning through vocabulary.

Collaborating with Peers

Every unit in ***Close Reading of Complex Texts*** involves students in collaborative conversations that promote authentic student participation. Talking with peers is an essential feature of close reading and one that supports the deepening of thinking. During each Read, students discuss Text-Dependent Questions with their peers. Partner Talk prompts in the Teacher's Edition provide pairs with opportunities to delve deeper into texts after each Read. The Connect Text feature on the **Analyze and Synthesize Across Texts** page of the Teacher's Edition encourages small groups to use academic language to discuss how each of the four texts they've read answers the Focus Question.

When collaborating, students hear the ideas of others and compare them to their own. Best of all, they learn to value and to communicate with others. The teacher is not driving these conversations; they are occurring between peers. Students are free to ask questions, challenge one another, and identify multiple perspectives regarding the same text or question, using the academic vocabulary they have recently learned and previously knew.

In addition, as students hear the thoughts of their peers and compare them to their own, they evaluate the depth of their thinking. They become aware of their own processing of the textual information, defined as metacognitive awareness. As metacognition develops so, too, does students' ability to understand, analyze, and control all of their cognitive processes that support learning.

Assessing Understanding and Differentiating Learning

Teachers assess student understanding and responses at multiple strategic points during the close reading process. Formative assessments can include teacher assessment of student text annotations and student responses to Text-Dependent Questions and prompts during Partner Talk and small and whole group discussions. Students' completion of graphic organizers and uses of Self-Monitoring Strategies also provide opportunities for assessment. In addition, the **Return to the Text** pages that follow Texts 1, 2, and 3 provide an opportunity for formative assessment of students' understanding of each text, especially as it relates to the Focus Question.

Writing prompts at the end of each unit provide teachers with a summative assessment. The writing responses focus students on demonstrating their ability to analyze and synthesize across texts. A rubric that allows both student self-assessment and teacher summative assessment appears at the end of every unit. Teachers can differentiate end-of-unit projects with the Differentiate and Extend activity on the **Write** page of each unit.

For students who struggle with doing a close reading of a text on their own, a close reading of a paragraph situated within a larger text that is being presented as a shared reading is very appropriate. By situating a close reading within a shared reading, teachers support students with an appropriate sized and complex text within a context they understand. The teacher may begin by reading the first paragraph or section orally as students read silently. Then the teacher can pose a question related to the material that was read. After collaboration that addresses the question, the teacher, continuing the shared reading, may continue reading a second section of the text, and when finished, again engage students in a discussion focused on the language or structures the author uses. After student collaboration, the teacher may say, *Now I want you to closely read the next section and identify the author's intent.*

As ***Close Reading of Complex Texts*** authors Diane Lapp, Barbara Moss, Maria Grant, and Kelly Johnson note in their book *Turning the Page on Complex Texts: Differentiated Scaffolds for Close Reading*, if it becomes obvious during close reading that students are not deeply comprehending the text, additional questions may need to be asked. If initial questions do not support students' developing this deep understanding, teachers may use the Scaffolded Support that accompanies many of the Text-Dependent Questions or create their own layered questions that serve as scaffolds to understanding. The questions should be asked about the areas of the text that seem to be holding the students back from comprehending. For example, if students are not able to infer a character's traits in a narrative text or identify reasons for the timeline of a historical event in an informational text, additional questions should push them to look at specific words, phrases, sentences, or patterns in the text.

At the conclusion of the text, teachers may offer an extension activity that promotes in-depth thinking about the topic. For example, students might do additional reading from texts related to the unit theme or research a topic connected to the theme. In addition, teachers can also work with smaller groups of students who may need additional scaffolded supports.

Using the Interactive Student Edition

The Interactive Edition of ***Close Reading of Complex Texts*** enhances the learning experience for students by allowing them to work independently on readings after classroom instruction and to make use of a personalized digital notebook.

The Notebook captures and saves student's annotations for each Read of the texts. In addition, the Interactive Edition allows students to work independently by providing instructional guidance throughout the texts through features such as Text-Dependent Questions and Think Alouds that model metacognitive thinking.

Through use of their Notebooks and saved annotations, students are able to review and revisit their thinking across multiple readings. They can reference their notes and make connections while crafting responses for their assignments. Interactive graphic organizers help students organize their written responses and develop their ability to read critically. When prompted to provide written responses, students are able to toggle between the texts and the Notebook. These responses serve as formative assessment in real time.

The Notebook allows teachers to interact with students and respond instantly—a virtual teacher-student conference. Teachers can easily view students' personalized notes and comment on student work without having to gather and redistribute materials. With the Interactive Edition, teachers gain immediate insight into students' understanding by reading, reviewing, and commenting on students' annotations, notes, and responses to assignments and can intervene with students as necessary.

The Interactive Edition is an optional purchase to be used along with the print edition as part of a blended solution. The Interactive Edition is accessed via Sadlier Connect, Sadlier's learning platform, at **SadlierConnect.com.**

Implementing the Program

Close Reading of Complex Texts can be used to supplement a core reading program or be integrated into a literature-based curriculum. Below is one example of how teachers may choose to pace the instruction. These ten days need not be successive and may alternate with other classwork, independent reading and writing, and instruction.

Suggested 10-Day Implementation Model Pacing Guide

Day 1	Day 2	Day 3	Day 4	Day 5
• Introduce the Unit Focus Question and four texts. • Introduce the Visual Text. • Have students "read" the Visual Text and annotate. • Have students answer Student Worktext questions independently. • Support partner, small group, or whole group discussion of Student Worktext questions.	• Introduce Text 1. • Have students conduct a First Read of Text 1, or parts of Text 1, and annotate. • Have students do a Second and Third Read of Text 1, or parts of Text 1, and annotate. • Ask Text-Dependent Questions with each Read. • Have students discuss Partner Talk prompts.	• Have students revisit Text 1 as necessary. • Have students review Text 1 annotations. • Have students work independently to answer Respond to Reading questions. • Assessment: Have students complete Comprehension Check. • Work with small groups or individual students for re-teaching and support as necessary.	• Introduce Text 2. • Have students conduct a First Read of Text 2, or parts of Text 2, and annotate. • Have students do a Second and Third Read of Text 2, or parts of Text 2, and annotate. • Ask Text-Dependent Questions with each Read. • Have students discuss Partner Talk prompts.	• Have students revisit Text 2 as necessary. • Have students review Text 2 annotations. • Assessment: Have students complete Comprehension Check. • Work with small groups or individual students for re-teaching and support as necessary.
Day 6	**Day 7**	**Day 8**	**Day 9**	**Day 10**
• Introduce Text 3. • Have students conduct a First Read of Text 3, or parts of Text 3, and annotate. • Have students do a Second and Third Read of Text 3, or parts of Text 3, and annotate. • Ask Text-Dependent Questions with each Read. • Have students discuss Partner Talk prompts.	• Have students revisit Text 3 as necessary. • Have students review Text 3 annotations. • Assessment: Have students complete Comprehension Check. • Work with small groups or individual students for re-teaching and support as necessary.	• Have students discuss the four texts collaboratively then complete Analyze and Synthesize Across Texts independently. • Work with small groups or individual students for re-teaching and support as necessary.	• Have students write first drafts of Writing About the Focus Question. • Work with small groups or individual students for re-teaching and support as necessary.	• Have students revise their writing. • Have students complete Self-Assess and Reflect. • Work with small groups or individual students for re-teaching and support as necessary.

Sources

Cervetti, G. N., Wright, T. S., Hwang, H. J. (2016). "Conceptual Coherence, Comprehension, and Vocabulary Acquisition: A knowledge effect?" *Reading and Writing: An Interdisciplinary Journal*, 29 (4), p. 761–779.

Duke, N. K., Pearson, P. D., Strachan, S. L., and Billman, A. K. (2011). "Essential elements of fostering and teaching reading comprehension." In A. E. Farstrup and S. J. Samuels (Eds.), *What research has to say about reading instruction* (4th ed., pp. 51–93). Newark, DE: International Reading Association.

Ericcson, K. A., Krampe, R. T., and Tesch-Romer, C. (1991). "The role of deliberate practice in the acquisition of expert performance." *Psychological Review* 100(3), 363–406.

Goff, D. A., Pratt, C., and Ong, B. (2005). "The relations between children's reading comprehension, working memory, language skills, and components of reading decoding in a normal sample." *Reading and Writing*, 18 (7–9), 583–616.

Hoffman, J. V., Sailors, M., Duffy, G. G., and Beretvas, S. N. (2004). "The effective elementary classroom literacy environment: Examining the validity of the TEX-IN3 observation system." *Journal of Literacy Research*, 36 (3), 303–334.

Lapp, D., Moss, B., Grant, M., Johnson, K. (2015). *A Close Look at Close Reading* Alexandria, VA: ASCD. *Turning the Page on Complex Texts* Bloomington, IN: Solution Tree Press.

Paige, D. D. (2011). "Engaging struggling adolescent readers through situational interest: A model proposing the relationships among extrinsic motivation, oral reading, fluency, comprehension, and academic achievement." *Reading Psychology*, 32(5), 395–425.

Shanahan, T. (2014). "Should we teach students at their reading level?" *Literacy Leadership*, 14–15.

Stone, J. C. (2007). "Popular websites in adolescents' out-of-school lives: Critical lessons on literacy." In M. Knobel and C. Lankshear (Eds.), *A new literacies sampler* (pp. 49–65). New York, NY: Peter Lang.

CONTENTS

Getting Started with Close Reading

Unit 1

Unit 2

Unit 3

Unit 4

Unit 5

Unit 6

Unit 7

Unit 8

Unit 9

Unit 10

GETTING STARTED

Getting Started with Close Reading

USING THIS UNIT

Getting Started with Close Reading introduces the essential elements of close reading that students need to learn and to practice in order to become successful critical readers of complex texts.

Before you teach units 1–10, have students complete this introductory unit. The activities included here provide focused instruction and practice with very brief texts. By learning and practicing each element individually first, students will be better able to practice and apply those elements simultaneously as they move through the units.

After students complete this unit, encourage them to refer back to it to support their work throughout units 1–10.

READING CLOSELY

Each unit of ***Close Reading of Complex Texts*** includes four texts—a Visual Text and Text 1, Text 2, and Text 3. The Visual Text is an image that begins each unit, and the three other texts are written texts. All texts in a unit relate to the unit Focus Question. Reading all four texts provides students with the opportunity to synthesize information from all of the texts in order to answer the Focus Question, but it is possible for them to closely read only the Visual Text and Text 1 to answer the Focus Question.

Students will be conducting multiple reads of the texts in order to gain a deeper understanding of them. Tell students that they will read an entire text during a First Read but may read or concentrate on only part of the text during subsequent reads.

1st READ

Tell students that in the First Read, they will try to understand what the text is about or what is happening.

With the class, read aloud the bulleted list of questions. Ask students to suggest other questions they might ask the first time they read a text.

After students have had a chance to independently complete the activity on page 6 of the Student Worktext, ask them to discuss their responses with partners or as a whole class.

READING CLOSELY

Close reading is reading a text more than once in order to understand its deeper meaning. You uncover the reasons authors choose particular words and phrases, include literary elements and plot points, or organize the text or introduce information a particular way. You draw connections between the ideas and details in the texts—and from specific texts to bigger topics.

You will read the texts in ***Close Reading of Complex Texts*** three times, with a different purpose each time.

1st READ

Determine what the text is about. Read to find out:

- What are the key ideas or major points?
- Who are the characters?
- Where does the action take place?
- What happens?

Read this excerpt from Johanna Spyri's novel *Heidi*.

Heidi

by Johanna Spyri

On a clear sunny morning in June two figures could be seen climbing the narrow mountain path. One was a tall strong-looking girl, and the other was a child whom she was leading by the hand. This child's cheeks were so glowing with heat that you could see their crimson blush even through the dark, sunburnt skin of her face. And this was hardly to be wondered at, for in spite of the hot June sun the child was clothed as if to keep off the bitterest frost. She did not look more than five years old, but what her natural figure was like it would have been hard to say. She appeared to be wearing two, if not three dresses, one over the other. On top of these a thick red woolen shawl was wound round about her, so that the little body presented a shapeless appearance. With her small feet shod in thick, nailed mountain-shoes, this odd little figure slowly and laboriously plodded her way up in the hot sunshine.

Who or what is the excerpt from *Heidi* telling the reader about?

Sample answer: a young girl who is being led up a mountain path by an older girl

PROFESSIONAL DEVELOPMENT

Text Complexity

What Is It? The term *complexity* refers to a text's level of difficulty. Complexity can be measured quantitatively. Qualitative measurement of complexity takes into account elements such as text structure, the author's style and use of language, tone, theme, the relationship of ideas within a text, the use of visual supports, and readers' prior knowledge and levels of reading and cognition.

Why Is It Important? Advancement in education depends on a student's ability to read complex texts independently. Therefore, teachers should be giving students increasingly complex texts to read and interpret.

GETTING STARTED

2nd READ

Focus on the language used by the author and the structure of the text. As you read, make a note of answers to the following questions:

- How is the text organized? Chronologically? In a problem-and-solution structure? As cause and effect? With headings or bulleted lists?
- How does the author's use of figurative language give you a greater understanding of what is happening in the text?
- What words or phrases are repeated? How does the repetition add to the text's meaning?
- What is the author's purpose?
- What message is the writer communicating through his or her choice of language or structure?

Reread the excerpt from *Heidi* on page 6. How is the text organized?

Sample answer: The excerpt is mainly a description. The author introduces the characters and setting, and then describes the little girl from head to toe.

3rd READ

Look for meaning by making inferences. Think about whether the text answers these questions:

- What inferences can I make from the text to help me understand what the author doesn't say explicitly?
- How can I connect any of the ideas in the text to another text I've read or something I've learned?
- What is the theme of the text?
- What larger point or message do the writer's ideas add up to?

Reread the excerpt from *Heidi* again. What inference can you make from the text?

Sample answer: The child must be uncomfortable in her pile of clothes. Her cheeks are "glowing with heat," and she is climbing the path "slowly and laboriously."

How Do I Use It? Challenge students constantly to read beyond their lexiles. Before you introduce a given text, read it and note vocabulary that will be new to students and passages they might find confusing. Formulate scaffolded questions and prompts to use when students need extra support, taking care to ask questions that can be answered from the text. In discussions following Second and Third Reads, refrain as much as possible from giving students information or answers; instead, have them make inferences from the text, share prior knowledge, or otherwise discover answers for themselves. Your questions should serve as scaffolds that push comprehension.

2nd READ

Tell students that in the Second Read they will be paying attention to how the author communicates ideas and builds the text.

Read aloud the bulleted list of questions with the class. Ask students to identify which questions relate to authors' use of language and which questions relate to text structure. Have students identify other questions they might ask when they read a text for language and structure.

After students have had a chance to independently complete the Second Read activity on page 7 of the Student Worktext, ask them to discuss their responses with their partners or as a whole class.

3rd READ

Tell students that they will make inferences during a Third Read. Explain that when a reader makes an inference, he or she uses the information that the author states in the text to understand what the author isn't saying directly.

Read the bulleted list of questions aloud with the class. Discuss how making connections with other texts and identifying the theme of a text can help readers understand texts better.

After students have had a chance to independently complete the Third Read activity on page 7 of the Student Worktext, ask them to discuss their responses with their partners or as a whole class.

ANNOTATING A TEXT

Explain to students that the annotations of skillful readers identify what they don't understand and point out major points they want to remember and use in discussions and writing. Caution students that overannotating will be confusing rather than helpful.

Review the bulleted list of annotations on Student Worktext page 8 with students. Encourage them to suggest other symbols to use when annotating text.

Read the excerpt from *Heidi* with the class. Point out the underlining under the references to time and place—"morning in June" and "mountain path,"—which indicate the setting. Discuss why the reader may have made these annotations during the First Read. **(During a First Read, the information tells the reader that the story is taking place in the summer somewhere on a mountain.)**

Have the class conduct a Second Read of *Heidi* and ask volunteers to identify which annotations and notes the reader likely made during the Second Read and explain why. **(The reader probably circled key words and phrases and made the note "nailed mountain shoes?" during the Second Read because they relate to the author's use of language.)**

Have students read *Heidi* a final time and suggest what annotation notes the reader made during the Third Read. **(The reader probably wrote "Little girl must feel weighed down and uncomfortable" in the Annotation Notes since that is an inference from the text.)**

ANNOTATING A TEXT

Skillful readers annotate as they read. When you annotate a text, you mark the text and write notes or questions in the margins. Annotating will help you keep track of your ideas and questions.

Just as you read with a purpose, you should annotate with a purpose. You can use the following symbols to help you organize your annotations:

- Underline key ideas and major points.
- Write a ? next to anything that is confusing, such as unfamiliar words or unclear information.
- Circle key words or phrases.
- Put an ! next to surprising or important information or information that helps you make a connection.

Read the excerpt from *Heidi* three times. Think about which annotations and notes the reader made during each read.

Heidi

by Johanna Spyri

On a clear sunny morning in June two figures could be seen climbing the narrow mountain path. One was a tall strong-looking girl, and the other was a child whom she was leading by the hand. This child's cheeks were so glowing with heat that you could see their crimson blush even through the dark, sunburnt skin of her face. And this was hardly to be wondered at, for in spite of the hot June sun the child was clothed as if to keep off the bitterest frost. She did not look more than
! five years old, but what her natural figure was like it would have been hard to say. She appeared to be wearing two, if not three dresses, one over the other. On top of these a thick red woolen shawl was wound round about her, so that the little body presented a shapeless appearance. With her small feet shod in thick, nailed
? mountain-shoes, this odd little figure slowly and laboriously plodded her way up in the hot sunshine.

ANNOTATION NOTES

An older girl is leading a younger girl up a mountain.
around five years old
June–Why is the girl so overdressed?
Little girl must feel weighed down and uncomfortable.
nailed mountain shoes?

PROFESSIONAL DEVELOPMENT

Annotations

What Is It? As they read, students mark the text and make notes in the margins, using a standard annotation system. For example, they might circle key words, underline major points, or highlight unclear passages and add question marks for questions or exclamation points for surprising facts. The teacher circulates while students read, noting where and how they are marking the text, and uses students' annotations to inform instruction and class discussion, to assess progress, and to note areas where additional support is needed.

Why Is It Important? Annotating a text establishes a personal connection between the individual student and the text.

GETTING STARTED

Read the following excerpt from the monograph "The Principles of Scientific Management" three times. Make annotations and write your notes on the lines each time you read.

Sample annotations are indicated.

The Principles of Scientific Management

by Frederick Winslow Taylor

President Roosevelt in his address to the Governors at the White House, prophetically remarked that "The conservation of our national resources is only preliminary to the larger question of national efficiency."

The whole country at once recognized the importance of conserving our material resources and a large movement has been started which will be effective in accomplishing this object. As yet, however, we have but vaguely appreciated the importance of "the larger question of increasing our national efficiency."

! We can see our forests vanishing, our water-powers going to waste, our soil being carried by floods into the sea; and the end of our coal and our iron is in sight. But our larger wastes of human effort, which go on every day through such of our acts as are blundering, ill-directed, or inefficient, and which Mr. Roosevelt refers to as a lack of "national efficiency," are less visible, less tangible, and are but vaguely appreciated.

ANNOTATION NOTES

Roosevelt—conserving resources is a first step

prophetically = foretelling the future

efficiency in what?

National resources aren't just material resources.

human effort = work

People aren't concerned about efficiency because they can't SEE the waste.

Making notes helps the reader to stay focused, to read every word and line, and to stick with a text they find challenging. Using a standard system enables students to compare their work. Annotations also serve to guide the next reading. Observing students as they annotate enables you to observe and assess students' reading and cognitive abilities.

How Do I Use It? Introduce annotation by modeling it for your students. Explain your annotation system and caution students against overannotating. Guide them as they annotate short practice paragraphs. Select the best examples of student annotations, and have students explain why they annotated as they did. Then have students annotate texts independently.

Tell students to read the "The Principles of Scientific Management" excerpt three times, making appropriate annotations and notes for each read. Remind them of the purpose of each read:

1st READ

Determine what the text is about.

2nd READ

Focus on the language used by the author and the structure of the text.

3rd READ

Look for meaning by making inferences.

Refer students to pages 6–7 for questions they might ask during each read. Circulate through the class as students read and annotate the text, making note of any difficulties they have.

Throughout the units, students will return to their annotations to answer text-dependent questions, respond to readings, converse with their peers, participate in class discussions, and collaborate. Tell them to review their annotations and notes and make sure they are clear so that when they return to them, they will be useful.

Students gain and expand their thinking though their conversations with their peers. Ask volunteers to explain the annotations and notes they made.

SELF-MONITORING STRATEGIES

Texts that are worthy of a close reading are often challenging. Throughout the year, as students become more adept at reading texts closely, the texts can become even more complex. However, in order for students to gain a deeper understanding of a text, they must have a basic understanding of the topic being shared and they must have the needed reading skills. Self-Monitoring Strategies allow students to work independently to gain that basic understanding.

Review the Self-Monitoring Strategies on Student Worktext page 10 with students. Model using a Self-Monitoring Strategy for the excerpt from *The Life of Abraham Lincoln,* Vol. 1.

Think Aloud *The author says Lincoln's childhood home was "the ordinary one of the poorer western pioneer" and that descriptions by others of asqualid and wretched house are "overdrawn." Then she quotes Dr. Graham, who says that the idea that the Lincolns lived in an "open shed" is "all stuff."* Overdrawn *means "exaggerated," and* stuff *in this context means "nonsense." I can conclude that Tarbell's purpose is to correct an incorrect idea about Lincoln's childhood.*

Have students read the excerpt from *The Life of Abraham Lincoln,* Vol. 1 and complete page 10 of the Student Worktext.

Ask volunteers to explain what strategies they used and how using the strategies improved their understanding of the text.

SELF-MONITORING STRATEGIES

As you read, you can keep track of what you do and do not understand to help you better comprehend what you're reading. The process is called "self-monitoring."

✔Self-Monitoring Strategies

- ☐ **Visualize.**
  Picture in your mind the people or other characters, places, and events in the text.
- ☐ **Ask yourself questions.**
  Clarify what you read by asking questions such as:
  Does what I just read make sense?
  Are there words I don't know?
  What happened?
- ☐ **Draw conclusions.**
  Based on details in the text, draw conclusions about the topic or what the characters or subjects do or say.
- ☐ **Reread to clarify.**
  Go back to certain confusing parts to see if reading more slowly or more carefully helps you understand the text.

Read the excerpt from *The Life of Abraham Lincoln,* Vol. 1. In the Self-Monitoring Strategies box, put a checkmark next to the strategies you use as you read.

The Life of Abraham Lincoln, Vol. 1

by Ida M. Tarbell

The home into which the child came was the ordinary one of the poorer western pioneer—a one-roomed cabin with a huge outside chimney, a single window, and a rude door. The description of its squalor and wretchedness, which are so familiar, have been overdrawn. Dr. Graham, whom there is no better authority on the life of that day, and who knew Thomas Lincoln well, declares energetically that "It is all stuff about Tom Lincoln keeping his wife in an open shed in a winter. The Lincolns had a cow and calf, milk and butter, a good feather bed—for I have slept on it." The Lincoln home was

PROFESSIONAL DEVELOPMENT

Self-Monitoring Strategies

What Is It? As students read independently, they pause at intervals to check comprehension. Self-Monitoring Strategies include visualizing, asking questions, drawing conclusions, and rereading to clarify.

Why Is It Important? Self-Monitoring Strategies allow students to work independently and to better understand what they are reading. Visualizing helps students focus on details in the text. Asking questions provides invaluable preparation for tests and writing assignments. Drawing conclusions builds confidence for participation in class discussions. Rereading to clarify increases comprehension and focuses attention. All these Self-Monitoring Strategies build good study habits.

undoubtedly rude, and in many ways uncomfortable, but it sheltered a happy family, and its poverty affected the new child but little. He grew to be robust and active and soon learned how endless are the delights and interests the country offers to a child.

SUMMARIZING

By summarizing a text, you can show that you understand what you have read. In general, a summary provides answers to questions such as *Who?* or *What?* A summary of any text should include only significant information and leave out unimportant details. This chart works well for summaries of both literature and informational text.

Summary Chart

	Literature	Informational Text	
Who?	the characters	the people or subjects	Abraham Lincoln's family, Dr. Graham
What?	the conflict or problem	the topic or problem	question of the quality of Abraham Lincoln's childhood home
Where?	the place characters are in	the location or region events occur	exact location is not given
When?	the era, year, or time	the date, year, or time	time of Lincoln's early years
How?	the plot or major events	the events, steps, or processes	Author says Lincoln's childhood home was not that bad. Lincoln authority agrees.

Write a 2–3 sentence summary of *The Life of Abraham Lincoln*, Vol. 1 excerpt on page 10. Use the Summary Chart to organize your thoughts.

Sample answer: The author claims that Lincoln's home was not wretched as often reported. A quotation from Dr. Graham, who knew the Lincolns, confirms her claim. She goes on to say that, despite their poverty, the Lincolns were a "happy family," and young Abraham enjoyed his childhood.

GETTING STARTED

SUMMARIZING

Summarizing requires students to use text evidence to support their ideas. It also provides them with a means to demonstrate that they understand the major points and key details of a text and to self-assess their comprehension.

Have students complete the activity on Student Worktext page 11. Ask volunteers to explain how the Summary Chart helped them write their summaries.

As a class, discuss how students were able to summarize the excerpt from *The Life of Abraham Lincoln*, Vol. 1 while leaving out some important details. (Dr. Graham gives a list of some things the Lincolns had, but I didn't need to include those details. The important point is that Graham agreed with the author's claim.)

Ask volunteers to read their summaries aloud.

How Do I Use It? Introduce Self-Monitoring Strategies by discussing the value of independence in reading. Model each self-monitoring strategy by reading a text out loud and then applying the strategy. For English learners or less fluent readers, introduce, practice, and apply only one strategy at a time. For example, show students how to visualize the settings, characters, or actions in a text and then have them read and visualize independently. Repeat the process with the other strategies, using a different text for each strategy.

READING A VISUAL TEXT

Discuss with the class the different types of images they see regularly. Ask volunteers to provide an example and explain what the purpose of the image is. Encourage students to tell whether they think their example images merit a closer look and tell them to explain their answers.

Before students complete the exercises on Student Worktext page 12, direct their attention to the Visual Text, "Science, Technology, Engineering, and Math (STEM) Event, Denver, Colorado." Provide support before they begin analyzing the image independently. Use such prompts as:

- Start by looking at the entire image. Think about what might be happening. Next, examine the details. Look for clues that might help you understand what the image means.
- Then, look at the entire image again. How did the details add to your comprehension of the Visual Text?

Have students complete the activity on Student Worktext page 12. Discuss their answers.

READING A VISUAL TEXT

Like written texts, images can make you think about bigger ideas in ways you may not have thought about them before.

Images—paintings, drawings, and photographs—can communicate information in ways words cannot. They can provide viewers with a scene in a single instant. In this way, an image is a "visual text." Like written texts, visual texts often deserve a closer look—or two.

Look at the Visual Text and think about what information the image is communicating to its viewers.

Science, Technology, Engineering, and Math (STEM) Event, Denver, Colorado

Now answer the following questions about the Visual Text. Review the image or parts of the image as many times as necessary.

1. What is your first impression of what is going on in this photograph?
   Sample answer: It looks like a group of students is doing an experiment or giving a demonstration of some kind.
2. What details in the image make you think that?
   Sample answer: A group is gathered around a tub of water. It looks like there are objects being placed in the water. The image's caption says the setting is a science event.
3. What is the photographer's message?
   Sample answer: The photograph shows that students are interested in science and that science can be fun.

PROFESSIONAL DEVELOPMENT

Visual Text

What Is It? Visual elements such as photographs, illustrations, and diagrams need to be interpreted correctly in order for readers to comprehend their full meaning.

Why Is It Important? Interpreting Visual Texts is a critical reading skill. With the proliferation of electronic communications, visual literacy is a critical life skill.

How Do I Use It? Have students view the Visual Text three times, first identifying what it shows, then focusing on details that give meaning, and finally looking for greater meaning by making inferences.

UNIT 1

Focus Question How can we better prepare for earthquakes?

Texts for Close Reading

Unit 1 • 13

GENRE STUDY

Discuss with students the genres of "Earthquake and Fire: San Francisco in Ruins," "Earthquake Science in the U.S. Before 1906 to Today," and "You're a *what*? Seismologist."

Remind students that *genre* refers to the format and features of a text and typically falls into one of two categories—literature or informational text. Literature is creative and may not rely on facts. Informational text has factual information.

With the class, list the features of newspaper articles and explanatory texts. Have students identify the shared characteristics of these genres. Both rely on factual information, are meant to impart knowledge to readers, and may include visuals to help readers understand information in the text. Then have students identify ways in which the genres differ.

Focus Question

Have students read the Focus Question on Worktext page 13. Tell students that the texts they will read will help them answer the question.

Texts for Close Reading

Have students read to themselves the summaries about the texts in this unit.

There is no need to explain what students should expect to find in their close readings or to do any pre-teaching about the subject matter.

TEXT COMPLEXITY

Disaster Supplies

- Style: documentary
- Knowledge demands: medium
- Levels of meaning: literal

San Francisco in Ruins

Quantitative: 1110L

Qualitative

- Structure: conventional
- Language: familiar
- Knowledge demands: medium
- Levels of meaning: literal/inferential

Earthquake Science in the U.S.

Quantitative: 1210L

Qualitative

- Structure: conventional
- Language: academic
- Knowledge demands: medium
- Levels of meaning: literal

You're a *what*?

Quantitative: 1060L

Qualitative

- Structure: conventional
- Language: familiar
- Knowledge demands: medium
- Levels of meaning: literal/inferential

Disaster Supplies

Set a Purpose

Explain to students that they will look at the image on page 14 to think about what supplies people might need in an emergency or disaster.

Visual Text Analysis

Remind students that an image can be analyzed as a text by looking at its details and making inferences. Direct students' attention to the image on Student Worktext page 14.

1. Have students record their immediate impressions after they look at the photograph. Lead them to discuss as a whole class, in small groups, or with a partner, what they think is happening in the photograph.

2. Encourage students to make notes of the details that support their observations in question 1. Have students explain as a whole class, in small groups, or with a partner, what the details tell them about what supplies people might need when they face disasters.

3. Have students return to the Visual Text and consider various types of emergency situations and how the supplies in the Visual Text might be required in each one.

Optional: Provide any additional information you feel is appropriate to enhance the discussion:

- First aid kits typically contain antibiotic ointment, gauze, sanitizer, cotton balls and swabs, needles, a bulb syringe, an instruction booklet, and contact information for family members.

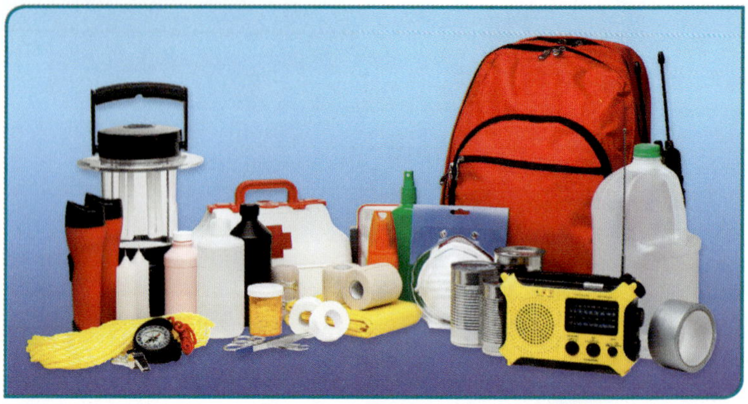

Disaster Emergency Supplies

Look at the Visual Text to answer the following questions. Review the image or parts of the image as many times as necessary.

1. What is happening in this image?
   Sample answer: The photograph shows things you would want to have if you were expecting a disaster or that you would take with you if you were responding to a disaster.

2. What details support your answer to the previous question?
   Sample answer: The photo shows a first aid kit, radio, water, canned food, rope, lantern, candles, compass, medical supplies, facemask, duct tape, flashlights, a tarp, and a backpack to put everything in. These supplies would be useful in an emergency.

3. When you look again, what are you thinking and feeling?
   Sample answer: I am thinking of what each of these items would be used for in an emergency. I am also thinking of any additional materials I might include in an emergency supply kit.

PROFESSIONAL DEVELOPMENT

Intertextual Analysis: Incorporating Information from a Visual Text

What is It? The focus question for each unit addresses the Visual Text as well as the written texts. Incorporating analysis of the Visual Text helps students make intertextual connections and comprehend each text more deeply.

Why Is It Important? Given the focus on close reading, the Visual Text may get overlooked, but Visual Text analysis can greatly enrich comprehension for all learners. Visual Texts can be an aid in the visualization strategy, and can include details, events, ideas, and perspectives not found in written texts.

✔ Self-Monitoring Strategies you used to help you check your understanding as you read.

☐ Visualize. ☐ Draw conclusions. ☐ Ask yourself questions. ☐ Reread to clarify.

Read the text to learn what happened during the San Francisco earthquake of 1906. Make annotations in the text and write your notes in the Annotation Notes column.

Sample annotations and notes appear throughout the text.

Earthquake and Fire: San Francisco in Ruins

After the earthquake and fire of 1906, the three San Francisco newspapers—the Call, *the* Chronicler, *and the* Examiner*—published an edition together. This was the lead article on the day after the disaster.*

1 Death and destruction have been the fate of San Francisco. Shaken by a tremblor at 5:13 yesterday morning, the shock ? lasting 48 seconds, and scourged by flames that raged diametrically in all directions, the city is a mass of smoldering ruins. At six o'clock last evening the flames seemingly playing with increased vigor, threatened to destroy such sections as their fury had spared during the earlier portion of the day. Building their path in a triangular circuit from the start in the early morning, they jockeyed as the day waned, left the business section, which they had entirely devastated, and skipped in a dozen directions to the residence portions. As night fell they had made their way over into the North Beach section. Springing anew to the south, they reached out along the shipping section down the bay shore, over the hills and across toward Third and Townsend streets.

2 Warehouses, wholesale houses, and manufacturing concerns fell in their path. This completed the destruction of the entire district known as the "South of Market Street." How far they are reaching to the south across the channel cannot be told as this part of the city is shut off from San Francisco papers.

3 After darkness, thousands of the homeless were making their way with their blankets and scant provisions to Golden Gate Park and the beach to find shelter. Those in the homes on the hills just north of the Hayes Valley wrecked section piled ! their belongings in the streets. Express wagons and automobiles were hauling the things away to the sparsely settled sections.

ANNOTATION NOTES

1st Read:
A fire begins because of an earthquake, and then spreads in all directions across the city.

2nd Read:
includes chronology and geography of events

figurative language—*raged, playing, jockeyed, left, skipped, reached out*

3rd Read:
The fire must have seemed unstoppable—the author portrays it as something alive that is devouring the city.

How Do I Use It? After completing the readings in each unit, return to the Visual Text. Have students apply any new understandings to the Visual Text. Ask:

What do you think about the objects in this photo now that you have learned more about the topic?

Does this image seem to have a purpose like that of the written texts, or is it different?

What connections did you make between this image and the events and situations described in the texts?

Encourage students to summarize the image in relation to the focus question when completing their graphic organizers.

San Francisco in Ruins

Tell students that they will read to learn what happened during the San Francisco Earthquake of 1906.

1st READ

Set a Purpose

Tell students they will be reading to find out what this text is about.

Have students read "Earthquake and Fire: San Franciso in Ruins" independently, annotating as they read. Circulate and make notes of students' markings, questions, and confusions. Your notes can be used to inform instruction and as data for informal assessment.

Text-Dependent Questions

1. What is this text about? (It describes the immediate effects of an earthquake in San Francisco. The earthquake caused buildings to fall, fires to break out, and many deaths.)

Scaffolded Support Use the following sentence frame as necessary to build comprehension.

The earthquake caused ________.

2. What are some details you noted about this historical event? (The cost in dollars and lives was high, the fire was still burning when the article was written, the army arrived to keep order.)

3. Vocabulary: Multiple-Meaning Words Discuss the multiple meanings of a familiar word.

Paragraph 10: What does *check* mean here? What other meanings does it have? (Here it means "to stop progress," but it can also mean "to examine," "to mark a box," or "to restrain.")

Partner Talk Have students discuss the effects of the earthquake.

San Francisco in Ruins

2nd READ

Set a Purpose

Tell students they will reread parts of the text to observe how the author's language reveals the message.

Text-Dependent Questions

1. What type of language does the author use to show the passage of time? (The text includes specific times in paragraph 1, then uses phrases such as "after darkness" in paragraph 3 and "at nine o'clock" in paragraph 9 to show time passed.)

2. What is the effect of the language used to describe the aftermath of the earthquake in the first four paragraphs? (The text uses powerful phrases such as, "a mass of smoldering ruins," "entirely devastated," "totally destroyed," and "crumbled into heaps," that convey a sense of the magnitude of the event.)

3. What purpose does the information about the newspaper offices in paragraph 5 serve? (People depended on newspapers for information. Paragraph 5 lets the audience know that it will be difficult to get news in the usual way.)

Think Aloud *In paragraph 6 the text explains the cost of the damage at $200,000,000. I wondered what it would cost to rebuild the city today. This article was written in 1906, so I can conclude that in today's dollars, the cost would be much, much higher.*

Partner Talk Have students discuss the language of the text and its effects.

ANNOTATION NOTES

1st Read:
Details show the effects of the fire on buildings and people.

2nd Read:
words synonymous with "destroyed": *fell in their path, shut off, wrecked, in ruin, crumbled into heaps*

3rd Read:
Everybody, including the author, has given up on saving the city.

The city must have lacked protections against fire. Were the buildings made mostly of wood?

Everybody in San Francisco is prepared to leave the city. The belief is firm that San Francisco will be totally destroyed.

4 Downtown everything is ruin. Not a business house stands. Theaters are crumbled into heaps. Factories and commission houses lie smoldering on their former sites.

Looking Down Sacramento Street, local photographer Arnold Genthe's photograph shows "the results of the earth quake, the beginning of the fire and the attitude of the people."

5 All of the newspaper plants have been rendered useless. The "Call" and the "Examiner" buildings, excluding the "Call's" editorial rooms on Stevenson Street, being entirely destroyed.

6 ! It is estimated that the loss in San Francisco will reach from $150,000,000 to $200,000,000. These figures are in the rough and nothing can be told until partial accounting is taken.

7 On every side, there was death and suffering yesterday. Hundreds were injured, either burned, crushed or struck by falling pieces from the buildings. One died while on the operating table at Mechanics' Pavilion, improvised as a hospital for the comfort and care of 300 of the injured.

8 The number of dead is not known, but it is estimated that at least 500 met their death in the horror.

9 At nine o'clock, under a special message from President Roosevelt, the city was placed under martial law. Hundreds of troops patrolled the streets and drove the crowds back while hundreds more were set at work assisting the fire and police departments. The strictest orders were issued. In true

PROFESSIONAL DEVELOPMENT

Think-Aloud Modeling: Purposeful Partner Talk

What Is It? Purposeful partner talk is productive conversation between two students who are analyzing a text to increase comprehension.

Why Is It Important? Purposeful partner talk requires students to use academic language to further develop their speaking and listening skills, and to understand a text from a different point of view. These skills will serve students well not only in an academic setting, but in life in general.

military spirit the soldiers obeyed. During the afternoon ! three thieves met their death by rifle bullets while at work in the ruins. The curious were driven back at the breasts of the horses that the cavalrymen rode. The crowds were forced from the level district to the hilly section beyond to the north.

10 The water supply was entirely cut off, and maybe it was just as well. The lines of fire department would have been absolutely useless at any stage. Assistant Chief Dougherty supervised the work of his men and early in the morning it was seen that the only possible chance to save the city ? lay in effort to check the flames by use of dynamite. During the day a blast could be heard in any section at intervals of only a few minutes, and buildings not destroyed by fire were blown to atoms. But through the gaps the flames jumped, and although the failures of the heroic efforts of the police firemen and soldiers were at times sickening, the work was continued with a desperation that will live as one of the features of the terrible disaster. Men worked like fiends to combat the laughing, roaring, onrushing fire demon.

Ruins after San Francisco earthquake, 1906/Genthe

ANNOTATION NOTES

1st Read:
description of the death and injury

Water supply is cut off while fires continue to burn.
How does dynamite help combat a fire?

2nd Read:
Look up "martial law"—something to do with war?

keeping order—"drove the crowds back," "strictest orders"

3rd Read:
report is from first day of fire; reader does not know how it will end

How Do I Use It? Use language frames and various productive conversation techniques, such as restating, adding on, and extending, to model purposeful partner talk before partners discuss "Earthquake and Fire: San Francisco in Ruins" on Student Worktext pages 15–17. For example: *After rereading the text, I've determined ________. The details ________ in paragraph ________ support my idea. I agree with your statement that ________. However, I'd like to add ________.*

San Francisco in Ruins

3rd READ

Set a Purpose

Tell students they will read to make inferences about the text.

Text-Dependent Questions

1. What inference can you make about the population's reaction to the fire? **(The text describes people "making their way" to find shelter and "everyone is prepared to leave the city." It seems as if people remained calm and organized considering the circumstances.)**

2. Why do the authors include the details about the military in paragraph 9? **(The authors want the audience to understand that the crowds got in the way of the people fighting the fire. Also, thieves found opportunity in the chaos. The crowds and disorder added to the immediate danger caused by the fire.)**

3. Vocabulary: Figurative Language Discuss the literal and associative meanings of words used to describe the fire.

Paragraph 10: Why might the author have used *demon* to describe the fire? **(I know that *demon* means "an evil spirit." The author uses *demon* to help the reader visualize something powerful and terrible.)**

Partner Talk Have students discuss what inferences they made about what it was like in San Francisco after the earthquake.

Return to the TEXT

Respond to Reading

You may want to check students' understanding by having them complete pages 18–19 in the Student Worktext.

1. Remind students to review their annotations and recall discussions they've had in order to complete the summary charts. Remind students that only evidence from the text should be included in the summary chart.

As students complete their summary charts, circulate and note which students struggle to identify the correct text evidence. Some students may benefit from small group instruction.

2. Remind students to include only the most important information in their summaries.

Have students work indepedently to complete page 18 of their Worktexts.

COLLABORATE When finished, have students exchange summaries with their partners and share their insights.

Return to the TEXT

Respond to Reading: Earthquake and Fire: San Francisco in Ruins

Review your annotations and notes.
Think about how they can help you summarize the text.

1. Use this chart to help you summarize the text.

Summary Chart		
	Informational Text	
Who?	the people or subjects	residents, business owners, firefighters, and military troops
What?	the topic or problem	A massive earthquake causes a huge fire that devastates an entire city.
Where?	the location or region events occur	San Francisco
When?	the date, year, or time	1906
How?	the events, steps, or processes	Firefighters try to put out the blaze while residents flee with their belongings and troops enforce martial law.

2. Write a 2–3 sentence summary of the news report "Earthquake and Fire: San Francisco in Ruins."

The San Francisco fire of 1906 was so widespread and destructive that people at the time believed the city would not survive. On the second day, the city was in smoldering ruins, there were hundreds of dead and thousands homeless, and the water system was entirely cut off. President Roosevelt put the city under martial law as police, firefighters, and soldiers worked heroically to contain the flames.

PROFESSIONAL DEVELOPMENT

Annotations: Self-Monitoring Strategy

What Is It? Annotations record a reader's thoughts, ideas, and understandings while reading. Annotations include underlining or highlighting text, circling key words and ideas, recording important or surprising information, marking places of confusion, or noting questions.

Why Is It Important? Annotating is a **Self-Monitoring Strategy** that allows readers to record their initial thoughts and questions about a text. Annotating is a metacognitive strategy that allows a reader to self-monitor comprehension. Annotations also provide the teacher with valuable information regarding what students do and do not understand. They can help to pinpoint areas of confusion to be dealt with during a scaffolded close

Return to the TEXT

3. What sort of problems did the earthquake and the fire cause? Support your answer with evidence from the text.
   Sample answer: In paragraph 4, the text states that "Downtown everything is ruin." The earthquake and fire caused "at least 500" deaths, the complete destruction of huge areas of the city, countless injuries, and from "$150,000,000 to $200,000,000" worth of damage. In paragraph 9, the text states that "three thieves met their death by rifle bullets," and, in paragraph 10, that the water supply was cut off.

4. How did hospital staff, police, and firefighters respond to the disaster? Provide text evidence to support your answer.
   Sample answer: The hospital staff members were heroic and took care of "300 of the injured," including doing surgeries at Mechanics' Pavilion (paragraph 7). In paragraph 9, troops patrolled the streets and held back crowds. Despite the failures of their "heroic efforts," the soldiers, firefighters, and police fought the fires "with a desperation" (paragraph 10).

5. What is the effect of the use of language in this news report? Provide text evidence to support your answer.
   Sample answer: The use of figurative language makes the fire seem alive. In paragraph 1, the flames were "seemingly playing" as they "threatened to destroy" sections of the city. Phrases such as "building their path" and "springing anew" in paragraph 1 make the flames seem like they are planning and deliberating. Later the flames "jumped" through gaps. In paragraph 10, the flames are "laughing, roaring, onrushing fire demon."

REFLECT What sections of the text did you visualize to make sure you understood?
Sample answer: I visualized paragraph 10 because I couldn't figure out how using dynamite to blow up buildings would stop the fire. Once I visualized a pile of brick and rubble in the fire's path, I understood.

Return to the TEXT

Encourage students to refer back to the text and their annotations and notes to help them answer the questions.

3. Students will need to scan several paragraphs (3, 6, 9–10) to collect details to answer this question.

4. You can support students by directing them to details about the makeshift hospital in paragraph 7 and police and firefighters in paragraphs 9 and 10.

5. Suggest that students look for examples of figurative language to describe the fire in the first paragraph and in the last paragraph.

Have students work independently to complete page 19 of their Worktexts.

REFLECT Remind students that visualizing is a **Self-Monitoring Strategy** and that they made annotations and notes about confusions they may have had. Suggest that they review their annotations and think about any words, phrases, or sections that they visualized to check their comprehension of the text.

reading of the text and any subsequent instruction. Annotations also can be used for informal assessment.

How Do I Use It? Model annotating for students using a small section of "San Francisco in Ruins" on Student Worktext page 15. *When I read this text for the first time, I want to understand what happened in San Francisco after the earthquake, so I'll make some annotations that will help me do that. I'm not sure what* diametrically *in the first paragraph means, so I'll write a question mark next to the word. It describes how the flames moved through the city. I see the word part* dia- *but it doesn't help me understand what the word means. I'll come back to it and look it up if the text doesn't give me any more clues.*

Return to the TEXT

Stop and Assess

Use the following to assess your students' understanding of the text.

Item 1 answers indicate:	
2	two ways that people reacted to the fire with two pieces of evidence as support.
1	one way in which people reacted to the fire with only one piece of supporting evidence.
0	a lack of understanding about reactions and no relevant textual evidence.

Item 2 answers indicate:	
2	a logical interpretation about the author's purpose with at least two pieces of supporting evidence.
1	a logical interpretation of the author's purpose with only one piece of supporting evidence.
0	no understanding or misunderstanding of the author's purpose and no relevant evidence.

Item 3 answers indicate:	
2	an understanding of how the diction reflects meaning with supporting evidence.
1	some understanding of how the diction might reflect meaning but no textual evidence.
0	little or no understanding of how this diction reflects the meaning of the text.

Option: If you choose not to work with Texts 2 and 3 and to conclude the unit here, use the Visual Text and "Earthquake and Fire: San Francisco in Ruins" to answer the Focus Question: How can we better prepare for earthquakes?

Return to the TEXT

Comprehension Check: Earthquake and Fire: San Francisco in Ruins

Answer the questions to demonstrate an understanding of what the text means.

1. What inference can you make about ways in which people caught in the San Francisco earthquake and fire of 1906 reacted? Cite at least two pieces of text evidence to support your answer.

Sample answer: Thousands of people were just concerned with surviving and went to the park and the beach "to find shelter." Some people left the city and others stayed to help save lives and stop further destruction. Still others were "curious" onlookers. Paragraph 3 describes wagons and cars hauling belongings to parts of the city that were less affected as "everybody" prepared to leave. Paragraphs 7, 9, and 10 show examples of people who helped: doctors, soldiers, police, and firefighters.

2. Why does the report include horrific details of human suffering?

Sample answer: The report is intended to inform readers who are not in San Francisco of the scope of the destruction and suffering. The report doesn't just include facts and statistics. The writing appeals to all the senses in order to make a strong impression on readers.

3. Explain the effect of the sentences in paragraphs 4 and 5 and the single sentence in paragraph 8.

Sample answer: The sentences in paragraphs 4 and 5 are short and to the point because they don't need a lot of description to show the devastation. Short sentences can be more powerful. The single-sentence paragraph (paragraph 8) emphasizes that the loss of so much human life was the worst thing about the fire.

20 • Unit 1

PROFESSIONAL DEVELOPMENT

Academic Language: ELL

What Is It? Academic Language is difficult language that falls into two categories: general academic and domain-specific language. Academic Language is formal language, vocabulary and sentence structure used in books and formal discussions, including classroom discussions. Domain-specific language is vocabulary and idioms from a specific field of knowledge.

Why Is It Important? Academic Language is necessary for school and professional success. Knowledge of domain-specific language may be necessary to understand unfamiliar but essential topics—for example, technology and medicine—in everyday life.

TEXT 2

Read to find out why people want to understand earthquakes. If you need to read any sections more than once, note the reason in the Annotation Notes column.

Sample annotations and notes appear throughout the text.

Earthquake Science in the U.S. Before 1906 to Today

1 The 1906 earthquake marked the dawn of modern scientific study of the San Andreas fault system in California. Before 1906, earthquake research in the U.S. had advanced slowly compared to efforts in Japan and Europe. The first seismographs in the U.S. were installed in 1887, at the Lick Observatory (Mount Hamilton, California) and at the University of California at Berkeley. Around the turn of the century, a small number of geology professors working for the U.S. Geological Survey contributed some of the earliest observations of earthquake-related features. They also compiled the earliest lists of historic earthquakes in the U.S. At the time, we didn't know how and where they occurred, or the hazard they would present to our west- ? ward-bound, expanding nation. The theory of plate tectonics was still more than a half-century away.

The 1906 Earthquake Spawns a Flurry of Scientific Investigation

2 When the 1906 earthquake struck on April 18, nearly all scientists in California began to assemble observations of the earthquake and its effects. Professor Andrew C. Lawson, chairman of the geology department at the University of California, Berkeley, took the first steps that led to the Governor's order, three days later, to appoint a State Earthquake Investigation Commission. The Commission, headed by Lawson, would unify the work of scientific investigations then under way. ! This launched the first integrated, government-commissioned scientific investigation into earthquakes in the U.S.

Professor Andrew Lawson of UC Berkley coauthored the Lawson report in 1908.

ANNOTATION NOTES

1st Read:
Vigorous scientific research into earthquakes was motivated by the San Francisco earthquake of 1906.

2nd Read:
The first paragraph is about *before* the 1906 earthquake.

Subheading expresses the main idea.

seismograph = machine to measures earthquakes

3rd Read:
connection between disaster and the government releasing funds for research

Earthquake Science

Tell students that they will read to find out why people want to understand earthquakes.

1st READ

Set a Purpose

Tell students they will be reading to find out what the text is about.

Have students read "Earthquake Science in the U.S. Before 1906 to Today" independently, annotating the text as they read. Circulate and note students' markings, especially questions and confusions.

Text-Dependent Questions

1. What were the big ideas shared in this text? (The text shares information about a commission to study the damage from the San Francisco earthquake and the improvements in earthquake science that resulted.)

Scaffolded Support Use the following scaffolded question and sentence frame as necessary to build comprehension.

What was the State Earthquake Investigative Commission?

Their report showed ________.

Think Aloud *When I reread paragraph 7, I saw that seismographs are instruments that "measure the shaking intensity" at sites in California. If we can measure, we can better understand. If we better understand, we can better prepare.*

Partner Talk Have students discuss developments in earthquake science.

How Do I Use It? ELL students have both advantages and disadvantages when encountering Academic Language. Large words and complex English syntax may be intimidating. On the other hand, many Romance languages (Spanish, Portuguese, and French, for example) have more words and word parts in common with complex Latin-based vocabulary than with Anglo-Saxon based informal language. In scientific texts, point out word parts that may be familiar to Romance-language speakers. For example, ask, *Do you see the word parts* geo- *and* -ology *in* geology*? It looks like* geología *in Spanish or* géologie *in French. The parts mean "earth" and "description." What other word parts do you recognize in the Academic Language in this text?*

Earthquake Science

2nd READ

Set a Purpose

Tell students they will read to determine how the text's structure and language support its message.

Text-Dependent Questions

1. How is the text organized? (The text is chronological, tracing the development of earthquake science from the 1906 earthquake through today.)

2. How does the bulleted list in paragraph 8 support your understanding of the whole text? (The list summarizes the big questions that researchers are better prepared to answer today than they were in 1906. The questions address the prevention of earthquake damage in the future.)

3. Vocabulary: Figurative Language Discuss the difference between literal and figurative language.

Paragraph 1: What is the meaning of the phrase "the dawn of modern scientific study"? (This figure of speech means that the 1906 San Francisco earthquake was like the beginning of a new day in the way earthquakes were studied.)

Partner Talk Have students discuss the text's structure and how it reflects and supports the author's purpose.

TEXT 2

ANNOTATION NOTES

1st Read:
relationship of 1906 event to studies and events that happened later

2nd Read:
"exhaustive compilation"—The report covered everything that had been learned.

3rd Read:
Scientists can't prevent earthquakes, but they can predict them.

There was damage during the 1989 earthquake, but it was not as devastating.

3 The Commission's final report, known as the Lawson report, was an exhaustive compilation of detailed reports from more than twenty scientists. It looked at the earthquake's damage and the movement on the San Andreas fault. It also explored the seismograph records of the earthquake from around the world, and the underlying geology in northern California.

The Investigations Pay Off

4 The 1906 earthquake and the Lawson report demonstrated the importance of accurate, widespread, and repeated observations of earthquakes, their effects, and the faults on which they occur. The report provided the basis for much of what is now known about earthquakes in California.

5 Maps included in the report clearly showed that some of the strongest shaking in 1906 occurred in the soft sedimentary soils of China Basin and in the present Marina district. These ! two San Francisco neighborhoods would, some 83 years later, again (and for the same reason) be shaken hard and damaged in the 1989 earthquake.

6 Geological observations carried out after the earthquake by people who walked the entire length of the earthquake rupture (often through poison oak-covered hills) showed where and how much the fault had slipped. Maps of surveys carried out during 1906–1907 also documented the earth movement. This information plays a key role in our current models of how much (and when) the San Andreas is expected to slip in the next earthquake.

Greater Understanding and Reduction of Earthquake Hazards

7 Since 1906, a vigorous earthquake research program has developed in the U.S. Today, seismographs measure the shaking intensity at over 1000 sites in California. Instruments and repeated surveys track the plate motion and the related stressing and distortion of Earth's crust (which causes earthquakes) throughout California. Data from these instrument networks are analyzed with the aid of computers. From these observations, scientists have formed a detailed picture of the location and activity of the hundreds of faults that make up the San Andreas fault system. They have achieved a growing understanding of which faults are likely to produce strong

22 • Unit 1

PROFESSIONAL DEVELOPMENT

Self-Monitoring Strategies: Reread to Clarify

What Is It? Active readers employ a variety of **Self-Monitoring Strategies** while reading to ensure and deepen comprehension. One such strategy is rereading to clarify. Reading again allows for more attention to language, connections, and themes.

Why Is It Important? Rereading is a key strategy for basic comprehension. Good readers reread sentences or paragraphs when they do not understand language or ideas. Good text analyzers reread entire passages to understand connections between ideas, the overall text structure, and the major themes.

TEXT 2

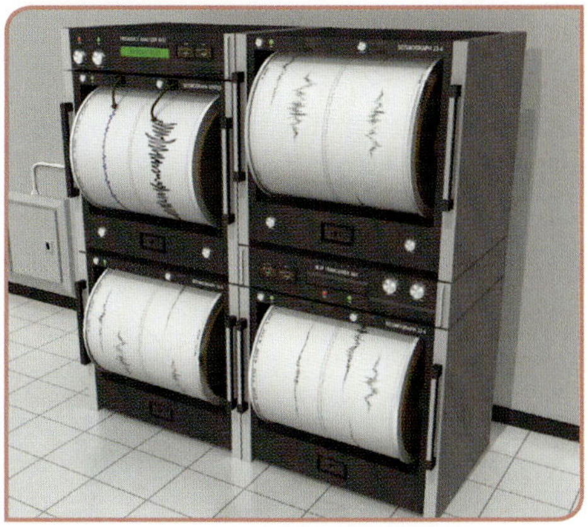

A seismograph is an instrument that measures earthquake movements.

earthquakes. They have helped us understand what the long-term probabilities for occurrence are, and how intense the shaking from them is likely to be.

Significant Advances . . . and Challenges for the Future

!

8 Of course, there are still major questions about earthquakes for which we really have no answers at this time. Probably the most asked question is "Exactly when will the next damaging earthquake happen?" At present, we cannot answer this more precisely than by stating the long-term probabilities for large earthquakes. But when one considers how much we have learned since 1906 about the other important questions—

- Where is a strong quake likely to happen?
- How probable is it?
- How intense will the shaking be?
- How well will our infrastructure fare?
- Where should we avoid building critical structures?
- How do we design and build earthquake-resistant structures?

—it is clear that tremendous progress has been made.

ANNOTATION NOTES

1st Read:
Scientists have a better understanding of earthquakes but still cannot predict them.

2nd Read:
lists the advances in earthquake science over time

present state of the science/what is still needed

3rd Read:
Connection between new technologies and new knowledge—the more scientists know, the more able they are to predict quakes.

How Do I Use It? Model rereading for language comprehension when reading aloud. Identify your behavior by saying, for example, *Wait, I'm not sure I understood that sentence (or word, or phrase). Let me read it again.* During close-reading instruction, students will reread entire passages as part of the assignment. Instruct students and model how to follow annotations and annotation notes to focus rereading on parts of the text marked as important or confusing. Provide the option of a partial reread, in which students choose which parts to reread to identify those places in the text critical to comprehension.

Earthquake Science

3rd READ

Set a Purpose

Tell students they will read to make inferences about the text.

Text-Dependent Questions

1. What is one positive outcome of the San Francisco earthquake? (The scientific research and knowledge that it "spawned" has led to a "growing understanding" of faults and the probability of earthquake occurrence. The disaster inspired new technologies and a federal commitment to an ongoing earthquake research program.)

2. What area of San Francisco is most likely to experience another earthquake? Why? (The soft sedimentary soils near China Basin and the Marina district and their nearness to the San Andreas fault make these neighborhoods most vulnerable.)

3. What kinds of work do seismologists in California perform? (They conduct surveys to track plate motion, analyze data to constantly update the map of the fault system, and measure shaking intensity at more than 1,000 sites throughout the state.)

4. Vocabulary: Homophones Discuss pairs of homophones suggested by the text (i.e. site, role, intense)

Paragraph 8: What does *fare* mean here? What is its homophone? (*Fare* means "to get along" in this context. *Fair* is its homophone.)

Partner Talk Have students discuss inferences they can draw from the kinds of research into earthquakes that are underway.

Return to the TEXT

Stop and Assess

Use the following to assess your students' understanding of the text.

	Item 1 answers indicate:
2	how Lawson advanced our understanding of earthquakes, with at least two pieces of supporting evidence.
1	that Lawson advanced our understanding of earthquakes, with one piece of text evidence.
0	a lack of understanding about Lawson's contributions and no evidence from the text.

	Item 2 answers indicate:
2	at least two ways in which scientists monitor Earth's crust with evidence from the text.
1	one way in which scientists monitor Earth's crust with evidence from the text.
0	no understanding of how scientists monitor Earth's crust in California today.

	Item 3 answers indicate:
2	an inference about scientific progress, with at least two pieces of text evidence as support.
1	one piece of text evidence about scientific progress.
0	a lack of understanding about scientific progress based on this text.

Return to the TEXT

Comprehension Check: Earthquake Science in the U.S. Before 1906 to Today

Answer the questions to demonstrate an understanding of what the text means.

1. How did Lawson and his colleagues influence our understanding of earthquakes? Cite text evidence in your answer.
   Sample answer: Lawson and his colleagues studied everything about the 1906 San Francisco earthquake. In paragraphs 3–6, the article describes how they surveyed the damage, explored seismograph records from around the world, studied the soils in different areas, "walked the entire length of the earthquake rupture," and "documented the earth movement." These findings "provided the basis for much of what is now known about earthquakes in California."

2. How do scientists monitor Earth's crust in California today? Cite text evidence in your answer.
   Sample answer: Paragraph 7 explains that today seismographs "measure the shaking intensity at over 1000 sites in California," and scientists analyze all the data they collect "with the aid of computers." They now know that the San Andreas fault is really a system of hundreds of faults, and they know which ones are "likely to produce strong earthquakes."

3. In general, what does this article suggest about scientific progress? Give text evidence to support your answer.
   Sample answer: The article suggests that progress happens slowly over time, such as the steady progress from 1906 to now. A disaster may motivate investigation. After the 1906 earthquake, the government started to fund research. In paragraph 4, it says that "accurate, widespread, and repeated observations" by a team of experts can lead to a much greater understanding of earthquakes. Technology can aid analysis. This report shows how seismographs and computers have played a role in earthquake science.

PROFESSIONAL DEVELOPMENT

Teacher Observation: Guide to Note-taking for Teachers

What Is It? As students work independently or in small groups, circulate and listen in on conversations while making notes on which students are having difficulty with comprehension and which students display higher levels of knowledge or skill.

Why Is It Important? Your students have different levels of reading skill and differing abilities to understand scientific concepts, sequence historical events, and otherwise grasp the contents of a reading selection. They also have different life experiences. Your notes can help you form small groups in which students' skills complement each other.

Read to find out more about the job of studying earthquakes. You may want to read some sections more than once and make different annotations and Annotation Notes each time.
Sample annotations and notes appear throughout the text.

You're a *what?* Seismologist

by Sara Royster

1 Unlike many people, Graham Kent isn't afraid of earthquakes. He studies earthquakes as a seismologist and director of the Seismological Laboratory at the University of Nevada, Reno.

2 Seismology is the scientific study of earthquakes and related phenomena, such as volcanic eruptions. Earthquakes occur when the tectonic plates that make up Earth's crust shift and release energy in the form of waves. These seismic waves, which move through Earth's molten core, can cause destruction on the surface by damaging structures, warping roads and bridges, and injuring living things.

3 Graham's work is about more than just earthquakes, though. Seismologists also apply what they learn from studying Earth's structure and other geological events, such as tsunami.

What they do

4 Seismologists' tasks vary, depending on their area of focus. Some seismologists conduct research; others directly observe earthquakes. Still others use their expertise in practical ! applications.

5 ***Research.*** Research seismologists study the internal structure of Earth and try to determine factors that contribute to or foretell an earthquake. Their work helps guide engineering and building practices to improve safety wherever earthquakes are common.

6 ***Applications.*** Some seismologists apply their knowledge to commercial or other uses. For example, they may use sound waves to aid the energy industry in finding oil deep under Earth's crust.

7 Seismology also can help detect nuclear explosions. These explosions create seismic waves that can be identified at great distances, so seismologists help monitor whether countries are complying with nuclear test bans.

ANNOTATION NOTES

1st Read:
Text blends definitions and information with one man's personal experience.

2nd Read:
Title is kind of jokey—the tone is informal.

The headings give main ideas and the subheadings give details.

3rd Read:
This job seems challenging, exciting, and useful.

How Do I Use It? As you form pairs for partner talk or small groups for collaborative work, match students' needs and abilities to encourage students to help each other.

You're a *what?*

Tell students that they will read to find out more about the job of studying earthquakes.

1st READ

Set a Purpose

Explain to students that they will read to find out what the text is about. Have students read "You're a *what?* Seismologist" independently, annotating the text.

Text-Dependent Questions

1. What is this text about? (The text describes the job seismologists do. They conduct research, observe earthquakes, guide engineers and builders to improve safety, work for companies such as those in the energy industry, and/or determine compliance with nuclear test bans.)

2. How does someone become a seismologist? (Seismologists need "a range of interests," problem-solving skills, science and math education, and a knowledge of data analysis software, and they need to study and train.)

3. How can seismology be dangerous? (Seismologists might work around dangerous equipment, in difficult terrain, or in extreme weather.)

Partner Talk Have students discuss what a seismologist might do during a typical day at work.

You're a *what?*

2nd READ

Set a Purpose

Tell students they will examine the purpose of some of the author's word choices.

Text-Dependent Questions

1. How does the author's choice of words in paragraphs 2 and 3 contribute to your understanding? (The author relies on geological terms such as *phenomena, volcanic eruptions, crust,* and *energy,* which helps me understand that a seismologist has to have a firm science background.)

2. What does Graham mean by "You need to be a bit of an explorer, a bit of an engineer"? (He means that the job has two sides to it: part science and part adventure.)

Partner Talk Have students discuss the impact of informal and domain specific language on tone.

3rd READ

Set a Purpose

Tell students they will read to make inferences about the text.

Text-Dependent Questions

1. For whom is the author writing? (The author is writing to people who might be interested in seismology.)

2. Does the author give a fair and balanced evaluation of this job? Give reasons for your answer. (Yes. She shows both pros and cons. She is realistic about the "long hours" and "difficulties" as well as the rewards.)

Partner Talk Have students discuss what the author thinks about seismologists.

TEXT 3

ANNOTATION NOTES

1st Read:
Details show how to become a seismologist and what the job might be like.

Reread benefits and downsides of being a seismologist—some downsides seem like benefits.

2nd Read:
Paragraph 8—Author uses quotations to give the text life and personality.

toolset—not a literal toolset but knowledge and skills

3rd Read:
Seismology might seem like a narrow field of study but it takes different kinds of background knowledge and a broad range of skills—seems like a job for someone who likes studying and adventure.

How they prepare

Seismologists don't necessarily sit in front of instruments and computers all day; many work out in the field.

8 To become a seismologist, Graham suggests also having a range of interests. "You need to be a bit of an explorer, a bit of an engineer," he says. "It's important to have a wide toolset and be able to take in all kinds of information and make something useful out of it."

9 ***Skills.*** Critical thinking and problem-solving skills are essential for seismologists. Their work often involves collecting and analyzing data to develop solid conclusions.

10 ? ***Education.*** Coursework usually includes subjects such as geology, math, and physics. Knowledge of data analysis software is also important.

What to expect

11 Working as a seismologist can be interesting and rewarding, but, like any job, seismology has its frustrations and difficulties, too.

12 ! ***Work environment.*** Seismologists work primarily in areas of the United States where earthquakes are common, such as the West Coast. Those in the energy industry may be employed in oil-rich states, such as Texas.

13 Seismologists usually work for long, irregular periods, including nights and weekends. Other working conditions vary, depending on the focus.

14 ! Research seismologists spend much of their time in the lab, usually at a computer. Seismologists who focus on observation often trek long distances, sometimes in extreme weather and through difficult terrain, to find suitable locations for collecting data. And those in the energy industry may work around complex, dangerous drilling equipment.

PROFESSIONAL DEVELOPMENT

Self-Monitoring: Visualize

What Is It? Visualization is a **Self-Monitoring Strategy** that encourages students to imagine a described scene using their senses.

Why Is It Important? Visualization can help students understand lengthy or difficult descriptions or complex action sequences. It can also enhance reading enjoyment and motivation for reluctant readers.

Comprehension Check: You're a *what?* Seismologist

Answer the questions to demonstrate an understanding of what the text means.

1. Write a summary of the text in your own words.
   Sample answer: Graham Kent is a seismologist in Nevada. In paragraphs 4–10, the author gives information about what it takes to be a seismologist and uses Kent's career as an example of one that is both interesting and rewarding. In paragraphs 13 and 14, he shows that it can also be difficult and dangerous. The job requires critical thinking, math and science skills, and a sense of adventure. Many seismologists work for energy industries. Some work in labs, and others work out in the field.

2. What connection can you make between the "wide toolset" needed to be a seismologist and the work a seismologist does? Use specific examples from the text in your answer.
   Sample answer: The "wide toolset" includes education in "geology, math, and physics" and "knowledge of data analysis software" (paragraph 10), "critical thinking and problem-solving skills" (paragraph 9), the patience to spend "long, irregular periods" (paragraph 13) in labs and in front of computers, and the physical ability to trek long distances in difficult conditions (paragraphs 13–14).Seismologists have to have a thorough knowledge of their complicated subject, and they have to be able to collect data in the real world and manipulate data using computers.

3. Does the text present a positive view of the job of a seismologist? Why or why not? Use evidence from the text to support your opinion.
   Sample answer: The tone is mostly neutral, but the author describes the benefits of the work seismologists do. They "improve safety wherever earthquakes are common."

Return to the TEXT

Stop and Assess

Use the following to assess your students' understanding of the text.

	Item 1 answers indicate:
2	the ideas and details of the various parts of the text and how they are connected.
1	a main idea of the text but not an understanding of how the parts work together as a whole.
0	no understanding of the text's main ideas and details.

	Item 2 answers indicate:
2	an understanding of this figurative phrase supported by at least two pieces of text evidence.
1	a limited understanding of the phrase's meaning with only one piece of text evidence as support.
0	a lack of understanding or a misunderstanding of the meaning of this figurative phrase.

	Item 3 answers indicate:
2	the text presents a generally positive view, with at least two pieces of text evidence as support.
1	the text presents a generally positive view, but text evidence is weak.
0	a lack of understanding of the author's perspective and no relevant supporting evidence from the text.

How Do I Use It? Use visualization with texts that have rich descriptions and vivid scenes. Encourage students to make text-text and text-self connections. Model using a Think Aloud: *As I read the end of paragraph 2, I visualize the enormous power that can warp "roads and bridges." I picture an urban highway that has been bent, twisted, and broken. It seems so out of control. And it must be incredibly loud.* Make difficult words more accessible by providing images from the Internet, your own sketches, or realia, and encourage students to make sketches of their own to help them understand words and ideas.

Return to the Focus Question

Explain to students that they will fill out a graphic organizer that helps them answer the Focus Question: How can we better prepare for earthquakes?

CONNECT TEXTS Have small groups of students discuss how each text they read helps them answer the Focus Question.

Scaffolded Support You may provide the following sentence frames to support students in their use of academic language:

> In the text ________,
> the author/photographer
> makes the point that ________.
> He/she does this by ________.

Remind students to use their annotations and summaries to support their answers. They can also reread portions of the texts if necessary.

Have students complete their graphic organizers individually.

REFLECT Remind students that each text provides different information about better preparing for earthquakes. Ask, *how did reading all four texts give you a greater understanding of how people can prepare for these disasters?*

ANALYZE and SYNTHESIZE ACROSS TEXTS

Return to the Focus Question: How can we better prepare for earthquakes?

Review your answers to questions about the texts as well as your annotations and Annotation Notes, and think about the discussions you've had about the texts. How does that information help you answer the Focus Question?

Use the graphic organizer to organize information about the texts.

1. In the appropriate box below, record the details that help you answer the Focus Question.
2. Make connections between those details to answer the Focus Question. Write your answer in the box provided.

Disaster Supplies (Visual Text)
Sample answer: Gather supplies, equipment, and tools that may save lives in an emergency.

Earthquake Science in the U.S.
Sample answer: Measure and map data over time, develop tech to collect information and analyze it.

San Francisco in Ruins
Sample answer: Understand more about the potential dangers during and after an earthquake.

You're a *what*?
Sample answer: Encourage people to become seismologists, develop technology, provide more funding.

How can we better prepare for earthquakes?
Sample answer: Making scientifically based predictions and planning for possible disaster are essential. San Francisco had no plan in the event of a major earthquake and was devastated when one hit. That's why it's so important to make sure dedicated people are working to understand plate tectonics in order to predict when earthquakes will happen.

REFLECT How did making connections between the four texts enable you to answer the Focus Question?

Sample answer: The texts build on one another. The first is about the earthquake that spawned the research described in the second text. The third text has information about modern earthquake research. The Visual Text has information about what I can do.

PROFESSIONAL DEVELOPMENT

Scaffolding: Sentence Frames

What Is It? Frames are open-ended cloze sentences, or sentence models, with a blank or open ending that students complete.

Why Is It Important? Sentence frames provide scaffolding to help students answer questions. The provided words or phrases can act as guidelines for students' thinking or research within the text. The sentence frame provides a model for constructing a response to a question.

How Do I Use It? It is best to generate frames during planning. Frames should guide students back to what the text says in order to build greater meaning. A thoughtful frame has two components: a "hint" within the provided part of the sentence,

WRITE

Writing About the Focus Question

Now that you have answered the Focus Question using all four texts, expand on your thinking and communicate your ideas through your writing.

USE EVIDENCE

- Explain how people can better prepare for earthquakes. Use at least one piece of evidence from the Visual Text and at least two pieces of evidence from Texts 1, 2, and 3 to support your answer.
- If you need more room, use additional paper.

MONITOR

- Use the Writing Checklist as you write to make sure your writing meets all the necessary criteria.
- Use the rubric on page 30 when you have completed a first draft of your writing to help you evaluate, revise, and edit your work.

WRITING CHECKLIST ✓

Does my writing . . .

- ☐ answer the Focus Question?
- ☐ have a clear organizational structure?
- ☐ cite the correct amount of text evidence?
- ☐ correctly use language, spelling, and conventions?

and a blank that is somewhat open-ended but elicits an answer that is a step in formulating an answer to a text-dependent question. In the frame *Sara Royster uses Graham's words to* ________, the phrase "Graham's words" is a hint, a reference to the quotations in the text, which students can use to locate the details to support their answer. The word *uses* gives students several options for answering, including *to give her article realism and variety, to create a friendly, casual tone,* or *to offer an example of a successful seismologist.* Multiple students' answers can lead the class to a greater understanding of what it takes to be a seismologist.

Writing About the Focus Question

USE EVIDENCE Remind students that they should use their graphic organizers as well as their annotations in the texts to write their responses.

Allow students to revisit the texts as frequently as they need to in order to support comprehension and to respond to the Focus Question.

MONITOR After students have completed their responses, have them review the Writing Checklist and revise their writing response.

DIFFERENTIATE AND EXTEND

In addition to or instead of the writing response, consider having students complete one of the following assignments:

Write Beyond Have students imagine that they are seismological research interns. Have them write emails home describing their work. Emails should include facts from the unit texts.

Interview Have students use information from Text 1 to write a reporter's interview with a person on-site during the disaster.

Research Have students choose and research another famous earthquake such as Tokyo 1923, Chile 1960, China 1976, or Indonesia 2004.

Create a Visual Text Have students create diagrams that show how earthquakes occur along the San Andreas fault.

SELF-ASSESS and REFLECT

SELF-ASSESS Have students use the Writing Rubric on page 30 to self-assess their writing response and write a final version. Tell them to assign themselves a score from 1–4 (with "4" being the highest) for each category in the first column.

Use the Writing Rubric on Student Worktext page 30 to assess each student's writing. Record points for each category in the first column of the rubric. Have students remove the page from their Student Worktexts and place it in their writing portfolios, along with the drafts and final versions of their responses.

SELF-ASSESS and REFLECT

Focus Question: How can we better prepare for earthquakes?

This is the rubric that your teacher will use to assess your writing. Refer to it as you revise your work. After you have finished the final version of your response, assess your response and record your points for each category on the "Student" line in the first column.

	Accomplished (4 points)	Competent (3 points)	Developing (2 points)	Beginning (1 point)
RESPONSE Score: Student ____ Teacher ____	The response answers the question effectively and with insight.	The response answers the question effectively.	The response partially responds to the question but does not adequately address it.	The response addresses the texts but does not address the question.
ORGANIZATION Score: Student ____ Teacher ____	The main idea is convincingly stated. Ideas are organized in cohesive paragraphs that support the main idea.	The main idea is clearly stated. Ideas are organized in logical paragraphs.	The main idea is weak. Ideas are organized in a somewhat logical and cohesive way.	The main idea is missing. The organization of the paragraphs is not logical.
TEXT EVIDENCE Score: Student ____ Teacher ____	Response includes more than one piece of appropriate text evidence from each text. Evidence supports the main idea in a thorough way.	Response includes one piece of text evidence from each text. Evidence supports the main idea clearly.	Response does not include at least one piece of text evidence from each text. Text evidence does not adequately support the main idea.	Response does not contain relevant evidence.
LANGUAGE Score: Student ____ Teacher ____	Writing includes precise and sophisticated vocabulary related to the topic.	Writing includes appropriate vocabulary related to the topic.	Writing includes imprecise and inaccurate vocabulary.	Writing does not include vocabulary that appropriately reflects the topic of the response.
SPELLING AND CONVENTIONS Score: Student ____ Teacher ____	Response includes correct spelling, grammar, and punctuation consistently.	Response includes mostly correct spelling, grammar, and punctuation.	Response has many errors in spelling, grammar, and punctuation.	Response's errors in spelling, grammar, and punctuation make it extremely difficult to understand the response.

UNIT 2

Focus Question How have views on equality and athletics changed over time?

Texts for Close Reading

Unit 2 • 31

GENRE STUDY

Discuss with students the genres of "The Future of Physical Education," "Title IX: A Sea Change in Gender Equity in Education," and "Senate Resolution 462."

Remind students that *genre* refers to the format and features of a text and typically falls into one of two categories—literature or informational text. There are many subgenres of informational text with overlapping characteristics. Identifying text purpose and even where a text is published can help to distinguish subgenres. With the class, list the features of a magazine article, an explanatory text, and a resolution. Have students identify the characteristics shared among these genres as well as the differences.

Focus Question

Have students read the Focus Question on Worktext page 31. Tell students that the texts they will read will help them answer the question.

Texts for Close Reading

Have students read to themselves the summaries about the texts in this unit.

There is no need to explain what students should expect to find in their close readings or to do any pre-teaching about the subject matter.

TEXT COMPLEXITY

Playing Dodge Ball
- Style: documentary
- Knowledge demands: low
- Levels of meaning: inferential

The Future of Physical Education

Quantitative: 1060L

Qualitative
- Structure: conventional
- Language: academic
- Knowledge demands: medium
- Levels of meaning: literal

Change in Gender Equity

Quantitative: 1090L

Qualitative
- Structure: conventional
- Language: academic
- Knowledge demands: high
- Levels of meaning: literal

Senate Resolution 462

Qualitative
- Structure: conventional
- Language: academic
- Knowledge demands: high
- Levels of meaning: literal

Playing Dodge Ball

Set a Purpose

Explain to students that they will look at the image on page 32 to understand how views on equality and athletics have changed over time.

Visual Text Analysis

Remind students that an image can be analyzed as a text by looking at its details and making inferences. Direct students' attention to the image on Student Worktext page 32.

1. Have students record their immediate impressions after they look at the image. Lead them to discuss as a whole class, in small groups, or with a partner what they think is happening in the photograph.

2. Encourage students to make note of the details that support their observations in question 1. Have students explain as a whole class, in small groups, or with a partner what details they noted and what those details tell them about how views on equality and athletics have changed over time.

3. Tell students to record their thoughts and feelings about the image. Have them discuss how these reactions deepen their understanding of the Visual Text.

Provide any additional information you feel is appropriate to enhance the discussion as necessary to support your students:

- Dodge ball was invented in Africa over 200 years ago as a deadly activity used to train warriors.
- The National Dodgeball League is a professional league founded in the U.S. in 2004. NDL teams are open to both men and women.

VISUAL TEXT

High School Students Playing Dodge Ball in Gym

Look at the Visual Text to answer the following questions. Review the image or parts of the image as many times as necessary.

1. What is happening in this photograph?

Sample answer: Kids in a gym are playing a game that looks like dodge ball. A young woman is supervising.

2. What details support your answer to the previous question?

Sample answer: I can see boys and a girl in matching clothes. There is a woman with a whistle who looks like a coach. There are several balls and the kids are in motion.

3. When you look again, what are you thinking and feeling?

Sample answer: The game seems intense because the players look determined, but the coach looks calm so it must be a friendly game. I wonder if it is boys against girls because the boys are on one side, and on the opposite side, only a girl is in the photo.

32 • Unit 2

PROFESSIONAL DEVELOPMENT

Intertextual Analysis: Incorporating Information from a Visual Text

What Is It? Close-reading techniques can be applied to visual texts in order to gain deeper meaning from them and to connect them with other texts.

Why Is It Important? Visual texts may contain information that cannot easily be transmitted through words. There are many historical examples of powerful images that changed public opinion where written reports could not. Being able to analyze images—including images intended to influence viewers—is a critical citizenship skill.

TEXT 1

✔ Self-Monitoring Strategies you used to help you check your understanding as you read.

☐ Visualize. ☐ Draw conclusions. ☐ Ask yourself questions. ☐ Reread to clarify.

Read the text to learn about the early role of sports in the classroom. Make annotations in the text and write your notes in the Annotation Notes column.

Sample annotations and notes appear throughout the text.

The Future of Physical Education

by Dudley Allen Sargent

Dudley Allen Sargent was the director of the Hemenway Gymnasium at Harvard University from 1879 to 1919.

1 As a preliminary step to a sane consideration of physical education in the colleges, the subject must receive the necessary attention in the elementary and preparatory schools. Here ? children must be allowed more freedom of movement—to run, jump, climb, swim, dive, skate, and play. This is the age in which the elementary work in the so-called heavy gymnastics should be begun. And every effort should be made to teach children the correct way of doing things. In regard to group or class gymnastics, elect those exercises, which children most delight in. Then get them to imitate the instructor as to the accuracy, order, rhythm, and harmony of the movements.

2 The work begun in the elementary schools should be carried on progressively through the secondary schools. Take advantage ! of the boy's innate desire at this time to test his strength and courage. Every effort should be made to enrich the routine work in gymnastics and physical training. Introduce group contests, antagonistic exercises, and field, track and water sports and games.

3 The ability and character of the men chosen for physical instructors during the secondary-school period should be superior to that of any other instructor. More than any other teaching staff, they can exert more influence for good or evil at this time. As this is the period when the boy's character and physique is forming, every effort should be made to apply the teachings of the classroom and lecture hall. Hygiene, ethics, economics, and religion should be applied to the practice of the field, track, and gymnasium. Long and careful training,

ANNOTATION NOTES

1st Read:
Argument: Physical education should be taught from an early age and continued throughout all years of school.

2nd Read:
begins with clear claim

repeated use of *should*—what they need to do

In paragraph 1 he refers to "children," but in paragraph 2 it's just boys.

3rd Read:
Author is speaking only of boys but advice applies today to girls as well.

How Do I Use It? Reference the Visual Text frequently when comparing across texts during unit instruction. Make specific comparisons that allow students to make connections, such as, *What similarities are there in the authors' arguments for equality in athletics?* Encourage students to provide text evidence when supporting connections to the Visual Text. For example, *I know Title IX broke down barriers for girls and women because I can see in the photograph not only a girl athlete, but also a woman coach.*

The Future of Phys. Ed.

Tell students that they will read to learn about the early role of sports in the classroom.

1st READ

Set a Purpose

Tell students they will be reading to find out what this text is about.

Have students read "The Future of Physical Education" independently, annotating as they read. Circulate and make notes of students' markings, questions, and confusions. Your notes can be used to inform instruction and as data for informal assessment.

Text-Dependent Questions

1. What is the main idea of this text? (Physical education early in life builds "better scholars" and men "prepared with vigor, zeal, and earnestness to fight the battles of the weak.")

2. Why does the author believe physical education should start early? (He states that instructors can make use of a young boy's "innate desire . . . to test his strength and courage," and that this is "when the boy's character and physique is forming.")

3. **Vocabulary: Multiple-Meaning Words** Discuss contextual meanings of familiar words and phrases.

Paragraph 4: What does "regime" refer to in this sentence: "If time cannot be found for such a regime in the present overcrowded curriculum, then the mental requirements to enter college should be reduced." (Regime refers to the emphasis on physical training and body-building in college.)

Partner Talk Have students discuss ways in which participating in sports affects a person's future.

The Future of Phys. Ed.

2nd READ

Set a Purpose

Tell students they will read to understand how the author uses language to make his argument.

Text-Dependent Questions

1. How does the author describe the kinds of activities that will build a strong character? (In paragraph 3, he directs instructors to use "long and careful," "rough and strenuous," and "hard, exciting" activities to build students' characters.)

Scaffolded Support Use the following scaffolded question and sentence frames as necessary to build comprehension.

What kinds of activities does Sargent suggest?

Sargent believes training should be ________ and ________, games should be ________ and ________, and contests should be ________. He claims these kinds of activities provide ________ and ________.

2. What criticism does the author level at some individual college athletes? (In paragraph 5, he says that some college athletes use "intentional foul tactics" and play in a "dirty, brutal" way just to help their team "win victories.")

3. How does the author convey the benefits of starting physical education early? (In paragraph 6, the author shares "a catalogue of virtues to attribute to physical education," which include "alertness," "perseverance," "rapid and responsible exercise of judgment," and "obedience.")

Partner Talk Have students discuss how the author uses language to present his views.

TEXT 1

ANNOTATION NOTES

1st Read:
Playing sports at secondary school is important for college and life.

physical fitness just as important as mental fitness

2nd Read:
reread paragraph 3: basic principles of self-government and civic righteousness

3rd Read:
Physical fitness from a young age makes old age better.

Colleges should hold athletes and physical instructors to a higher moral standard.

rough and strenuous games, hard, exciting contests—these all afford the best possible opportunity for building the basic ? principles of self-government and civic righteousness.

4 When a boy comes to college, he should enter well trained in body as well as mind. At the present time, an ambitious boy is likely to neglect his physique. Instead, he may overapply himself mentally in the hope of taking a high stand in scholarship. The adoption of this measure would tend to place the greater part of physical training and body-building where it belongs, that is, in the homes and preparatory schools. If time cannot be found for such a regime in the present overcrowded curriculum, then the mental requirements to enter college should be reduced. With a good physique, a man may continue to increase his intellectual power and efficiency up to fifty or sixty years of age. With a poor physique he is liable to break down at any time. That remains true even though his early years may be replete with fine mental attainments.

5 All of the intentional foul tactics, and dirty, brutal play in which individual college athletes have indulged in their team contests, have frequently been unhesitatingly condoned by the college. That's because such tactics enabled the team to win victories. But all of these mistaken methods, in the best institutions at least, are slowly passing away. I believe that students throughout the country are awaking to a sense of ! their moral and ethical as well as intellectual responsibility to the community. They are learning that they cannot afford to have a man on an athletic team who will not play fair. The moral standard of the team must measure up to that of the individual men who make it.

6 These are some of the lessons which the college student is slowly learning through his athletic experiences. When these later-day experiences have been preceded by the preparatory-school drills in the sports, games, and physical activities to which we have referred, we shall have a catalogue of virtues to attribute to physical education. Among these will be increased powers of attention; increased development of the will; greater accumulation of energy; greater accuracy in execution; alertness; quickness of perception; and perseverance. These virtues will also include rapid and responsible exercise of judgment; patience; obedience; self-control; loyalty; courage of convictions; and willingness to serve any cause that makes for the betterment of man.

PROFESSIONAL DEVELOPMENT

Productive Conversation: Providing Appropriate Wait Time

What Is It? Wait time is intentional silence after asking a question or giving a prompt.

Why Is It Important? Wait time allows students to think and/or look through the text for supporting evidence. Comfortable, frequent wait time takes pressure off students who may read or respond at a slower pace.

How Do I Use It? Be consistent in the use of wait time. For questions posed to the class, provide a lengthy pause even if some students are ready to answer immediately. A good way to gauge wait time is to ask students to indicate when they have an answer and allow enough time for 80 percent of students to

These, I say, are some of the virtues that may be developed through physical activities. Again, I say conduct and character are not to be molded through self-denial and the practice of ! inhibitions only. They are wrought out largely through daring, doing, and achieving.

This illustration shows a football match between Yale and Princeton in 1879. At the time, only men were allowed to attend these schools.

7 ? When the college authorities throughout the land recognize these latent possibilities in athletics, and when college students recognize the significance of mental training as well as physical training as a preparation for their life's work, this recognition of the unity of mind and body will make for the unity of college education in general. In other words, both parties will realize ! that it is the whole man that is to be educated. The college as a whole must assume the responsibility for the job. When this time comes our institutions of learning will not only turn out better scholars but men better prepared with vigor, zeal and earnestness to fight the battles of the weak. They will be better able to meet the game of the unprincipled strong; and wrestle with the great moral, social, political, and financial problems that await them in the world at large as soon as their college days are over.

ANNOTATION NOTES

1st Read:
Physical education is about both the body and the mind.

2nd Read:
catalogue of virtues = long list of virtues to make his main point

latent = dormant, waiting to be developed

3rd Read:
Education of the "whole man" will improve society as a whole, too.

Physical health and courage are reflected in moral courage.

respond. When asking a single student to respond, hold back on calling on another student too quickly. Gently quiet other students who volunteer. Make it a classroom guideline that when you call on one student, that student will be the first to respond. Have peers practice wait time by assigning small groups and partners a period of silence before discussing a question or prompt. A classroom timer may be effective.

The Future of Phys. Ed.

3rd READ

Set a Purpose

Tell students they will read to understand the author's argument.

Text-Dependent Questions

1. In paragraph 3, Sargent states that secondary school physical education teachers "exert more influence for good or evil" than other teachers. What does he mean? (A boy's "character and physique is forming" at this time; physical education teachers can apply "hygiene, ethics, economics, and religion" to their instruction where other teachers can't.)

2. According to the author, how does one develop virtues and character? (In paragraph 6, the author states that "self-denial and the practice of inhibitions only" won't develop character, but "daring, doing, and achieving" through "physical activities" will.)

Think Aloud *In paragraph 7, Sargent states that men who have trained both their "mind and body" are better able to "wrestle" many of the "great moral, social, political and financial problems that await them in the world." I conclude that the author's view is that early physical education benefits not only the student, but all of society.*

Partner Talk Have students discuss how early physical education might contribute to an individual's wider life.

Return to the TEXT

Respond to Reading

You may want to check students' understanding by having them complete pages 36–37 in the Student Worktext.

1. Remind students to review their annotations and recall discussions they've had in order to complete the summary chart. Remind students that only evidence from the text should be included in the summary chart.

As students complete their summary charts, circulate and note which students struggle to identify the correct text evidence. Some students may benefit from small group instruction.

2. Remind students to include only the most important information in their summaries.

Have students work independently to complete page 36 of their Worktexts.

COLLABORATE When finished, have students exchange summaries with their partners and share their insights.

Return to the TEXT

Respond to Reading: The Future of Physical Education

Review your annotations and notes.
Think about how they can help you summarize the text.

1. Use this chart to help you summarize the text.

Summary Chart

	Informational Text	
Who?	the people or subjects	students (boys)
What?	the topic or problem	when physical education and sports should begin
Where?	the location or region events occur	elementary and preparatory schools, secondary school, college
When?	the date, year, or time	written some time around 1900
How?	the events, steps, or processes	Physical activity and sports should begin early: they teach many virtues, which keep the mind as healthy as the body.

2. Write a 2–3 sentence summary of *The Future of Physical Education.*

Sample summary: Physical education is as important as academics. Engaging in physical activity and sports at an early age prepares a student, physically and mentally, for college. The author says, "When a boy comes to college, he should enter well trained in body as well as mind." Physical education tests and builds a young man's character, and a "catalogue of virtues" developed through physical activity will last beyond college.

PROFESSIONAL DEVELOPMENT

Collaboration: Whole Class

What Is It? Whole-class work involves all students working on a specific task as a group. Depending on class size and ability, whole-class collaboration may consist of call-and-response contributions or monitored discussions.

Why Is It Important? While whole-class instruction may not address targeted differentiation, the size and diversity of a full-class group can nonetheless be a tool to help students model, self-monitor, and observe.

Return to the TEXT

3. According to the author, what kind of physical education should children receive in elementary school? Support your answer with evidence from the text.

Sample answer: In paragraph 1, the author states that children should do activities that they delight in, such as "run, jump, climb, swim, dive, skate, and play."

4. Based on information in the text, in what ways does the continuous study of physical education help boys? Provide text evidence to support your response.

Sample answer: Through physical education, a boy would know about "hygiene, ethics, economics, and religion" and about "self-government and civic righteousness" (paragraph 3). As stated in paragraph 4, he would be sound in "body as well as mind" into his adult life.

5. Explain how the author's words and phrases define physical education. What inferences can you make based on the author's description of physical education?

Sample answer: Physical education fulfills a "boy's innate desire...to test his strength" and become a man, which means that sports and games are a natural part of development. The author explains that excellent physical education instructors can make a big difference in a boy's development. In college is where he learns how to become a "whole man," through "mental training as well as physical training." I infer that the author believes that physical strength and mental strength are related.

REFLECT What questions did you ask yourself about the text to make sure you understood the text?

Sample answer: As I read paragraph 5, I asked myself why the colleges would condone "foul tactics" and "dirty, brutal play." I read on and saw that it was because they could win with these strategies.

How Do I Use It? To facilitate collaboration, whole-class work should not function as a lecture. A teacher serves as both a participant and a moderator. Before lessons, plan the types of questions you might ask in a monitored collaborative discussion, including scaffolding where needed. Be flexible in order to accommodate unexpected developments, including difficulties and new areas of student inquiry.

Return to the TEXT

Encourage students to refer back to the text and their annotations and notes to help them answer the questions.

3. You can support students by directing them to paragraph 1.

4. Support students by directing them to paragraphs 3 and 4. Have them note the author's ultimate goals for students beyond physical prowess and ability in sports.

5. Suggest that students review the text again, looking for words or phrases that describe how the author defines and views physical education.

Have students work independently to complete page 37 of their Worktexts.

REFLECT Remind students that asking yourself questions is a **Self-Monitoring Strategy** and that they made annotations and notes about confusions they may have had. Suggest that they review their annotations and think about any words, phrases, or sections that they asked themselves questions about to check their comprehension of the text.

Return to the TEXT

Stop and Assess

Use the following to assess your students' understanding of the text.

Item 1 answers indicate:	
2	the author believes early physical education forms habits that affect one's whole life. Two pieces of text evidence support the answer.
1	the author believes early physical education benefits one's whole life. Supporting evidence is insufficient.
0	a lack of understanding of why the author believes physical education should begin early.

Item 2 answers indicate:	
2	terms that physical education creates ethical men. Two pieces of text evidence support the answer.
1	terms that physical education creates ethical men. Only one piece of text evidence supports the answer.
0	a lack of understanding of the main argument or no terms supporting the main argument are provided.

Item 3 answers indicate:	
2	that physical education was not widely respected when the text was written. Two pieces of text evidence support the answer.
1	that physical education was not widely respected. Supporting text evidence is insuffient.
0	no understanding of how physical education was viewed when Sargent wrote the text and no text evidence is cited.

Option: If you choose not to work with Texts 2 and 3 and to conclude the unit here, use the Visual Text and "The Future of Physical Education" to answer the Focus Question: How have views on equality and athletics changed over time?

Return to the TEXT

Comprehension Check: The Future of Physical Education

Answer the questions to demonstrate an understanding of what the text means.

1. What was most likely the author's purpose in starting his article with a description of elementary school physical education?

Sample answer: In paragraph 1, the author sets the foundation for his argument that physical education is a lifelong pursuit. He continues his argument by stating that it must begin "in the elementary and preparatory schools" as "a preliminary step" and continue on to "physical education in the colleges" in order to form lasting habits for one's whole life.

2. What terms does the author use to support his main argument? Use details from the text to support your answer.

Sample answer: The words *moral* and *virtue* are used several times and the words *ethics* and *ethical* are also included the article. Sargent's main argument is that physical education is part of the education of the "whole man." He believes men will have to fight "evil" and the "unprincipled strong." In order to do so, they will need to have a strong character, which a strong body helps to build. His use of these terms reminds his audience that sports is more than just simple games.

3. Was physical education widely respected at the time that Sargent wrote his article? Support your answer with evidence from the text.

Sample answer: The text indicates that physical education was not important at the time. In paragraph 4, Sargent says that "an ambitious boy is likely to neglect his physique" because he overapplies himself mentally. In paragraph 5, he also points out that some college athletes are allowed to cheat in order to win, which shows a lack of moral virtues, which is part of proper physical education as he defines it.

PROFESSIONAL DEVELOPMENT

Annotations: Key Words and Phrases

What Is It? Annotations are marks that students make as they read the text, such as highlighting, underlining, and circling key words. Students add annotations in layers as they read and reread.

Why Is It Important? Making annotations helps keep students' attention focused on specific words. Students can mark places of confusion, note questions to ask, or write their own reactions to text information. Making personal marks on a page makes the reading experience personal.

How Do I Use It? As you introduce Text 2, model how to annotate by underlining *Title IX* in the title and then circling *civil rights*

Read to find out about federal legislation for equal rights in education. If you need to read any sections more than once, note the reason in the Annotation Notes column.
Sample annotations and notes appear throughout the text.

Title IX: A Sea Change in Gender Equity in Education

Athletic competition builds character in our boys. We do not need that kind of character in our girls.

—Connecticut judge, 1971

No person in the United States shall, on the basis of sex, be excluded from participation in, be denied the benefits of, or be subject to discrimination under any educational programs or activity receiving federal financial assistance.

—From the preamble to Title IX of the Education Amendments of 1972

Title IX increased girls' opportunities to participate in school sports programs, but its mandate was much broader.

1 Civil rights laws have always been a powerful mechanism for effecting social change in the United States. They represent a national commitment to end discrimination. They also establish a mandate to bring the excluded into the mainstream. These laws ensure that the federal government delivers on the ! Constitution's promise. It's a promise of equal opportunity so that every individual has the right to develop his or her talents.

2 Title IX of the Education Amendments of 1972 supports this national agenda. It prohibits sex discrimination in federally assisted education programs. Modeled on Title VI of the Civil Rights Act of 1964 prohibiting race, color, and national origin

ANNOTATION NOTES

1st Read:
Title IX is a law.
It's modeled after past laws that fought discrimination.

The laws were passed in the 1960s and 1970s.

2nd Read:
Quotations at start of passage show contrasting points of view about the topic.

mandate = authority to carry out a policy

3rd Read:
Once one law against discrimination passed, others quickly followed.

laws in paragraph 1. Then think aloud to demonstrate that annotations can be used to keep track of key facts and clear up confusions. *Paragraph 1 explains that civil rights "ensure that the federal government delivers on the Constitution's promise." I'm going to reread the paragraph to make sure I understand what "promise" the article's talking about, since this promise seems to inspire all civil rights laws. I think the answer is in this sentence: "It's a promise of equal opportunity so that every individual has the right to develop his or her talents." This looks like a very important idea, so I'll mark it, and then keep it in mind as I continue reading.*

Change in Gender Equity

Tell students they will read to learn about federal legislation for equal rights in education.

1st READ

Set a Purpose

Tell students they will be reading to find out what this text is about.

Have students read "Title IX: A Sea Change in Gender Equity in Education" independently, annotating the text as they read. Circulate and note students' markings, especially questions and confusions.

Text-Dependent Questions

1. What is the main idea of this text? (Title IX, which "prohibits sex discrimination in federally assisted education programs," created "profound changes in American education" and "made a positive difference" in many Americans' lives.)

2. What role did the women's civil rights movement play in the creation of Title IX? (It "focus[ed] attention on inequities" for girls in education, which led to "a higher education bill with provisions regarding sex equity.")

3. Vocabulary: Domain-Specific Words Discuss making connections to meanings of known words.

Paragraph 6: In physics, *momentum* is the impetus gained by a moving object. Explain what "As the women's civil rights movement gained momentum" means. (It's referring to a time when the women's civil rights movement was starting to make gains in a way that couldn't be stopped.)

Partner Talk Have students discuss how the percentage of female college graduates changed after Title IX became law.

Change in Gender Equity

2nd READ

Set a Purpose

Tell students they will read to understand how the text's structure and language support its message.

Text-Dependent Questions

1. How does the report establish a credible voice in the text? (The report uses academic language such as *mandate, civil rights legislation,* and *gender discrimination,* and provides statisics in paragraph 7 to support the main idea.)

2. How does the report guide readers through the text? (The report uses subheadings to introduce and emphasize the main idea of each section.)

Scaffolded Support Use the following scaffolded question and sentence frame as necessary to build comprehension.

How is information organized? Each section has a ________ that tells readers ________.

3. How important are the statistics provided in paragraph 7? Why? (The statistics are very important because without them, some readers may not be convinced that Title IX helped all Americans, not just girls.)

Think Aloud *The report mentions different "Titles" and legislation in paragraph 2, and I don't clearly understand what is what. As I slowly reread the paragraph, I see that Title IX was written in 1972 and was modeled on Title VI, which was written in 1964 and prohibits "race, color, and national origin discrimination."*

Partner Talk Have students discuss the language used to describe civil rights laws.

ANNOTATION NOTES

1st Read:
Title IX has made a difference for women—"improvements in educational and related job opportunities."

2nd Read:
"snapshot" report = a quick look at key moments

report uses statistics to support argument with facts

3rd Read:
Saying U.S. is "a world leader in opening the doors of higher education to women" suggests other countries will follow the example.

discrimination, it was followed by three other pieces of civil rights legislation. These prohibited disability discrimination, age discrimination, and disability discrimination by public entities.

3 Twenty-five years after its passage, we recognize and celebrate Title IX. This legislation has brought about profound changes in American education. It has resulted in improvements in educational and related job opportunities for millions of young Americans. While no study has been done on the full impact of Title IX, this "snapshot" report suggests that Title IX has made a positive difference in the lives of many Americans.

Women now make up the majority of students in America's colleges and universities.

4 Substantial progress has been made, for example, in overcoming the gap between men and women in completing four years of college. In 1971, 18 percent of female high school graduates were completing at least four years of college. This was in comparison to 26 percent of their male peers. Today, that education gap no longer exists. Women now make up the majority of students in America's colleges and universities. They also make up the majority of those receiving master's degrees. Women are also entering business and law schools in record numbers. Indeed, the United States stands alone as a world leader in opening the doors of higher education to women.

5 As this report makes clear, many barriers have been brought down that once prevented girls and women from choosing the educational opportunities and careers they would have liked to pursue. The history of this progress begins 25 years ago with the passage of Title IX.

The Legislative Road to Title IX

6 As the women's civil rights movement gained momentum in the late 1960s and early 1970s, Americans began to focus attention on inequities that inhibited the progress of women

PROFESSIONAL DEVELOPMENT

Think-Aloud Modeling

What Is It? Remind students that close reading is not a passive activity. Skilled readers employ a variety of **Self-Monitoring Strategies** to ensure they fully comprehend a text's meaning. Model the use of one of these strategies with a Think Aloud to verbally "walk" through the thought process.

Why Is It Important? Think Alouds that model a **Self-Monitoring Strategy** demonstrate how to read closely. Frequent modeling of a variety of strategies demonstrates that some strategies work better than others for specific comprehension challenges. This exposure will help your students internalize and employ the strategies more often on their own.

TEXT 2

and girls in education. The issue of sex bias in education moved into the public policy realm when Representative Edith Green (Oregon) introduced a higher education bill with provisions regarding sex equity. The hearings that Green held were the first ever devoted to this topic. They are considered the first legislative step toward the enactment of Title IX.

In the 1960s and 1970s, rallies and marches showed support for equal rights for women.

Everyone Benefits from Title IX

7 Title IX prohibits institutions that receive federal funding from practicing gender discrimination in educational programs ! or activities. Because almost all schools receive federal funds, Title IX applies to nearly everyone. The Office for Civil Rights in the U.S. Department of Education is charged with enforcing the civil rights and regulations in education, extending protection to

- about 51.7 million elementary and secondary school students;
- about 14.4 million college and university students;
- almost 15,000 school districts;
- more than 3,600 colleges and universities;
- more than 5,000 proprietary schools; and
- thousands of libraries, museums, vocational rehabilitation agencies, and correctional facilities.

ANNOTATION NOTES

1st Read:
two key points:
(1) there is a legal history behind the law; and
(2) the law does not affect only women

2nd Read:
Subheads reinforce key points.

statistics show law's relevancy and far reach

inequities = opposite of equity

3rd Read:
Text suggests that everyone benefits when discrimination is eliminated.

Law has impact on how funding is provided to schools even today.

How Do I Use It? Use the Think Alouds provided in the lessons. Use additional Think Alouds at points in the text where you predict a comprehension challenge, or when you note one or more students are struggling. Keep your Think Alouds brief and focused on a particular challenge.

Change in Gender Equity

3rd READ

Set a Purpose

Tell students they will read to make inferences about the text.

Text-Dependent Questions

1. Does the article present Title IX in a positive or negative light? Provide text evidence to support your opinion. (In pargraphs 4 and 5, the text refers to the "progress" in women's civil rights that have resulted from Title IX. This puts the legislation in a very positive light.)

Scaffolded Support Use the following scaffolded sentence frame and question as necessary to build comprehension.

Title IX helped to bring about progress in ________.

Does the word *progress* have a positive or negative connotation?

2. How does ensuring equity for one group help all people? (In paragraph 7, the article explains that Title IX "prohibits institutions that receive federal funding from practicing gender discrimination," and that "almost all schools receive federal funds," Title IX helps "nearly everyone.")

3. Vocabulary: Multiple-Meaning Words Discuss contextual meaning of familiar words and phrases.

Paragraph 7: What does *charged* mean in the phrase "charged with enforcing"? (In this context, *charged* means "officially responsible for.")

Partner Talk Have students discuss the effects of Title IX they see in their own school.

Stop and Assess

Use the following to assess your students' understanding of the text.

Item 1 answers indicate:	
2	the quotations show contrasting attitudes about females participating in sports. Two pieces of text evidence support the answer.
1	the quotations show contrasting attitudes about females in sports, but text evidence is insufficient.
0	a lack of understanding of the purpose of the two quotations. No supporting text evidence is cited.

Item 2 answers indicate:	
2	Title IX opened doors for women and cites laws and statistics to back the claim. Two pieces of text evidence support the answer.
1	Title IX opened doors for women and cites laws and statistics to back the claim, but text evidence is lacking.
0	no understanding of how Title IX affected women and cites no supporting text evidence.

Item 3 answers indicate:	
2	that as Title IX ended discrimination in schools, more girls participated in all programs. Two pieces of text evidence support the answer.
1	that Title IX ended discrimination in schools so more girls participated in all programs, but supporting text evidence is lacking.
0	a lack of understanding of the impact Title IX had on education. No supporting text evidence is cited.

Return to the TEXT

Comprehension Check: Title IX: A Sea Change

Answer the questions to demonstrate an understanding of what the text means.

1. What is the purpose of the two quotations at the beginning of the text? Why are those quotations included at the beginning of the passage?
   Sample answer: The quotations show a contrast in attitudes about the participation of females in sports. They prepare the reader for the possibility that not everyone agreed with the change.

2. What claim does the text make about Title IX? What support does the text provide for the claim? Use details from the text to support your answer.
   Sample answer: The text claims that Title IX opened doors for women, including repeatedly "overcoming the gap between men and women in completing four years of college." It cites past laws (paragraphs 2 and 6) and statistics (paragraphs 4 and 7) as factual evidence to support its claim.

3. What inference can you draw about the effect Title IX had on education in the United States? Cite evidence to support your answer.
   Sample answer: As stated in paragraph 2, Title IX ended discrimination in all educational activities. Therefore, I can infer that public institutions everywhere saw an increase in participation by females in subject areas that had been thought of as male domains. That led to more women working at jobs in those areas.

PROFESSIONAL DEVELOPMENT

Visual Supports: Visual Learners

What Is It? Visual learners prefer pictorial information such as maps, diagrams, and images over verbal descriptions.

Why Is It Important? Visual learners benefit from visual supports in many contexts, including when background knowledge is limited or when a text includes unfamiliar or difficult vocabulary. When you include a variety of visual supports as differentiated scaffolding prior to, during, and after a text reading, you provide visual learners with the tools they need to best comprehend the text.

Read to find out about the Senate's call in May 2016 for equal pay for female soccer players. You may want to read some sections more than once and make different annotations and Annotation Notes each time.

Sample annotations and notes appear throughout the text.

Senate Resolution 462

by Senator Patty Murray

1 Urging the United States Soccer Federation to immediately eliminate gender pay inequity and treat all athletes with the same respect and dignity.

2 • Whereas title IX of the Education Amendments of 1972 (20 U.S.C. 1681 et seq.) (referred to in this preamble as "title IX") requires schools and institutions of higher education to provide the same opportunities for girls as they do for boys;

3 • Whereas 6 years after the date of enactment of title IX, the approximate percentage of girls playing team sports increased from 4 percent to 25 percent, a sixfold increase;

4 • Whereas the participation of girls in team sports results in lifelong improvements to the educational, work, and health prospects of the girls;

5 • Whereas the United States Women's National Team has won 3 Federation Internationale de Football Association (commonly referred to as "FIFA") Women's World Cups, 4 Olympic Gold Medals, and 7 Confederation of North, Central America, and Caribbean Association Football (commonly referred to as "CONCACAF") Gold Cups;

6 • Whereas the United States Women's National Team is ranked first in the world as of the date of adoption of this resolution;

7 • Whereas the 2015 final Women's World Cup match generated an audience of approximately 750,000,000 viewers worldwide and more than 25,000,000 viewers in the United States, the largest audience of any soccer game shown in the United States on English language television;

8 • Whereas the members of the United States Women's National Team are some of the most visible athletes in the world and serve as an inspiration and as role models to young athletes across the United States and worldwide;

ANNOTATION NOTES

1st Read:
The Senator believes that the U.S. Women's National Team is not getting paid fairly.

She builds her case by citing title IX, health benefits of sports, and showing team accomplishments.

2nd Read:
first paragraph is continuation of title

Paragraphs are not full sentences.

"whereas" similar to "because"

3rd Read:
wide viewer audience = bigger economic opportunities for sponsors

How Do I Use It? Preview the visuals and text layout for "Senate Resolution 462" to anticipate where visual learners will need support. Provide background information as necessary to help them access content in the image. Make use of visual learners' skills to pull meaning from images for the class.

Senate Resolution 462

Students will read to find out about the Senate's call for equal pay for female soccer players.

1st READ

Set a Purpose

Explain to students that they will be reading to find out what this text is about. Have students read "Senate Resolution 462" independently, annotating the text.

Text-Dependent Questions

1. What is the main idea of the text? (Sample answer: The main idea is that, despite the fact that the women on the U.S. Women's National Soccer Team are "ranked first in the world" as of the adoption of the resolution, and are "some of the most visible athletes in the world," they are "paid less than similarly situated members" of the men's team. The text outlines why gender pay inequity must end.)

2. What connection exists between the Equal Pay Act of 1963 and this resolution? (Sample answer: The Equal Pay Act stated that "women deserve equal pay for equal work.")

Partner Talk Have students discuss why Senator Murray urged the passing of Resolution 462.

Senate Resolution 462

2nd READ

Set a Purpose

Students will read to learn how the author structures and supports her message.

Text-Dependent Questions

1. How does Senator Murray convey the abilities of the United States Women's National Team? **(She lists what they have won and mentions that the team was "ranked first in the world" when the resolution was adopted.)**

2. What does Senator Murray outline in paragraphs 13–16? **(She details what needs to be done to ensure that women athletes are paid fairly.)**

Partner Talk Have students discuss how the details in the text affected their comprehension.

3rd READ

Set a Purpose

Tell students they will reread to make inferences from the text.

Text-Dependent Questions

1. Why is Title IX relevant to this resolution? **(Title IX resulted in more girls participating in sports.)**

2. What can you infer about Senator Murray's opinion on gender pay inequity? **(I believe she thinks gender pay inequity is unfair and insulting. This resolution is a call for equal pay for women, and in paragraph 14, she states that "all athletes" should be treated with "respect and dignity.")**

Partner Talk Have students discuss connections between this resolution and Text 1.

TEXT 3

ANNOTATION NOTES

1st Read:
This resolution demands equal pay for the women's team.

2nd Read:
Equal Pay Act (1963) and the Civil Rights Act (1964) cited to support demand

urges, *supports*, and *instructs* = call to action

almost entire text is one sentence

3rd Read:
Senate resolution shows support for women's soccer team but does not take any action. We do not know the outcome.

The U.S. Women's National Team won the 2015 Women's World Cup.

9 • Whereas the members of the United States Women's National Team, despite the international success of the members, are consistently paid less than similarly situated members of the United States Men's National Team for doing the same job, regardless of the performance of the teams;

10 • Whereas, in 1963, Congress passed and President Kennedy signed the landmark Equal Pay Act of 1963 (29 U.S.C. 201 note; Public Law 88–38) (referred to in this preamble as the "Equal Pay Act"), unequivocally affirming that women deserve equal pay for equal work;

11 • Whereas the enactment of the Equal Pay Act laid the groundwork for title VII of the Civil Rights Act of 1964 (42 U.S.C. 2000e et seq.) and title IX, which together vastly expanded opportunities for girls and women at school and work;

12 • Whereas unequal pay on the basis of gender violates generally held beliefs regarding equality and fundamental fairness; Now, therefore, be it

13 *Resolved*, That the Senate—

14 (1) urges the United States Soccer Federation to immediately end gender pay inequity and to treat all athletes with the respect and dignity those athletes deserve;

15 (2) supports an end to pay discrimination based on gender and the strengthening of equal pay protections; and

16 (3) instructs the Secretary of the Senate to submit a copy of this resolution to the United States Soccer Federation.

PROFESSIONAL DEVELOPMENT

Text Complexity: High-Knowledge Demands

What Is It? Some texts have a concentration of domain-specific vocabulary and concepts that demand higher-order thinking from readers. Even the best readers must read slowly and closely, and additional domain-specific knowledge might be needed to achieve full comprehension.

Why Is It Important? The ability to work through complex texts and meet high knowledge demands without discouragement is essential to students in education, in training for jobs that require technical knowledge, and in meeting the demands of a complex world.

Comprehension Check: Senate Resolution 462

Answer the questions to demonstrate an understanding of what the text means.

1. What argument does the author make in paragraph 8?
What evidence does she give to support the argument?
Is the evidence convincing? Support your answer with details from the text.
Sample answer: She claims that the U.S. Women's National Team are some of the most visible athletes in the world and serve as role models. She lists the awards the team has won, cites their "first in the world" ranking in paragraph 6, and their huge television audience in paragraph 7. This evidence proves that they are some of the most visible athletes in the world. It is likely that the team would also inspire others because of these accomplishments.

2. What language and tone does the Senator take in paragraphs 12–16?
Give specific examples from the text.
Sample answer: The Senator has a no-nonsense tone and tells how she expects the problem to be resolved. She uses strong verbs, such as *urges, supports,* and *instructs.* She asks the United States Soccer Federation to act "immediately." She considers the treatment of the team a violation of basic rights and wants athletes to be treated with "respect and dignity."

3. What conclusions can you draw about gender equity in sports today based on this resolution? Cite evidence to support your answer.
Sample answer: Since the issue only reached the highest level of government in May 2016, I can conclude that gender inequity in sports still exists, and there is more work to be done before this issue is resolved.

How Do I Use It? Help students comprehend the meanings of the details and fit those details into a bigger picture. For "Senate Resolution 462," suggest that students "translate" each bulleted point and record the gist of the idea, using their own words, on a separate piece of paper. Have students identify and define unknown words and phrases and apply this knowledge to determining the text's main idea and purpose. Visual learners might use a main idea graphic organizer that allows them to identify the main idea and list supporting details.

Return to the TEXT

Stop and Assess

Use the following to assess your students' understanding of the text.

Item 1 answers indicate:	
2	the author cites convincing evidence that the U.S. Women's National Team are visible positive role models. Two pieces of text evidence support the answer.
1	the author cites evidence that the U.S. Women's National Team are visible positive role models, but text evidence is insufficient.
0	no understanding of the author's claim. No text evidence is cited.

Item 2 answers indicate:	
2	that the Senator uses a no-nonsense tone in the last five paragraphs. Two pieces of text evidence support the answer.
1	that the Senator uses a no-nonsense tone, but supporting text evidence is insufficient.
0	the reader doesn't understand the Senator's tone in the last five paragraphs. No text evidence is cited.

Item 3 answers indicate:	
2	that the issue of gender inequity in sports is being dealt with in a serious way, with logical supporting text evidence.
1	that the issue of gender inequity in sports is being dealt with in a serious way, but text evidence is weak.
0	no understanding of how gender inequity in sports is perceived or being dealt with today.

Return to the Focus Question

Explain to students that they will fill out a graphic organizer that helps them answer the Focus Question: How have views on equality and athletics changed over time?

CONNECT TEXTS Have small groups of students discuss how each text they read helps them answer the Focus Question.

Scaffolded Support You may provide the following sentence frames to support students in their use of academic language:

> In the text ________,
> the author/artist makes
> the point that ________.
> He/she does this
> by ________.

Remind students to use their annotations and summaries to support their answers. They can also reread portions of the texts, if necessary.

Have students complete their graphic organizers individually.

REFLECT Remind students that each text provides different information about how views on equality and athletics have changed over time. Ask, *How did reading all four texts give you a greater understanding of those changes?*

ANALYZE and SYNTHESIZE ACROSS TEXTS

Return to the Focus Question: How have views on equality and athletics changed over time?

Review your answers to questions about the texts as well as your annotations and Annotation Notes, and think about the discussions you've had about the texts. How does that information help you answer the Focus Question?

Use the graphic organizer to organize information about the texts.

1. In the appropriate box below, record the details that help you answer the Focus Question.
2. Make connections between those details to answer the Focus Question. Write your answer in the box provided.

Playing Dodge Ball (Visual Text)
Sample answer: Both boys and girls play sports in today's high schools.

Change in Gender Equity
Sample answer: Women gained the right to participate in publicly funded education programs.

The Future of Physical Education
Sample answer: Sports help develop boys' moral and physical strength.

Senate Resolution 462
Sample answer: Women athletes are not paid as much as men for the same sports-related jobs.

How have views on equality and athletics changed over time?
Sample answer: In the past, only boys and men could participate in athletics. Title IX was passed so girls and women had the same opportunities in schools and athletics. Later, a resolution was passed to end pay discrimination for women on the U.S. soccer team.

REFLECT How did making connections between the four texts enable you to answer the Focus Question?

Sample answer: The texts show how public attitudes about women in education and sports changed over time. Until laws and resolutions were passed for gender equity, only men were allowed to participate in sports and afforded more educational opportunities.

46 • Unit 2

PROFESSIONAL DEVELOPMENT

Differentiation: Multiple Graphic Organizers

What Is It? Graphic organizers are flow charts, grids, and other diagrams used to organize and connect ideas. Using multiple graphic organizers can be an effective strategy for tackling complex informational texts with high knowledge demands.

Why Is It Important? Using multiple graphic organizers helps students connect ideas in multiple ways. For example, a branching graphic organizer might help students identify main ideas and details, while a two-column grid or Venn diagram might help students compare those ideas. The more connections students make, the more deeply they will comprehend what they read.

Writing About the Focus Question

Now that you have answered the Focus Question using all four texts, expand on your thinking and communicate your ideas through your writing.

USE EVIDENCE

- Explain what you have learned about how views on equality and athletics have changed over time. Use at least one piece of evidence from the Visual Text and at least two pieces of evidence from Texts 1, 2, and 3 to support your answer.
- If you need more room, use additional paper.

MONITOR

- Use the Writing Checklist as you write to make sure your writing meets all the necessary criteria.
- Use the rubric on page 48 when you have completed a first draft of your writing to help you evaluate, revise, and edit your work.

WRITING CHECKLIST ✔

Does my writing . . .

- ☐ answer the Focus Question?
- ☐ have a clear organizational structure?
- ☐ cite the correct amount of text evidence?
- ☐ correctly use language, spelling, and conventions?

How Do I Use It? Select one graphic organizer format that serves the main purpose of a reading, such as exploring structure. In addition, select another graphic organizer format that focuses on a different aspect, such as language. Then have students compare the two organizers. For "Title IX: A Sea Change in Gender Equity in Education," the second organizer might be a simple two-column chart designed to compare what life was like for girls and women before and after the passage of Title IX. This helps students recognize the profound and far-reaching effects of this one law.

Writing About the Focus Question

USE EVIDENCE Remind students that they should use their graphic organizers as well as their annotations in the texts to write their responses.

Allow students to revisit the texts as frequently as they need to in order to support comprehension and to respond to the Focus Question.

MONITOR After students have completed their responses, have them review the Writing Checklist and revise their writing response.

DIFFERENTIATE AND EXTEND

In addition to or instead of the writing response, consider having students complete one of the following assignments:

Write Beyond Have students write a letter to the editor that details their response to "The Future of Physical Education."

Create a Visual Text Using images from magazines or online sources, have students create a visual display that answers the Focus Question.

Make a Plan Have students identify a situation in which they believe equality has not been legally ensured or enforced. Then, have them draft a bill outlining the changes they believe necessary to ensure equity for all.

Research Have students write a one-page biography on a female professional athlete of their choice.

SELF-ASSESS and REFLECT

SELF-ASSESS Have students use the Writing Rubric on page 48 to self-assess their writing response and write a final version. Tell them to assign themselves a score from 1–4 (with "4" being the highest) for each category in the first column.

Use the Writing Rubric on Student Worktext page 48 to assess each student's writing. Record points for each category in the first column of the rubric. Have students remove the page from their Student Worktexts and place it in their writing portfolios, along with the drafts and final versions of their responses.

SELF-ASSESS and REFLECT

Focus Question: How have views on equality and athletics changed over time?

This is the rubric that your teacher will use to assess your writing. Refer to it as you revise your work. After you have finished the final version of your response, assess your response and record your points for each category on the "Student" line in the first column.

	Accomplished (4 points)	Competent (3 points)	Developing (2 points)	Beginning (1 point)
RESPONSE Score: Student ____ Teacher ____	The response answers the question effectively and with insight.	The response answers the question effectively.	The response partially responds to the question but does not adequately address it.	The response addresses the texts but does not address the question.
ORGANIZATION Score: Student ____ Teacher ____	The main idea is convincingly stated. Ideas are organized in cohesive paragraphs that support the main idea.	The main idea is clearly stated. Ideas are organized in logical paragraphs.	The main idea is weak. Ideas are organized in a somewhat logical and cohesive way.	The main idea is missing. The organization of the paragraphs is not logical.
TEXT EVIDENCE Score: Student ____ Teacher ____	Response includes more than one piece of appropriate text evidence from each text. Evidence supports the main idea in a thorough way.	Response includes one piece of text evidence from each text. Evidence supports the main idea clearly.	Response does not include at least one piece of text evidence from each text. Text evidence does not adequately support the main idea.	Response does not contain relevant evidence.
LANGUAGE Score: Student ____ Teacher ____	Writing includes precise and sophisticated vocabulary related to the topic.	Writing includes appropriate vocabulary related to the topic.	Writing includes imprecise and inaccurate vocabulary.	Writing does not include vocabulary that appropriately reflects the topic of the response.
SPELLING AND CONVENTIONS Score: Student ____ Teacher ____	Response includes correct spelling, grammar, and punctuation consistently.	Response includes mostly correct spelling, grammar, and punctuation.	Response has many errors in spelling, grammar, and punctuation.	Response's errors in spelling, grammar, and punctuation make it extremely difficult to understand the response.

INTRODUCE THE UNIT

UNIT 3

Focus Question Why do people value the animals in their lives?

Texts for Close Reading

GENRE STUDY

Discuss with students the genres of *The Call of the Wild*, "Faithful and True," and "Spending on Pets."

Remind students that *genre* refers to the format and features of a text and typically falls into one of two categories—literature or informational text. Literature is a creative work that doesn't necessarily rely on facts, and informational text contains factual information.

The Call of the Wild is a traditional fictional novel with an unusual point of view, while both "Faithful and True" and "Spending on Pets" are informational. Ask students to identify elements of literature that might be found in an informational text and vice versa.

Focus Question

Have students read the Focus Question on Worktext page 49. Tell students that the texts they will read will help them answer the question.

Texts for Close Reading

Have students read to themselves the summaries about the texts in this unit.

There is no need to explain what students should expect to find in their close readings or to do any pre-teaching about the subject matter.

TEXT COMPLEXITY

Farmer working

- Style: documentary
- Knowledge demands: low
- Levels of meaning: literal

The Call of the Wild

Quantitative: 1080L

Qualitative

- Structure: conventional
- Language: narrative
- Knowledge demands: medium
- Levels of meaning: inferential

Faithful and True

Quantitative: 1120L

Qualitative

- Structure: conventional
- Language: familiar
- Knowledge demands: medium
- Levels of meaning: literal

Spending on Pets

Quantitative: 1050L

Qualitative

- Structure: conventional
- Language: academic
- Knowledge demands: low
- Levels of meaning: literal

Farmer working

Set a Purpose

Explain to students that they will look at the image on page 50 to gain a deeper understanding about relationships between humans and animals.

Visual Text Analysis

Remind students that an image can be analyzed as a text by looking at its details and making inferences. Direct students' attention to the image on Student Worktext page 50.

1. Have students record their immediate impressions after they look at the photo. Lead them to discuss as a whole class, in small groups, or with a partner what they think is happening in the photo.

2. Encourage students to list details that support their observations in their answers to question 1. Have students explain as a whole class, in small groups, or with a partner what conclusions they drew from the information in the photo.

3. Tell students to record their thoughts and feelings about the image. Have students discuss how these reactions deepen their understanding of the Visual Text.

Provide any additional information you feel is appropriate to enhance the discussion as necessary to support your students:

- People began domesticating animals with the advent of agriculture between 8000 and 2500 BCE.
- In general, we make a clear distinction between livestock—cows raised for milk production and other animals raised for slaughter—and pets.

VISUAL TEXT

Farmer working and tending to one of his animals

Look at the Visual Text to answer the following questions. Review the image or parts of the image as many times as necessary.

1. What is happening in this image?
   Sample answer: A farmer is caring for a calf.

2. What details from the image support your answer to the previous question?
   Sample answer: The man is wearing work clothes—gloves, heavy jacket, and high rubber boots. He's kneeling next to the calf on the straw-covered ground in front of what might be a barn, and he's touching the calf's face gently.

3. What inferences can you draw from the image?
   Sample answer: The man seems to feel kindly toward the animal, because he is being very gentle and smiling. Also, the calf must be used to this man as it is standing there very calmly.

PROFESSIONAL DEVELOPMENT

Intertextual Analysis: Incorporating Information from a Visual Text

What Is It? To incorporate information from a visual text, students follow a process similar to close reading. The first look at the image is the equivalent of the first read. Its purpose is to describe what the image shows. On the second "read," students look at visual details and composition. On the third "read," students analyze the message the image is trying to convey.

Why Is It Important? Because so much of what we learn is now conveyed by images, analyzing visual elements is a critical comprehension skill. Our comprehension of images

✔ Self-Monitoring Strategies you used to help you check your understanding as you read.

☐ Visualize. ☐ Draw conclusions. ☐ Ask yourself questions. ☐ Reread to clarify.

Read the text to learn about a relationship between a dog and his master. Make annotations in the text and write your notes in the Annotation Notes column.

Sample annotations and notes appear throughout the text.

The Call of the Wild

by Jack London

In this novel excerpt, the dog Buck is sold as a pack animal to a prospector in Alaska.

1 Love, genuine passionate love, was his for the first time. ? This he had never experienced at Judge Miller's down in the sun-kissed Santa Clara Valley. With the Judge's sons, hunting and tramping, it had been a working partnership; with the Judge's grandsons, a sort of pompous guardianship; and with the Judge himself, a stately and dignified friendship. But love that was feverish and burning, that was adoration, that was madness, it had taken John Thornton to arouse.

2 This man had saved his life, which was something; but, ? further, he was the ideal master. Other men saw to the welfare of their dogs from a sense of duty and business expediency; he saw to the welfare of his as if they were his own children, because he could not help it. And he saw further. He never forgot a kindly greeting or a cheering word, and to sit down for a long talk with them ("gas" he called it) was as much his delight as theirs. He had a way of taking Buck's head roughly between his hands, and resting his own head upon Buck's, of shaking him back and forth, the while calling him ill names that to Buck were love names. Buck knew no greater joy than that rough embrace and the sound of murmured oaths, and at each jerk back and forth it seemed that his heart would be shaken out of his body so great was its ecstasy. And when, released, he sprang to his feet, his mouth laughing, his eyes eloquent, his throat vibrant with unuttered sound, and in that fashion remained without movement, John Thornton would reverently exclaim, "God! you can all but speak!"

ANNOTATION NOTES

1st Read:
Buck is completely devoted to John Thornton because he saved his life and is an "ideal master."

2nd Read:
lots of emotional words: *love, passionate, kindly, cheering, ecstasy, laughing*

3rd Read:
Buck may have felt some friendship and a sense of duty toward his former owners, but he loves Thornton.

How did Thornton save Buck's life?

also enhances our comprehension of the verbal texts they accompany. For example, advertising imagery and copy can interact in complex ways to affect viewers.

How Do I Use It? Prompt students to try to identify the main idea of an image from the title and any labels. Then analyze the image's details and structure. For example, in the Visual Text for this unit, a man kneels next to a calf. The man wears clothing meant for working in the outdoors: rubber boots, a heavy jacket, leather gloves, and a cap. From these details, students should infer that the man is a farmer.

The Call of the Wild

Tell students that they will read to learn about a relationship between a dog and his master.

1st READ

Set a Purpose

Tell students they will be reading to identify the characters and setting.

Have students read the excerpt from *The Call of the Wild* independently, annotating as they read. Circulate and make notes of students' markings, questions, and confusions. Your notes can be used to inform instruction and as data for informal assessment.

Text-Dependent Questions

1. What is this text about? (This text is about a dog, Buck, and his relationship with his master, John Thornton.)

2. What is the main setting? (a camp in the wilderness of "the Northland")

Scaffolded Support Use the following scaffolded question and sentence frame as necessary to build comprehension.

What words in the text give you clues to the location?

The author uses the words ________ to identify the location.

Think Aloud *I'm confused about who is telling the story, so I will reread to clarify. The narrator describes feeling love for the first time, from a man named John Thornton. He talks about past masters and how John compares to them. The story is being told from the point of view of the dog, Buck.*

Partner Talk Have students discuss the relationship between the dog and his master.

The Call of the Wild

2nd READ

Set a Purpose

Tell students they will read to see how the author shows a relationship through language.

Text-Dependent Questions

1. What is the effect of the words the author uses to describe Buck's feelings? (Sample answer: "Genuine passionate love," "no greater joy," and "adoration" are examples of terms the author uses to characterize Buck's feelings toward Thornton. The description helps the reader understand the depth and intensity of the dog's feelings.)

2. What tone does London's language establish? (Sample answer: The tone is very emotional and intense.)

Scaffolded Support Use the following scaffolded question and sentence frame as necessary to build comprehension.

How do London's words make you feel?

The language gives the reader a feeling of ________.

3. Vocabulary: Figurative Language Discuss figurative meanings of familiar words.

Paragraph 6: What might "things born of fire and roof" mean in this sentence? (Sample answer: "Fire and roof" are symbols for living in a person's home as a pet, having warmth and shelter.)

Partner Talk Have students discuss how language helps create the text's point of view.

ANNOTATION NOTES

1st Read:
Buck is in the Northland. He has been abandoned before, so he fears Thornton will leave him. He watches Thornton's every move and responds to it.

2nd Read:
Point of view is the narrator's, but the narrator is usually seeing through Buck's eyes.

3rd Read:
Paragraph 6 hints that Buck has another side—foreshadowing?

Sled dogs are tough, loyal animals trained to pull heavy loads through harsh conditions.

3 Buck had a trick of love expression that was akin to hurt. He would often ! seize Thornton's hand in his mouth and close so fiercely that the flesh bore the impress of his teeth for some time afterward. And as Buck understood the oaths to be love words, so the man understood this feigned bite for a caress.

4 For the most part, however, Buck's love was expressed in adoration. While he went wild with happiness when Thornton touched him or spoke to him, he did not seek these tokens. He would lie by the hour, eager, alert, at Thornton's feet, looking up into his face, dwelling upon it, studying it, following with keenest interest each fleeting expression, every movement or change of feature. Or, as chance might have it, he would lie farther away, to the side or rear, watching the outlines of the man and the occasional movements of his body. And often, such was the communion in which they lived, the strength of Buck's gaze would draw John Thornton's head around, and he would return the gaze, without speech, his heart shining out of his eyes as Buck's heart shone out.

5 For a long time after his rescue, Buck did not like Thornton to get out of his sight. From the moment he left the tent to when he entered it again, Buck would follow at his heels. His transient masters since he had come into the Northland had bred in him a fear that no master could be permanent. He was afraid that Thornton would pass out of his life. Even in the night, in his dreams, he was haunted by this fear. At such times, he would shake off sleep and creep through the chill to the flap of the tent where he would stand and listen to the sound of his master's breathing.

6 But in spite of this great love he bore John Thornton, which seemed to bespeak the soft civilizing influence, the strain of the primitive, which the Northland had aroused in him, remained alive and active. Faithfulness and devotion,

PROFESSIONAL DEVELOPMENT

Productive Conversation: Clear Up Confusions

What Is It? Productive Conversation is class or small-group discussion with a specific goal, such as clearing up confusions. The teacher provides sentence frames and other prompts that lead students to sequence events, understand points of view, and otherwise clarify the meaning of the text.

Why Is It Important? Productive Conversation clears up confusion by helping readers identify the details that cause confusions and search for clarity using a close reading of the text. Productive Conversation also builds speaking and listening skills that enable students to share and build on each other's knowledge.

things born of fire and roof, were his; yet he retained his ! wildness and wiliness. He was a thing of the wild, come in from the wild to sit by John Thornton's fire. Because of his very great love, he could not steal from this man, but from any other man, in any other camp, he did not hesitate an instant; while the cunning with which he stole enabled him to escape detection.

7 Thornton alone held him. The rest of mankind was as nothing. Chance travelers might praise or pet him; but he was cold under it all, and from a too demonstrative man he would get up and walk away. When Thornton's partners, Hans and Pete, arrived on the long-expected raft, Buck refused to notice them till he learned they were close to Thornton; after that he tolerated them in a passive sort of way, accepting favors from them as though he favored them by accepting.

8 For Thornton, however, his love seemed to grow and grow. He, alone among men, could put a pack upon Buck's back in the summer travelling. Nothing was too great for Buck to do, when Thornton commanded. One day (they had grubstaked themselves from the proceeds of the raft and left Dawson for the headwaters of Tanana) the men and dogs were sitting on the crest of a cliff which fell away, straight down, to naked bed-rock three hundred feet below. John Thornton was sitting near the edge, Buck at his shoulder. A thoughtless whim seized Thornton, and he drew the attention of Hans and Pete to the experiment he had in mind. "Jump, Buck!" he commanded, ? sweeping his arm out and over the chasm. The next instant ! he was grappling with Buck on the extreme edge, while Hans and Pete were dragging them back into safety.

9 "It's uncanny," Pete said, after it was over and they had caught their speech.

10 Thornton shook his head. "No, it is splendid, and it is terrible, too. Do you know, it sometimes makes me afraid."

11 "I'm not hankering to be the man that lays hands on you while he's around," Pete announced conclusively, nodding his head toward Buck.

12 "By Jingo!" was Hans's contribution. "Not mineself either."

ANNOTATION NOTES

1st Read:
The dog is loyal to Thornton and no one else.

2nd Read:
"fire and roof" = Thornton gave him warmth and shelter

Dialogue gives a sense of the time and place.

3rd Read:
Paragraph 8 does not say how Buck responded to Thornton's experiment. I infer from the next action that he tried to jump.

How Do I Use It? Identify parts of the text readers have annotated with question marks or seem to be having difficulty comprehending. For example, in *The Call of the Wild*, the excerpt references events that happened previously in the novel, but about which students can make some limited inferences. Prompt partners to supply each other with missing information, as in the following:

Before coming to Thornton, Buck lived with ________.

His relationship with Judge Miller was ________.

Thornton rescued Buck, so I can infer that Buck's situation must have been ________.

The Call of the Wild

3rd READ

Set a Purpose

Tell students they will read to make inferences about the characters from their relationship.

Text-Dependent Questions

1. What can you infer about Thornton's character? (Sample answer: He is kind and caring.)

Scaffolded Support Use the following scaffolded question as necessary to build comprehension.

What dialogue or actions tell you about Thornton's character?

2. What can you infer about Buck's character? (Sample answer: Buck is deeply devoted to Thornton, but he has a wild side that does not care about other people.)

Scaffolded Support Use the following scaffolded question as necessary to build comprehension.

What actions and descriptions tell you about Buck's character?

Think Aloud *Paragraph 8 does not explicitly say what Buck did after John yelled "Jump, Buck!" But, because of what I know about how loyal Buck is to John and because John was then "grappling with Buck on the extreme edge," I can infer that Buck did try to jump off the cliff.*

Partner Talk Have students discuss how Thornton's and Buck's character traits bond them to each other.

Respond to Reading

You may want to check students' understanding by having them complete pages 54–55 in the Student Worktext.

1. Remind students to review their annotations and recall discussions they've had in order to complete the summary chart. Remind students that only evidence from the text should be included in the summary chart.

As students complete their summary charts, circulate and note which students struggle to identify the correct text evidence. Some students may benefit from small group instruction.

2. Remind students to include only the most important information in their summaries.

Have students work independently to complete page 54 of their Worktexts.

COLLABORATE When finished, have students exchange summaries with their partners and share their insights.

Return to the TEXT

Respond to Reading: The Call of the Wild

Review your annotations and notes.
Think about how they can help you summarize the text.

1. Use this chart to help you summarize the text.

Summary Chart

	Literature	
Who?	the characters	a dog named Buck and his new master, John Thornton
What?	the conflict or problem	Buck is completely devoted to Thornton, who rescued him.
Where?	the place characters are in	the introduction says Alaska
When?	the era, year, or time	?
How?	the plot or major events	Buck watches and obeys Thornton's every move and ignores or steals from others.

2. Write a 2–3 sentence summary of the excerpt from *The Call of the Wild.*

Sample summary: Buck, a dog, has a new master in Alaska. Buck completely adores his master, who rescued him. He watches his every move and obeys his every command, while he ignores other men and will even steal from them.

54 • Unit 3

PROFESSIONAL DEVELOPMENT

Teacher Observation: Scaffolding

What Is It? Scaffolds are questions, cues, prompts, and direct instruction teachers provide to students to help them answer difficult questions and arrive at new concepts. Scaffolding in class discussion often begins with questions about information given explicitly in a text and progresses to questions that require students to make increasingly complex inferences.

Why Is It Important? Scaffolded questions arranged in logical order help students develop the higher-order thinking skills they need to derive the full meaning from a text. Scaffolding can also clear up confusion and help students visualize what is happening in a narrative or grasp a concept presented in an explanatory text.

Return to the TEXT

3. How do Buck and Thornton show their feelings toward each other? Use text evidence to support your answer.

Sample answer: Buck and Thornton are affectionate and attentive to each other. Thornton cares for Buck and treats him lovingly, giving him "kindly greetings," "cheering words," and "long talks." He also shakes him by the head, which Buck loves. Buck gives Thornton "feigned bites" and sits or lies next to Thornton at all times, "looking up into his face."

4. How does London organize the text? Provide text evidence to support your answer.

Sample answer: The paragraphs show different aspects of Buck's relationship to Thornton. Paragraphs 1 through 4 show the affection between them. Paragraph 5 hints at Buck's past and how it affects his feelings. Paragraphs 6 and 7 hint at another side to Buck, a wild side that does not care about people.

5. What does the text reveal about Buck other than his love for Thornton? Show text evidence for your answer.

Sample answer: The text talks about Buck's wild side, and his disregard for people who aren't Thornton. Paragraph 6 says "the strain of the primitive ... remained alive and active." It tells how Buck "did not hesitate an instant" to steal from other men in camp. He only "tolerated" Thornton's partners. One of the partners says he wouldn't want to be around if someone laid hands on Thornton, implying that Buck would savagely attack.

REFLECT What conclusions did you draw from the text to make sure you understood?

Sample answer: Because the text did not say outright what happened when Thornton told Buck to jump, I reread paragraph 8. I concluded that Buck tried to jump since it says Thornton had to "grap[ple] with Buck on the extreme edge, while Hans and Pete were dragging them back to safety."

Return to the TEXT

Encourage students to refer back to the text and their annotations and notes to help them answer the questions.

3. Refer students to paragraphs 2, 3, and 4. Have them note the specific language the author uses to describe Buck's and Thornton's interactions.

4. Have students identify the main idea of each paragraph and then look for logical connections between ideas.

5. Refer students to paragraphs 6 and 7 and note how Buck behaves toward people other than Thornton.

Have students work independently to complete page 55 of their Worktexts.

REFLECT Remind students that drawing conclusions is a **Self-Monitoring Strategy** and that they made annotations and notes about confusions they may have had. Suggest that they review their annotations and think about any words, phrases, or sections they reread to draw conclusions to check their comprehension of the text.

How Do I Use It? Begin a series of questions with one that can easily be answered from the text, such as *How does Thornton show his affection for Buck?* Then use the answer in a prompt for the next question: *He teases him by calling him names, and also by* ________. Continue using answers to construct stems for succeeding questions or sentence frames: *Buck responded by* ________. *Thornton and his friends had to* ________. End the series with a higher-order question for discussion, such as, *Why does Thornton fear Buck's affection?*

Return to the TEXT

Stop and Assess

Use the following to assess your students' understanding of the text.

Item 1 answers indicate:	
2	Buck lived with the Judge's family and then with many masters in Alaska. Two pieces of text evidence support the answer.
1	identification of one part of Buck's past, but not both, with insufficient text evidence.
0	no identification of Buck's past, and no supporting evidence.

Item 2 answers indicate:	
2	Buck's previous distance and neglect led him to bond with Thornton, with two pieces of supporting evidence.
1	generalized understanding that Buck's past led him to bond with Thornton, with insufficient text support.
0	no understanding of the reasons for Buck's bonding, with no evidence.

Item 3 answers indicate:	
2	Thornton senses Buck's intense emotions and wild side, with two pieces of text support.
1	identification of Buck's wildness, but not Thornton's understanding, with insufficient text evidence.
0	no understanding of the question and no text evidence.

Option: If you choose not to work with Texts 2 and 3 and to conclude the unit here, use the Visual Text and *The Call of the Wild* to answer the Focus Question: Why do people value the animals in their lives?

Return to the TEXT

Comprehension Check: The Call of the Wild

Answer the questions to demonstrate an understanding of what the text means.

1. What inferences can you make about Buck's life before he came to live with John Thornton? Include details from the text to support your answer.
   Sample answer: Buck once lived with a man named Judge Miller and his family in the "sun-kissed Santa Clara Valley." He went "hunting and tramping" in a "working partnership." The phrase "His transient masters since he had come into the Northland" implies that he passed from one master to the next in Alaska. The text also says that Thornton "saved his life," so I can infer that Buck was in a dangerous situation.

2. How do Buck's previous relationships and experiences shape his current relationship with Thornton? Support your answer with evidence from the text.
   Sample answer: Buck's previous relationships were distant or even neglectful, which makes him love Thornton when he cares for Buck. The author says that Thornton "saved his life," and that his previous masters had been "transient." This hints that Buck's previous owners abandoned him or put him in some kind of danger. He contrasts Thornton's "kindly" and "cheering" ways with other men's "sense of duty and business expediency." The author also contrasts Thornton's love with the "working partnership," "pompous guardianship," and "stately and dignified friendship" Buck had with the Judge's family.

3. In paragraph 10, why does Thornton say that Buck's devotion "makes me afraid"? Use evidence from the text to support your answer.
   Sample answer: Buck's devotion, combined with his wild instincts and lack of care for others, could be dangerous for himself or others. Thornton thinks it is "terrible" that Buck obeyed his "thoughtless whim" to command him to jump off a cliff. Thornton's companions say they would not want "to be the man that lays hands on you while he's around," implying that Buck would attack anyone who would threaten Thornton.

PROFESSIONAL DEVELOPMENT

Text Complexity: Quantitative vs. Qualitative Features

What Is It? Quantitative features of text complexity are measurable and are based on word frequency, word length, number of syllables, and sentence length. Qualitative features of text complexity can't be measured by a formula and are based on language, structure, style, and levels of meaning.

Why Is It Important? Identifying the feature a student struggles to understand is critical for helping him or her achieve comprehension. The strategies for analyzing a quantitatively complex text are different from those used to decipher a qualitatively complex text.

Read to find out how dogs and human soldiers interact in wartime. If you need to read any sections more than once, note the reason in the Annotation Notes column.

Sample annotations and notes appear throughout the text.

Faithful and True Even to Death

by Matt McCrady

1 Of the thousands of veterans' stories archived with the Veterans History Project, the story of a Marine PFC known simply as Lucky stands out. Lucky didn't tell his own story for the project. Lucky left no letters or diaries, and no photo exists of him. In fact, the only remaining physical reminder of his service is an Honorable Discharge certificate. Yet after hearing Lucky's story, it's difficult to forget this quiet soldier who did his duty and was rewarded with nothing more than three pounds of food a day.

2 The thing about Lucky was that he wasn't even human. ! Lucky was one of the many dogs that have served in the military alongside human handlers. Lucky served during World War II.

Lucky was ranked a Private First Class.

3 Lucky was a German Shepherd. In other wars, dogs were Dobermans, Bull Terriers, Airedales, and sometimes even mutts. They were known as "war dogs," "devil dogs," "scout dogs," and "Red Cross dogs." But in every war, they have always been known as a soldier's most trusted companion. Corporal Richard Wolfe, a Vietnam veteran who served with a Military Police Scout and Sentry Dog company, expressed the special relationship between soldier and dog in this way. "It was a friend, it was actually your eyes and ears." By warning of imminent attacks and alerting to hidden enemies, scout dogs like Lucky saved lives and improved morale.

ANNOTATION NOTES

1st Read:
Lucky was a dog who served alongside a soldier in WWII.

2nd Read:
Introduction leads you to believe "Lucky" was a person, and then surprises you.

morale = feelings or attitudes

3rd Read:
Military Police Scout and Sentry Dog company—the use of dogs in the military is serious and highly organized.

How Do I Use It? The most rewarding close readings will come from texts with challenging qualitative features. Use the following questions to probe comprehension of "Faithful and True Even to Death":

- *How many main ideas are there? Are they stated or implied?*
- *Is the text organized simply or unconventionally (subplots, shifting points of view, disrupted chronology)?*
- *Are related ideas compared and contrasted directly? Is figurative language used? Is the tone easily identified?*
- *Are themes or deeper meanings stated or unstated? Are those themes familiar and simple, or new and challenging?*

TEXT 2

Faithful and True

Tell students that they will read to learn how dogs and human soldiers interact in wartime.

1st READ

Set a Purpose

Tell students they will be reading to find out what the article is about.

Have students read "Faithful and True Even to Death" independently, annotating the text as they read. Circulate and note students' markings, especially questions and confusions.

Text-Dependent Questions

1. What is the main idea of this text? (Sample answer: Dogs serve alongside soldiers in war.)

2. What types of jobs do dogs perform in the military during war? (Sample answer: They warn of attacks, improve morale, and do search-and-rescue for the wounded.)

3. Vocabulary: Definition from Context Use general knowledge and context to understand a word's meaning.

Paragraph 8: What type of job does the word *scout* suggest? (Sample answer: The context suggests "someone who detects what's ahead.")

Partner Talk Have students discuss how the dogs came to serve in the military and what their jobs were.

Faithful and True

2nd READ

Set a Purpose

Tell students they will read to analyze the structure of the text.

Text-Dependent Questions

1. From what sources did the author get the information for the article? (Sample answer: a Vietnam War veteran, a dog training guide, and Lucky's Honorable Discharge certificate)

Scaffolded Support Use the following scaffolded question and sentence frame as necessary to build comprehension.

What documents does the text cite?

The author includes quotations from ________ and ________.

2. What is the author's purpose in including the story about Lucky? (Sample answer: The story about Lucky acts as a frame for the information about war dogs. It helps give personal details about the topic.)

Think Aloud *I got a little confused when the text jumped between stories and times. Let me reread to see if I can get a sense of the overall structure of the text and figure out what the intention is. The story starts with Lucky, moves to the Vietnam veteran's story in paragraph 3, then back to Lucky. It explains war training in paragraphs 5 and 6 before coming back to Lucky. This emphasizes how many wars dogs have helped in and all the ways they can help.*

Partner Talk Have students discuss the transitions between ideas in the text.

TEXT 2

ANNOTATION NOTES

1st Read:
The dogs aren't brought up in the military—families lend their pets, who are then trained.

The dogs also do search and rescue.

2nd Read:
timeline moves around—WWII, Vietnam, WWI

3rd Read:
Dogs must be trained to go against lots of natural instincts, like barking at intruders.

4 Like many other civilians who wished to contribute their family pets to the war effort, Lucky's owner, Donald Walton, loaned him to the Marine Corps for the duration of the war. !

Dogs and soldiers worked side by side under the stressful conditions of battle.

5 While Lucky and other scout dogs were trained for more aggressive missions, the Red Cross dog of World War One was primarily what we would call a search and rescue dog. After a battle ended, the dog would be deployed to seek out the wounded on the battlefield, as described in Theodore F. Jager's 1917 training guide, *Scout, Red Cross, and Army Dogs.*

6 *The dogs are trained not to bark when they find a disabled soldier. They are taught to disregard dead soldiers. Each dog has a box containing first aid remedies and appliances tied to its neck. Upon locating a helpless soldier, the dog goes up close to him so that the box may be opened.*

7 Then the dog would return to camp and direct medical personnel where to find the wounded man.

8 Some thirty-five years later, not barking was a significant part of Lucky's training as a scout, as well. Walton relates that Lucky's handler would sleep with his hand resting under the dog's neck so that an inaudible vibration, instead of a bark, would warn him of an impending enemy sneak attack.

9 The goal of the dogs' education was to instill absolute willingness to follow orders and to protect their human companions. Captain William Putney, who was responsible for training the dogs used in World War II, describes a system whereby handler and dog trained as one. Beginning on the day they were assigned their dog, handlers worked so closely with their animal that they were effectively one entity. Every grueling physical test the handler went through, including live fire exercises, the dog went through right beside him. Because a dog handler often cannot speak while in the field, the dog had to become familiar with hand signals and low, almost inaudible whistles, as commands. The handlers also had the

PROFESSIONAL DEVELOPMENT

Classroom Management: Small-Group and Partner Work

What Is It? When you manage your classroom, you organize the flow of both work and students. One classroom management strategy is to move from whole-class instruction to small-group and partner work.

Why Is It Important? Small-group and partner discussions allow the teacher to circulate and give personal attention to more students. Small-groups and partner work provide opportunities for students to teach each other.

TEXT 2

responsibility for feeding and caring for their dog and, in short, bonding with it. In working together, they formed an unbreakable team. There is no doubt that what some dog handlers felt for their dogs was love.

10 The unnamed soldier who worked with Lucky during the war wrote the Waltons often. When the war came to a close, he wrote to them several times begging them to let him keep the dog. Tough as it was to tell him no, Donald Walton responded by saying that just as this soldier was going home to his family after discharge, Lucky needed to come home to his family.

11 Corporal Richard Wolfe also spoke at length about the bond between the handler and his dog, and the pain of that final separation. When asked whether he kept his dog after his tour was over, he says,

12 *I only wish that we could have. That was probably one of the saddest things I ever had to do was leave my dog. Because he had saved my life, and a lot of other people's lives. To have to leave him there was a sad, sad thing to do.*

13 Thankfully, Lucky's story has a happy ending. His reintroduction to civilian life was by all accounts successful. Lucky lived a long life for a German Shepherd. He was 14 when he died at home circa 1953, far away from the dangerous Pacific islands where he had risked his life years before.

Dogs continue to provide extra eyes and ears, rescue capabilities, and comfort to soldiers.

ANNOTATION NOTES

1st Read:
After wars, the dogs went home to their families.

2nd Read:
Lucky's story is the main story, with info from WWI and Vietnam to fill out details.

3rd Read:
Soldiers wanting to keep the dogs shows that they have bonded and love each other.

Faithful and True

3rd READ

Set a Purpose

Tell students they will read to make inferences about the relationships between human and dog soldiers.

Text-Dependent Questions

1. How did human soldiers feel about dog soldiers? (Sample answer: They cared about them deeply and depended on them.)

2. What events or circumstances helped foster this relationship? (Sample answer: The intense training and the stress of wartime helped bond the dogs and their handlers.)

Scaffolded Support Use the following scaffolded question and sentence frame as necessary to build comprehension.

How would people and dogs learn to work together?

The soldiers' and dogs' situations were ________.

3. Why did the author include the details about the dogs returning home? (Sample answer: This shows how attached the soldiers had become to their dogs.)

Partner Talk Have students discuss the value of the dogs to their handlers and to the war effort in general.

How Do I Use It? The most common management strategy is to open with the whole class, break into small groups, and then reassemble for sharing group findings and final class discussion. The teacher gets the whole class interested in the content, invites first impressions, and sets goals and guidelines for collaboration. Then, in small groups, students reread the material, ask and answer questions about details and inferences, and respond to each other's ideas. After this in-depth discussion, the final class discussion will be more active and meaningful.

Return to the TEXT

Stop and Assess

Use the following to assess your students' understanding of the text.

Item 1 answers indicate:	
2	an informational purpose, with two or more pieces of text evidence.
1	an informational purpose, but insufficient text support.
0	no identification of purpose, and no text support.

Item 2 answers indicate:	
2	a structure with a main story and supporting additional anecdotes that allow the author to include additional information, with text evidence to support each example.
1	a structure that tells a story but no identification of anecdotes or additional information, with some text evidence.
0	no understanding of the text structure, and no relevant evidence.

Item 3 answers indicate:	
2	a close bond between soldier and dog, with two or more text examples.
1	a bond between soldier and dog, with one text example.
0	no understanding of the relationship, with no evidence.

Return to the TEXT

Comprehension Check: Faithful and True Even to Death

Answer the questions to demonstrate an understanding of what the text means.

1. What is the author's purpose in writing this text? Provide text examples to support your answer.

Sample answer: The author's purpose is to tell about the roles that dogs played in wars, using the example of Lucky the German Shepherd. Paragraph 2 says that "Lucky was one of the many dogs that have served in the military." Paragraph 3 describes dogs' roles in war. Other paragraphs describe the dogs' training and how they lived after the war.

2. How does the text structure support the author's purpose? Provide examples from the text to support your answer.

Sample answer: The text structure follows the story of Lucky, and adds supporting details from a Vietnam War soldier and a World War I dog-training manual. After introducing Lucky and giving background information about dog soldiers, Corporal Wolfe adds the detail that the dogs were "your eyes and ears." After an introduction about Lucky's background, the training manual notes that he and others are trained "not to bark" and to obey orders. The details fill out the story to help inform readers about Lucky and war dogs in general.

3. What is the relationship between the dogs and their soldier handlers? Give examples from the text to support your answer.

Sample answer: The dogs and their handlers have a very tight bond. Paragraph 3 says that a war dog was its handler's "most trusted companion," while Corporal Wolfe defines the dog as "a friend." The text notes that "handlers worked so closely with their animals that they were effectively one entity." It also includes the details that many soldiers were very sad to have to say goodbye to their dogs, and that they "felt . . . love."

PROFESSIONAL DEVELOPMENT

Annotations: Important or Surprising Information

What Is It? Readers use exclamation points to mark words and passages they consider surprising or important. These items are usually, but not always, key details or part of the main idea of the passage. The teacher uses their annotations as the basis for discussion of concepts and building of comprehension.

Why Is It Important? When students annotate, they are focusing on the text. Observing students as they annotate enables you to identify which parts of the text grab students' attention. Such observation also enables you to identify students who are not distinguishing main ideas, who are not familiar with key words, or who lack background knowledge.

TEXT 3

Read to find out how people value their pets. You may want to read some sections more than once and make different annotations and Annotation Notes each time.
Sample annotations and notes appear throughout the text.

Spending on Pets: "Tails" from the Consumer Expenditure Survey

by Steven Henderson

1 Nearly three-quarters of U.S. households own pets. There are about 218 million pets in the United States, not including several million pet fish. Pet ownership crosses many demographic boundaries, with Americans of different ages and levels of wealth reporting spending on pets. Further, Americans spend a substantial amount of money on the care and feeding of their animals. Americans spent approximately $61.4 billion in total on their pets in 2011. On average, each U.S. household spent just over $500 on pets. This amounts to about 1 percent of total spending per year for the average household.

2 Expenditures on pets include pet food, pet purchases, supplies and medicine, pet services, and veterinarian services. The data shows the following:

- In 2011, households spent more on their pets annually than they spent on alcohol, residential landline bills, or men or boy's clothing.
- Average household spending on pet food alone was $183 in 2011. This was more than the amount spent on candy, bread, chicken, cereal, or reading materials.
- Even when spending at restaurants dropped during the recent recession, spending on pet food stayed constant.
- Married couples without children living at home spent the most on their pets.

3 Despite the difficult economic conditions brought on by the recession, families continued to spend consistently on their pets between 2007 and 2011. Although the amount that households spent on pets varied from year to year, the share of household spending on pets stayed relatively constant. It remained within a narrow range of 0.9 to 1.1 percent of total spending.

ANNOTATION NOTES

1st Read:
Americans spend a lot of money on their pets every year.

2nd Read:
Bullets include different types of facts: comparisons and specifics about who spends money.

3rd Read:
Comparisons imply that our pets are more important than the things we spend less on.

How Do I Use It? As you circulate among readers, note the items they are marking. If you see several students marking the same passages, discuss those passages with students, providing support as needed. Exclamation points that mark surprising facts provide good opportunities to motivate other students and to practice listening and speaking skills. Ask readers to explain what surprised them or why they think those words are important.

Spending on Pets

Tell students that they will read to understand how people value their pets.

1st READ

Set a Purpose

Explain to students that they will read the text to find out the facts included in the text. Have students read "Spending on Pets" independently, annotating the text.

Text-Dependent Questions

1. What is this text about? (This text is about how much Americans spend on caring for their pets.)

2. What types of figures does the text include? (The text includes the total spent on pets, and the average amount and its changes over time.)

Scaffolded Support Use the following sentence frames as necessary to build comprehension.

The figure $61.4 billion describes ________.

The figure of $500 describes ________.

2. Vocabulary: Multiple-Meaning Words Discuss contextual meanings of familiar words and phrases.

Paragraph 2, bullet 3: What does *constant* mean in this context? (It means "steady" or "continuing in the same way.")

Partner Talk Have students discuss what type of spending the data measures.

Spending on Pets

2nd READ

Set a Purpose

Tell students that they will read to analyze the text organization.

Text-Dependent Questions

1. What text structure does the author use? (Information is organized with paragraphs and bullets.)

2. How do the bullets help organize the text? (The bullets call out individual facts.)

Partner Talk Have students discuss how the author organizes ideas.

3rd READ

Set a Purpose

Tell students they will read to make inferences about people's relationships with their pets.

Text-Dependent Questions

1. What does the fact in paragraph 2, bullet 3 suggest? (Eating out is an unnecessary luxury, but pet food is necessary if you have a pet.)

2. What other fact from the text supports this inference? (Paragraph 3 says that during a recession, spending on pets remained constant.)

Scaffolded Support Use the following scaffolded questions as necessary to build comprehension.

What event does the bullet talk about?

Where else in the text is that event mentioned?

Partner Talk Have students discuss how other spending comparisons give clues to people's feelings about pets.

ANNOTATION NOTES

1st Read:
Spending on pets stayed constant even during hard times.

2nd Read:
Text uses argument/evidence structure: one sentence states a claim, and statistics back it up.

3rd Read:
People are willing to cut back on their own food before their pets' food.

Pet food consumption remains consistent, even when households cut back on other spending.

4 Household spending on pet food increased very slowly or remained relatively unchanged between 2007 and 2011. In 2007, annual pet food spending was $147, increasing to $163 in 2008, and then leveling off at $169 in 2009 and $165 in 2010. ? The amount climbed again by less than $20 to $183 in 2011. In contrast, people spent less at restaurants during and after the recession. Spending on meals away from home went from $2,668 in 2007 to its peak at $2,698 in 2008. It then dropped to $2,619 in 2009. Spending in this category further fell to $2,505 in 2010 before rising to $2,620 in 2011.

PROFESSIONAL DEVELOPMENT

Text-Dependent Questions

What Is It? Text-Dependent Questions are questions that can be answered only by referring back to the text. They keep students grounded in the text and reliant on only the content the author provides. Text-Dependent Questions require students to use evidence from the text to justify their answers.

Why Is It Important? Questions that focus on students' opinions and feelings take them away from the text. While we want to get students' reactions, we must first start with what they know using only the details in the text. This close examination of the text aids in comprehension and the development of skills students will need to understand and analyze other rigorous texts.

Return to the TEXT

Comprehension Check: Spending on Pets

Answer the questions to demonstrate an understanding of what the text means.

1. What points about Americans and their pets does the text suggest? Use evidence from the passage to support your answer.
   Sample answer: The text suggests that Americans are very devoted to their pets because they are willing to spend a lot of money on them. The text includes impressive statistics about total pet spending—"$61.4 billion in total." It also notes that people spend more on pets than on "men's or boy's clothing," or "candy, bread, chicken, cereal, or reading materials."

2. What was the author's purpose in describing, in paragraphs 3 and 4, spending during the economic recession? Use details from the text to support your answer.
   Sample answer: These paragraphs show that Americans continued to spend about the same amount on their pets even when the economy was bad. The text notes that "spending on pets stayed relatively constant." It also compares pet spending to how "people spent less at restaurants during and after the recession," to show that people cut back on other spending, but not on their pets.

3. How do the specific dollar figures and statistics support the purpose of the text? Provide examples to support your answer.
   Sample answer: The specific figures provide factual evidence to support the text's argument that people spend a lot on their pets. First, the text says that "Americans spent a substantial amount of money on . . . their animals," and then backs it up with the figure of $61.4 billion. The figures also show pet food spending over time, noting that it was "$163 in 2008, . . . $169 in 2009, and $165 in 2010" to support the idea that spending remained consistent.

How Do I Use It? Many students need support in identifying effective strategies in specific reading situations. Modeling these strategies will expand students' strategy repertoire. For example, support Text-Dependent Question 2 in the third read of Text 3 with a Think Aloud: *To answer this question, I reread paragraphs 3 and 4. I note that although households cut back on their spending during the recession, spending on pet items "remained constant." In fact, spending on pet food actually increased during that time while spending on meals away from home decreased. This shows me that people regarded restaurant spending as a luxury and pet food a necessity.*

Return to the TEXT

Stop and Assess

Use the following to assess your students' understanding of the text.

Item 1 answers indicate:	
2	an inference that Americans love their pets, with at least two pieces of text evidence.
1	an understanding that Americans love their pets, but insufficient text explanations for how they know.
0	no inference about people's relationship with pets, and no text evidence.

Item 2 answers indicate:	
2	an inference that people consider pet spending not optional, with two pieces of text support.
1	an inference that people value their pets, with insufficient text support.
0	no understanding of the meaning, and no text support.

Item 3 answers indicate:	
2	an understanding of the use of statistical support, with two pieces of text evidence.
1	a general sense of the value of statistical support, with insufficient evidence.
0	no understanding of statistical support, and no text evidence.

ANALYZE and SYNTHESIZE ACROSS TEXTS

Return to the Focus Question

Explain to students that they will fill out a graphic organizer that helps them answer the Focus Question: Why do people value the animals in their lives?

CONNECT TEXTS Have small groups of students discuss how each text they read helps them answer the Focus Question.

Scaffolded Support You may provide the following sentence frames to support students in their use of academic language:

> In the text ________ ,
> the author/photographer
> makes the point that ________ .
> He/she does this by ________ .

Remind students to use their annotations and summaries to support their answers. They can also reread portions of the texts, if necessary.

Have students complete their graphic organizers individually.

REFLECT Remind students that each text provides different information about people's relationships with animals. Ask, *how did reading all four texts give you a greater understanding of how and why people value animals?*

ANALYZE and SYNTHESIZE ACROSS TEXTS

Return to the Focus Question: Why do people value the animals in their lives?

Review your answers to questions about the texts as well as your annotations and Annotation Notes, and think about the discussions you've had about the texts. How does that information help you answer the Focus Question?

Use the graphic organizer to organize information about the texts.

1. In the appropriate box below, record the details that help you answer the Focus Question.
2. Make connections between those details to answer the Focus Question. Write your answer in the box provided.

Farmer working (Visual Text)
Sample answer: The farmer works with animals and also cares about them.

Faithful and True Even to Death
Sample answer: Some dogs and soldiers work side by side in war.

The Call of the Wild
Sample answer: A man forms a deep bond with his dog.

Spending on Pets
Sample answer: Americans show their love for pets in the large amount of money they spend on them.

Why do people value the animals in their lives?
Sample answer: People value animals partly for their usefulness, but mostly for their companionship. People who work closely with animals often form very strong bonds of friendship with them.

REFLECT How did making connections between the four texts enable you to answer the Focus Question?

Sample answer: The texts showed some working relationships, such as the farmer and calf and the war dogs and their handlers. But in every text, people demonstrated how much they loved the animals. Buck and Thornton dearly love each other. The soldiers bonded with their war dogs. And pet owners spend lots of money on food and other goods for their pets.

PROFESSIONAL DEVELOPMENT

Academic Language: Language Frames

What is It? Academic language is sometimes known as the "language of school." It differs from everyday spoken language, which is primarily social in nature. Academic language includes those more sophisticated and specific words used in books, in students' more formal writing, and the language of instruction used during lessons and classroom discussions.

Why Is It Important? Academic language is necessary for school success. It is the words and sentence structures used by educated adults and the language expected in college and in the workplace.

Writing About the Focus Question

Now that you have answered the Focus Question using all four texts, expand on your thinking and communicate your ideas through your writing.

WRITING CHECKLIST ✔

Does my writing . . .

- ☐ answer the Focus Question?
- ☐ have a clear organizational structure?
- ☐ cite the correct amount of text evidence?
- ☐ correctly use language, spelling, and conventions?

USE EVIDENCE

- Explain what you have learned about why people value the animals in their lives. Use at least one piece of evidence from the Visual Text and at least two pieces of text evidence from Texts 1, 2, and 3 to support your answer.
- If you need more room, use additional paper.

MONITOR

- Use the Writing Checklist as you write to make sure your writing meets all the necessary criteria.
- Use the rubric on page 66 when you have completed a first draft of your writing to help you evaluate, revise, and edit your work.

How Do I Use It? Focus on teaching words that may appear in rigorous texts but that students may be unfamiliar with or may not use in their everyday language. Examples in these texts include *expediency, communion, transient* (*The Call of the Wild*), *imminent, duration, inaudible* ("Faithful and True"), and *demographic* and *recession* ("Spending on Pets").

Scaffolded Support: Using discussion frames is an ideal way to assist students in using academic language (e.g., *The main idea of "Faithful and True" is* ________, or *Based on my reading, I conclude that* ________.)

Writing About the Focus Question

USE EVIDENCE Remind students that they should use their graphic organizers as well as their annotations in the texts to write their responses.

Allow students to revisit the texts as frequently as they need to in order to support comprehension and to respond to the Focus Question.

MONITOR After students have completed their responses, have them review the Writing Checklist and revise their writing response.

DIFFERENTIATE AND EXTEND

In addition to or instead of the writing response, consider having students complete one of the following assignments:

Write Beyond Have students write a letter from a military dog handler to the owner of the dog he works with, talking about their relationship.

Read Beyond Have students read the complete novel of *The Call of the Wild* or another classic novel about the bond between humans and animals such as *Old Yeller* or *The Black Stallion.*

Interview an Expert Have students interview an expert animal handler, e.g. a dog trainer or dairy farmer.

Debate an Issue Have students debate the question of whether war dogs should be discharged to their military handlers or their original owners.

SELF-ASSESS and REFLECT

SELF-ASSESS Have students use the Writing Rubric on page 66 to self-assess their writing response and write a final version. Tell them to assign themselves a score from 1–4 (with "4" being the highest) for each category in the first column.

Use the Writing Rubric on Student Worktext page 66 to assess each student's writing. Record points for each category in the first column of the rubric. Have students remove the page from their Student Worktexts and place it in their writing portfolios, along with the drafts and final versions of their responses.

SELF-ASSESS and REFLECT

Focus Question: Why do people value the animals in their lives?

This is the rubric that your teacher will use to assess your writing. Refer to it as you revise your work. After you have finished the final version of your response, assess your response and record your points for each category on the "Student" line in the first column.

	Accomplished (4 points)	Competent (3 points)	Developing (2 points)	Beginning (1 point)
RESPONSE Score: Student ______ Teacher ______	The response answers the question effectively and with insight.	The response answers the question effectively.	The response partially responds to the question but does not adequately address it.	The response addresses the texts but does not address the question.
ORGANIZATION Score: Student ______ Teacher ______	The main idea is convincingly stated. Ideas are organized in cohesive paragraphs that support the main idea.	The main idea is clearly stated. Ideas are organized in logical paragraphs.	The main idea is weak. Ideas are organized in a somewhat logical and cohesive way.	The main idea is missing. The organization of the paragraphs is not logical.
TEXT EVIDENCE Score: Student ______ Teacher ______	Response includes more than one piece of appropriate text evidence from each text. Evidence supports the main idea in a thorough way.	Response includes one piece of text evidence from each text. Evidence supports the main idea clearly.	Response does not include at least one piece of text evidence from each text. Text evidence does not adequately support the main idea.	Response does not contain relevant evidence.
LANGUAGE Score: Student ______ Teacher ______	Writing includes precise and sophisticated vocabulary related to the topic.	Writing includes appropriate vocabulary related to the topic.	Writing includes imprecise and inaccurate vocabulary.	Writing does not include vocabulary that appropriately reflects the topic of the response.
SPELLING AND CONVENTIONS Score: Student ______ Teacher ______	Response includes correct spelling, grammar, and punctuation consistently.	Response includes mostly correct spelling, grammar, and punctuation.	Response has many errors in spelling, grammar, and punctuation.	Response's errors in spelling, grammar, and punctuation make it extremely difficult to understand the response.

UNIT 4

Focus Question How does nature benefit us?

Texts for Close Reading

GENRE STUDY

Discuss with students the genres of "Solitude," "The Halcyon in Canada," and "Returning to the Fields."

Remind students that *genre* refers to the features and content of a text and typically falls into one of two categories—literature or informational text. Literature, which includes poetry, is a creative work that doesn't necessarily rely on facts, while informational texts are based on factual information.

The texts in this unit are of distinct genres. Have students identify features poems and essays might share and features which distinguish them. For example, the essays and the poem in this unit describe feelings about a special place. Essays are written in paragraphs; poems are usually written in stanzas.

INTRODUCE THE UNIT

Focus Question

Have students read the Focus Question on Worktext page 67. Tell students that the texts they will read will help them answer the question.

Texts for Close Reading

Have students read to themselves the summaries about the texts in this unit.

There is no need to explain what students should expect to find in their close readings or to do any pre-teaching about the subject matter.

TEXT COMPLEXITY

Woman Kayaker
- Style: documentary
- Knowledge demands: low
- Levels of meaning: literal

Solitude

Quantitative: 1070L

Qualitative
- Structure: conventional
- Language: archaic
- Knowledge demands: medium
- Levels of meaning: literal/ inferential

The Halcyon in Canada

Quantitative: 1000L

Qualitative
- Structure: conventional
- Language: familiar
- Knowledge demands: medium
- Levels of meaning: literal/inferential

Returning to the Fields

Qualitative
- Structure: verse
- Language: archaic
- Knowledge demands: high
- Levels of meaning: inferential

Woman Kayaker

Set a Purpose

Explain to students that they will look at the image on page 68 to begin thinking about ways in which nature benefits people.

Visual Text Analysis

Remind students that an image can be analyzed as a text by looking at its details and making inferences. Direct students' attention to the image on Student Worktext page 68.

1. Have students record their immediate impressions after they look at the image. Lead them to discuss as a whole class, in small groups, or with a partner, what they think is happening in the photograph.

2. Encourage students to make note of the details that support their observations in their answers to question 1. Have students explain as a whole class, in small groups, or with a partner what details they noted and what those details tell them about how people can benefit from nature.

3. Tell students to record their thoughts and feelings about the image. Have students discuss how these reactions deepen their understanding of the Visual Text.

Optional: Provide any additional information you feel is appropriate to enhance the discussion:

- While outdoor pastimes like boating, hiking, and camping remain popular, a study published in 2008 showed that the amount of time Americans spend outdoors has declined since the 1980s.
- Kayaks were developed by the Inuit, Yup'ik, and Aleut people in the northern reaches of North America.

VISUAL TEXT

Woman Kayaker in Moose Lake, Near Mendenhall Glacier, Southeast AK

Look at the Visual Text to answer the following questions. Review the image or parts of the image as many times as necessary.

1. What is happening in this photograph?
   Sample answer: A woman is floating in a kayak on a calm lake, enjoying the natural sights that surround her.

2. What details in the photograph support your answer to the previous question?
   Sample answer: The water is perfectly smooth which shows the kayak is not moving; there would be ripples if the kayaker were paddling or moving quickly. The setting is beautiful, and the sky above is blue and cloudless.

3. When you look again, what are you thinking and feeling?
   Sample answer: I think the woman is on the lake specifically to enjoy the natural surroundings. This scene makes me feel peaceful. I imagine that the air smells fresh and clean, and the only sounds to be heard are the sounds of nature.

68 • Unit 4

PROFESSIONAL DEVELOPMENT

Visual Text: ELL

What Is It? Incorporating information from a visual text can present extra challenges for English language learners and other students who have difficulty reading. Such students need help in "translating" from their visual impressions to verbal descriptions.

Why Is It Important? Students can absorb an image without verbalizing, but they need words to analyze the image and to describe it to others. Looking at images and talking about what they see helps students develop fluency in reading, writing, and speaking about nonverbal texts. Such activities also work the other way around: as they build fluency with

✔ Self-Monitoring Strategies you used to help you check your understanding as you read.

☐ Visualize. ☐ Draw conclusions. ☐ Ask yourself questions. ☐ Reread to clarify.

Read the text to learn about how the author feels about living alone in the woods. Make annotations in the text and write your notes in the Annotation Notes column.

Sample annotations and notes appear throughout the text.

Solitude

by Henry David Thoreau

Henry David Thoreau (1817–1862) was an American writer, philosopher, and naturalist. This excerpt is from a chapter in his memoir Walden; or, Life in the Woods, *which was first published in 1854.*

Henry David Thoreau

1 This is a delicious evening, when the whole body is one sense, and imbibes delight through every pore. I go and come with a strange liberty in Nature. As I walk along the stony shore of the pond in my shirt-sleeves, it is cool as well as cloudy and windy. I see nothing special to attract me, yet all the elements are unusually congenial to me. The bullfrogs trump to usher in the night, and the note of the whippoorwill is borne on the rippling wind from over the water. Sympathy with the fluttering alder and poplar leaves almost takes away my breath. Yet, like

ANNOTATION NOTES

1st Read:

The author lives alone in a house in the woods.

He feels free and at peace surrounded by nature.

2nd Read:

Poetic language makes the ordinary seem special—"the bullfrogs trump to usher in the night."

3rd Read:

Alone and surrounded by nature, Thoreau feels great inner peace and tranquility.

language, students are better able to create images from verbal descriptions.

How Do I Use It? Asking 5W questions about an image can help students form the words and sentences they need to describe what they see. For example, the Visual Text for this unit shows a person kayaking on a mountain lake. Start by pointing to items in the picture (sky, mountains, lake, kayak, paddle) and having students name them. Then ask questions such as, *What is the setting of the picture?, What is the person holding?,* and *What is he or she doing?* and have students write their answers. Work with students as they combine their answers into complete sentences.

Solitude

Tell students that they will read to learn about how the author feels about living alone in the woods.

1st READ

Set a Purpose

Tell students they will be reading to find out what the essay is about.

Have students read "Solitude" independently, annotating as they read. Circulate and make notes of students' markings, questions, and confusions. Your notes can be used to inform instruction and as data for informal assessment.

Text-Dependent Questions

1. What is the author's situation? (He's living alone in woods near a pond.)

Think Aloud *The author uses many unusual words to describe nature in paragraph 1, so I will visualize as I read. Hearing the "trump" of the bullfrogs makes them sound triumphant and friendly. Picturing the water "rippled but not ruffled" seems calm. I understand why he feels at peace in this location.*

2. How does Thoreau feel about the nature around him? What text evidence supports your answer? (He feels "sympathy" with nature, which is "congenial" to him.)

3. Vocabulary: Denotation and Connotation Discuss the literal and associative meanings of key words.

Paragraph 4: Is the connotation of the word *solitude* positive or negative? How do you know? (Positive, as his solitude is "companionable.")

Partner Talk Have students discuss the main idea of the essay.

Solitude

2nd READ

Set a Purpose

Tell students they will read to examine the tone expressed through the author's language.

Text-Dependent Questions

1. What kind of language does Thoreau use to describe nature in paragraph 1? (Paragraph 1 has many sensory words and phrases. The evening is "delicious," the air is "cool," and the bullfrogs "trump." The word *fluttering*, which Thoreau uses to describe the alder and poplar trees, appeals to the senses of both sight and sound.)

Scaffolded Support Use the following scaffolded question and sentence frame as necessary to build comprehension.

What word does Thoreau use to describe the evening and what sense does it appeal to?

The pond has a ________ ________ surface.

2. How does the tone of paragraph 4 compare or contrast with the tone of paragraph 1? (In paragraph 1, Thoreau describes nature using poetic language, and the tone is lyrical. In paragraph 4, he wants to make an intellectual point; the language is more formal, and the tone is more analytical.)

3. Vocabulary: Multiple-Meaning Words Discuss the contextual meaning of a familiar word.

Paragraph 5: What does the phrase "one is a mock sun" mean? (The phrase means that what looks like the second sun is not real.)

Partner Talk Have students discuss the author's use of language and its impact on tone.

ANNOTATION NOTES

1st Read:
The author finds that a person doesn't need other people to avoid loneliness; all he needs is the "beneficent society in Nature."

2nd Read:
"Society," "friendliness," "befriended," and "kindred" reveal the author's relationship with nature.

Thoreau gives some human emotions to elements of nature.

3rd Read:
Thoreau is saying that loneliness is a condition in the mind, not a situation. When we're connected with nature, we can't be lonely.

the lake, my serenity is rippled but not ruffled. These small waves raised by the evening wind are as remote from storm as the smooth reflecting surface. Though it is now dark, the mind still blows and roars in the wood. The waves still dash, and some creatures lull the rest with their notes. The repose is never complete. The wildest animals do not repose, but seek their prey now. The fox, and skunk, and rabbit, now roam the fields and woods without fear. They are Nature's watchmen.

2 When I return to my house I find that visitors have been there and left their cards, either a bunch of flowers, or a wreath of evergreen, or a name in pencil on a yellow walnut leaf or a chip. They who come rarely to the woods take some little piece of the forest into their hands to play with. One has peeled a willow wand, woven it into a ring, and dropped it on my table. I could always tell if visitors had called in my absence. I could tell either by the bended twigs or grass, or the print of their shoes, and generally of what sex or age or quality they were by some slight trace left, as a flower dropped, or a bunch of grass plucked and thrown away, even as far off as the railroad, half a mile distant.

3 I have never felt lonesome, or in the least oppressed by a sense of solitude but once. That was a few weeks after I came to the woods, when, for an hour, I doubted if the near neighborhood of man was not essential to a serene and healthy life. To be alone was something unpleasant. But I was at the same time conscious of a slight insanity in my mood, and seemed to foresee my recovery. In the midst of a gentle rain while these thoughts prevailed, I was suddenly sensible of such sweet and beneficent society in Nature. I found in the very pattering of the drops, and in every sound and sight around my house, an infinite and unaccountable friendliness all at once like an atmosphere sustaining me, as made the fancied advantages of human neighborhood insignificant, and I have never thought of them since. Every little pine needle expanded and swelled with sympathy and befriended me. I was so distinctly made aware of the presence of something kindred to me, even in scenes which we are accustomed to call wild and dreary.

4 I love to be alone. I never found the companion that was so companionable as solitude. We are for the most part more lonely when we go abroad among men than when we stay in

PROFESSIONAL DEVELOPMENT

Text Complexity: Reader and Task Factors

What Is It? The complexity of a given text depends on its readers, and readers vary greatly in their cognitive and reading skills, motivations, prior knowledge, life experiences, and familiarity with the tasks required of them. By analyzing students and their needs, the teacher can provide the appropriate scaffolding that supports full comprehension.

Why Is It Important? Complex texts are challenging for readers: they tend to have more domain-specific language and longer sentences and paragraphs than students' other readings. For students used to skimming and scanning, slowing down to read every word or line requires extra practice, as well as learning how to focus on content.

our chambers. A man thinking or working is always alone, let him be where he will. Solitude is not measured by the miles of space that intervene between a man and his fellows. The farmer can work alone in the field or the woods all day, hoeing or chopping, and not feel lonesome, because he is employed. But when he comes home at night he cannot sit down in a room alone, at the mercy of his thoughts. He must be where he can "see the folks," and recreate, and, as he thinks, remunerate himself for his day's solitude. Hence, he wonders how the student can sit alone in the house all night and most of the day without ennui and "the blues." He does not realize that the student, though in the house, is still at work in his field, and chopping in his woods, as the farmer in his, and in turn seeks the same recreation and society that the latter does, though it may be a more condensed form of it.

5 I have a great deal of company in my house; especially in the morning, when nobody calls. Let me suggest a few comparisons, that someone may convey an idea of my situation. I am no more lonely than the loon in the pond that laughs so loud, or than Walden Pond itself. What company has that lonely lake, I pray? And yet it has not the blue devils, but the blue angels in it, in the azure tint of its waters. The sun is alone, except in thick weather, when there sometimes appear to be two, but one is a mock sun. God is alone—but the devil, he is far from being alone. He sees a great deal of company. He is legion. I am no more lonely than a single mullein or dandelion in a pasture, or a bean leaf, or sorrel, or a horse-fly, or a bumblebee. I am no more lonely than the Mill Brook, or a weathercock, or the north star, or the south wind, or an April shower, or a January thaw, or the first spider in a new house.

ANNOTATION NOTES

1st Read:
A student's "field" is in his mind; that's why students can study alone for hours and not feel lonely.

The author has all the companionship he needs in nature.

2nd Read:
look up *remunerate*, *ennui*

"Let me suggest"—author is talking to reader

"I am no more lonely"—he is not lonely despite being alone

3rd Read:
There is a sacred quality in being alone and one with the nature that surrounds us.

How Do I Use It? As you prepare for close reading, identify words or passages for which your students might need scaffolding, Think Aloud modeling, or similar support. Suggest graphic organizers or annotation activities that help students connect words and ideas. For example, have students circle and draw lines to connect pronouns to their nouns and clauses to the words they modify. *At the end of paragraph 4, the author refers to "he" repeatedly. I scan back and see that the author has introduced "the farmer" and that is the "he" at the end of the paragraph. I wonder what type of farmer the author refers to. When I read again I realize the farmer is any farmer and the figure is used as an example.*

Solitude

3rd READ

Set a Purpose

Tell students they will read to understand the text's message.

Text-Dependent Questions

1. In paragraph 3, what emotional shift occurs within Thoreau? (Thoreau wonders whether being with other people is "essential to a serene and healthy life." But soon he is overcome with a sense of the "beneficent society in Nature.")

2. What is the main idea of paragraph 5? (Thoreau opens the paragraph with a contradiction: he says he has "a great deal of company" when nobody comes to visit. When Thoreau is alone, he feels himself most strongly as part of nature, like the loon, the lake, the sun, and the dandelion, all of which are alone but have no experience of loneliness.)

Scaffolded Support Use the following scaffolded question and sentence frame as necessary to build comprehension.

What does Thoreau compare himself to in this paragraph?

Thoreau is ________ than the loon in the pond.

3. Vocabulary: Figurative Language Discuss the use of hyperbole in Thoreau's descriptions of his mental states.

Paragraph 3: What word does Thoreau use to describe his mood in the first part of the paragraph, and why? (He says there is slight "insanity" in his mood. He is exaggerating to make the point that his thinking was off track.)

Partner Talk Have students discuss the central message of this essay.

Return to the TEXT

Respond to Reading

You may want to check students' understanding by having them complete pages 72–73 in the Student Worktext.

1. Remind students to review their annotations and recall discussions they've had in order to complete the summary chart. Remind students that only evidence from the text should be included in the summary chart.

As students complete their summary charts, circulate and note which students struggle to identify the correct text evidence. Some students may benefit from small group instruction.

2. Remind students to include only the most important information in their summaries.

Have students work independently to complete page 72 of their Worktexts.

COLLABORATE When they have finished, have students exchange summaries with their partners and share their insights.

Return to the TEXT

Respond to Reading: Solitude

Review your annotations and notes.
Think about how they can help you summarize the text.

1. Use this chart to help you summarize the text.

Summary Chart		
	Informational Text	
Who?	the people or subjects	Thoreau, the elements of nature
What?	the topic or problem	the value of solitude in nature; the difference between loneliness and solitude
Where?	the location or region events occur	cabin and surrounding woods
When?	the date, year, or time	not sure—intro says book was published in 1854
How?	the events, steps, or processes	The author describes being alone in nature and how nature offers a sense of friendship, so he is not lonely.

2. Write a 2–3 sentence summary of the excerpt from "Solitude."

Sample summary: The author, despite living alone in a house in the woods, never feels lonely as he has a "sweet and beneficent society in Nature." He's comforted by "every sound and sight around" his house, even the "the very pattering" of rain drops. According to the author, we feel loneliness when we aren't at peace internally and we are "at the mercy" of our thoughts.

PROFESSIONAL DEVELOPMENT

Productive Conversation: Adding On

What Is It? Productive conversation is partner talk or small-group discussion that centers on a specific topic and is designed to develop certain skills. Adding on elicits related ideas or connecting ideas already discussed.

Why Is It Important? Adding on is similar to how natural conversation works, and gives students practice contributing their own ideas to a discussion. It may also encourage reluctant speakers to join without the pressure of starting the discussion.

Return to the TEXT

3. What does the author mean when he says, "The repose is never complete" in paragraph 1? Cite evidence from the text to support your answer.
Sample answer: He means that, day and night, there is always some part of nature stirring and making noise; there is never total stillness or silence. Even when it's dark, the "waves still dash" and the "wildest animals" "seek their prey."

4. Did Thoreau ever feel lonely? If so, why, and how did he overcome the emotion? Cite evidence from the text to support your answer.
Sample answer: Yes, he did. In paragraph 3 Thoreau admits that he felt "oppressed by a sense of solitude but once" soon after he "came to the woods." At first, he believed being alone was "something unpleasant," but saw there was "a slight insanity" to that belief. It was a "gentle rain" that helped him recognize the "sweet and beneficent society in Nature" and the sense of loneliness went away.

5. According to the author, what is the farmer's experience of loneliness? Cite evidence from the text to support your answer.
Sample answer: The farmer doesn't feel lonely when working alone in the field because his companion is his employment; he's too busy to feel loneliness. But when his work is done and he's home, "he cannot sit down in a room alone" because he has nothing to distract his mind and he's "at the mercy of his thoughts."

REFLECT What words, phrases, or sections did you have to reread to make sure you understood the text?
Sample answer: I reread paragraph 5 because the ideas in that paragraph about nature, being alone, and loneliness are hard to grasp.

How Do I Use It? Use adding on during collaboration to draw out students' insights. To formalize the discussion and keep it on topic, call on individuals (whole-class/small group) or assign turns (small group/partner). Help students connect and flesh out ideas with questions such as, *Thoreau says that there is a difference between solitude and loneliness. Solitude is ________ and loneliness is ________. What visual image from the text could represent the idea? What is your response to that idea?*

Return to the TEXT

Encourage students to refer back to the text and their annotations and notes to help them answer the questions.

3. Suggest that students clarify the meaning of *repose* and reread paragraph 1. What words in the paragraph suggest the opposite of repose?

4. Have students scan the text for direct references to loneliness, which appear in paragraphs 3, 4, and 5.

5. Suggest that students reread paragraph 4 and compare Thoreau's description of the farmer to what he says about the student.

Have students work independently to complete page 73 of their Worktexts.

REFLECT Remind students that rereading is a **Self-Monitoring Strategy** and that they made annotations and notes about confusions they may have had. Suggest that they review their annotations and think about any words, phrases, or sections that they reread to check their comprehension of the text.

Stop and Assess

Use the following rubrics to assess your students' understanding of the text.

Item 1 answers indicate:	
2	Thoreau wanted to share his delight in nature and thoughts on loneliness. At least two pieces of text evidence support the answer.
1	Thoreau wanted to share his delight in nature or his thoughts on loneliness. Supporting text evidence may be insufficient.
0	no understanding of the author's purpose and no text evidence.

Item 2 answers indicate:	
2	Thoreau uses sensory language to describe nature and precise language to convey ideas. At least two pieces of text evidence support the answer.
1	Thoreau uses sensory language to describe nature or precise language to convey ideas. Supporting text evidence may be insufficient.
0	no understanding of Thoreau's use of language and no text evidence.

Item 3 answers indicate:	
2	Thoreau means that, when alone, he's aware that he is part of nature and not really alone. At least two pieces of text evidence support the answer.
1	a vague understanding of Thoreau's meaning and/or supporting text evidence is insufficient.
0	no understanding of Thoreau's meaning and no text evidence.

Option: If you choose not to work with Texts 2 and 3 and to conclude the unit here, use the Visual Text and "Solitude" to answer the Focus Question: How does nature benefit us?

Return to the TEXT

Comprehension Check: Solitude

Answer the questions to demonstrate an understanding of what the text means.

1. What is the author's purpose in writing this text?
   Cite at least two examples from the text to support your answer.
   Sample answer: The author's purpose is to share his sense of delight and comfort in nature and his thoughts and observations on solitude and loneliness. In paragraph 3, he says that when he became aware of the "beneficent society in Nature," he found "an infinite and unaccountable friendliness." In paragraph 4, he describes his solitude as "companionable" and goes on to give other examples of solitude that don't involve loneliness—the farmer busy at work and the student engrossed in his studies.

2. How does the author's choice of language enhance the text's meaning?
   Cite evidence from the text to support your answer.
   Sample answer: The author uses language that brings his experience of the beauty of nature to the reader. In paragraph 1, he describes the evening as "delicious." The bullfrogs "trump to usher in the night," and the whippoorwill's song is "borne on the rippling wind." Thoreau also noticed that even though Nature's "repose is never complete," it is peaceful; "waves still dash," yet creatures peacefully rest in the sound. In paragraph 3, he describes his inner experiences by saying he "doubted if the near neighborhood of man was not essential to a serene and healthy life," but that after he connected with nature, the "fancied advantages" of human neighbors seemed "insignificant."

3. What does Thoreau mean when he says in paragraph 5 that he has "a great deal of company . . . especially . . . when nobody calls"?
   Support your answer with evidence from the text.
   Sample answer: He means that when he is not distracted by other people, he is aware of how full the world is and that he is part of nature, too. He compares himself to elements of nature, including a loon, a lake, the sun, flowers, and insects, and notes that these things are all "alone" but not lonely and that he is "no more lonely" than any of them.

PROFESSIONAL DEVELOPMENT

Annotations: Annotation Notes

What Is It? As active readers, we mark up a text to aid comprehension. We also jot down notes in a reading journal or adjacent to the text. These notes reflect our personal ideas, feelings, questions about, and reactions to the text.

Why Is It Important? Readers who annotate are engaged readers. Connecting with a character, event, or theme is easier when readers make notes. Annotation notes allow readers to ask questions that they can answer later, and readers can refer to their notes when analyzing the text. Annotating deepens comprehension, and annotation notes facilitate a personal connection to the text.

TEXT 2

Read the text to learn what the author observed while fishing on a lake. If you need to read any sections more than once, note the reason in the Annotation Notes column.
Sample annotations and notes appear throughout the text.

? The Halcyon in Canada

by John Burroughs

1 Upon the lake you had the wildness and solitude at arm's length. You emerged and had a vantage-ground like that of a mountain peak, and could contemplate at your ease.

Upon the lake you had the wildness and solitude at arm's length.

2 Seated upon my raft and slowly carried by the current or drifted by the breeze, I had many a long, silent look into the face of the wilderness, and found the communion good. I was alone with the spirit of the forest-bound lakes, and felt its presence and magnetism. I played hide-and-seek with it about the nooks and corners, and lay in wait for it upon a little island crowned with a clump of trees that was moored just to one side of the current near the head of the lake.

ANNOTATION NOTES

1st Read:
The author is alone on the lake with nothing but nature and his thoughts.

2nd Read:
halcyon = a kingfisher

In the first paragraph, "you" pulls the reader in.

nature is hard to catch—he "played hide-and-seek with it" and "lay in wait for it"

3rd Read:
Like Thoreau, Burroughs seems to connect deeply with nature, but he seems to be more concerned with observing closely and describing what he sees.

How Do I Use It? Model writing annotation notes for the first paragraph of the "The Halcyon in Canada" on Student Worktext page 75. Read the title and a few sentences aloud and then think aloud as you jot down a note: *I'm not sure what* halcyon *in the title means so I'll put a question mark next to the word and look it up later. As I read, I notice words that give the setting—"[u]pon the lake," "[s]eated upon my raft," "the wilderness"—which seem important, so I'll underline them. I associate the word* communion *with religion. I'm going to circle it and watch for other language with religious overtones.*

The Halcyon in Canada

Tell students that they will read to learn what the author observed while fishing on a lake.

1st READ

Set a Purpose

Tell students they will be reading to find out what the essay is about.

Have students read "The Halcyon in Canada" independently, annotating the text as they read. Circulate and note students' markings, especially questions and confusions.

Text-Dependent Questions

1. What experience is the author describing, and where is it taking place? (Sample answer: The author describes his experience of fishing on a lake surrounded by wilderness. We know from the title that he is in Canada.)

2. What shift occurs between paragraphs 3 and 4? (Sample answer: In paragraph 3, the author is the observer describing the world around him. In paragraph 4, he becomes "an object of great interest to the loons." He becomes the thing observed.)

Scaffolded Support Use the following scaffolded question and sentence frame as necessary to build comprehension.

In paragraph 3, what does Burroughs do as he sits on his raft looking out onto the lake?

In paragraph 4, what does Burroughs say he became?

The loons would come out to _________ him.

Partner Talk Have students discuss Burroughs's experience on the lake.

The Halcyon in Canada

2nd READ

Set a Purpose

Tell students they will read to examine point of view in the essay and the author's use of figurative language.

Text-Dependent Questions

1. What is the point of view of this essay? How do you know? (Sample answer: The first paragraph is written in the second person—Burroughs uses "you." But then in the following paragraphs he switches to first person "I.")

2. Vocabulary: Figurative Language Discuss Burroughs's frequent use of personification to describe elements of nature.

Paragraph 3: To what does Burroughs compare the ducks, loons, and fish hawks? (Sample answer: He calls them "performers"—he is the audience watching what they do when the breeze picks up.)

3. How does Burroughs's use of figurative language affect your understanding of the text? (Sample answer: When Burroughs compares the lake to an ear and an eye and when he gives animal and human qualities to elements of nature, such as the wind "purring" and "sauntering like one on a Sunday walk," the scenes come alive, making it easier to relate to what he is experiencing.)

Partner Talk Have students discuss the author's use of language and how it reflects and supports his purpose.

TEXT 2

ANNOTATION NOTES

1st Read:
The author is aware of how nature's elements, such as the wind, water, and fish, interact.

It's better to fish while there is a wind.

2nd Read:
"Footsteps" and "sauntering" give human qualities to the wind.

The word "performers" implies that watching nature is like watching a play.

3rd Read:
Fishing just seems to be an excuse for Burroughs to be in nature.

I saw him leave his comrades and swim straight toward me.

3 Indeed, there is no depth of solitude that the mind does not endow with some human interest. As in a dead silence the ear is filled with its own murmur. And amid these aboriginal scenes one's feelings and sympathies become external to him, as it were, and he holds converse with them. Then a lake is the ear as well as the eye of a forest. It is the place to go to listen and ascertain what sounds are abroad in the air. They all run quickly thither and report. If any creature had called in the forest for miles about, I should have heard it. At times I could hear the distant roar of water off beyond the outlet of the lake. The sound of the vagrant winds purring here and there in the tops of the spruces reached my ear. A breeze would come slowly down the mountain, then strike the lake, and I could see its footsteps approaching by the changed appearance of the water. How slowly the winds move at times, sauntering like one on a Sunday walk! A breeze always enlivens the fish; a dead calm and all pennants sink, your activity with your fly is ill-timed. You soon take the hint and stop. Becalmed upon my raft,

76 • Unit 4

PROFESSIONAL DEVELOPMENT

Intertextual Analysis: Compare and Contrast Authors' Use of Language and Text Structure

What Is It? When students compare texts, they should compare not just the topic and major ideas, but how the authors' ideas are presented and the language used to express them.

Why Is It Important? Text structure and language can reveal deeper meanings about texts, especially when compared side-by-side. Language and structure can provide evidence for conclusions, connections, and contrasts.

How Do I Use It? When comparing structure and language, it is often helpful to physically set the two texts side-by-side. Use classroom displays to invite students to analyze how the text

I observed, as I have often done before, that the life of Nature ebbs and flows, comes and departs, in these wilderness scenes; one moment her stage is thronged and the next quite deserted. Then there is a wonderful unity of movement in the two elements, air and water. When there is much going on in one, there is quite sure to be much going on in the other. You have been casting, perhaps, for an hour with scarcely a jump or any sign of life anywhere about you, when presently the breeze freshens and the trout begin to respond, and then of a sudden all the performers rush in: ducks come sweeping by; loons laugh and wheel overhead, then approach the water on a long, gentle incline, plowing deeper and deeper into its surface, until their momentum is arrested, or converted into foam; the fish hawk screams; the bald eagle goes flapping by, and your eyes and hands are full. Then the tide ebbs, and both fish and fowl are gone.

4 Patiently whipping the waters of the lake from my rude float, I became an object of great interest to the loons. I had never seen these birds before in their proper habitat, and the interest was mutual. When they had paused on the Hudson during their spring and fall migrations, I had pursued them in my boat to ? try to get near them. Now the case was reversed; I was the interloper now, and they would come out and study me. Sometimes six or eight of them would be swimming about watching my movements, but they were wary and made a wide circle. One day one of their number volunteered to make a thorough ! reconnaissance. I saw him leave his comrades and swim straight toward me.

ANNOTATION NOTES

1st Read:
Burroughs observes cycles on the lake of no activity, and then sudden bursts of wind, the movement of bird and fish.

2nd Read:
interloper = trespasser, someone who becomes involved where they are not wanted

3rd Read:
As an "object of great interest" to the loons, the roles are reversed—Burroughs really is just a part of nature like everything he observes.

looks on the page: Are the paragraphs long and dense or short and well-spaced? Are there headings, illustrations, or features such as bullets, or is the text plain prose?

In "Solitude" and "The Halcyon in Canada," the authors share detailed observations of the natural world. Students might compare the descriptive language the authors use by compiling words and phrases in a T-chart. Both authors also share their thoughts on the nature of solitude, which students might consider most fruitfully in small group discussions that focus on the authors' use of language to convey concepts.

The Halcyon in Canada

3rd READ

Set a Purpose

Tell students they will read to understand the essay's meaning.

Text-Dependent Questions

1. What is the main idea of paragraph 3? (Sample answer: The main idea of paragraph 3 is that nature is constantly changing and that a change in one part of nature ripples out to cause changes in other parts.)

Scaffolded Support Use the following scaffolded sentence frame and question as necessary to build comprehension.

Burroughs says that the life of Nature _________ and _________.

What happens when the breeze "freshens"?

2. Why is observation important to Burroughs as a fisherman? (Sample answer: He knows that when the scene around him has been "deserted" by movement and other creatures, the fish are less likely to bite. So, he watches for the breeze to pick up before casting his line.)

Think Aloud *I wonder and ask myself about the relationship between the author and the animals. When I reread, paragraph 4, I notice that Burroughs describes himself as an "interloper," an intruder. The loons are "wary," and one makes a "reconnaissance" like a soldier. So, the relationship between man and nature can be uneasy.*

Partner Talk Have students compare the theme of the essay to the theme of Thoreau's "Solitude."

Stop and Assess

Use the following rubrics to assess your students' understanding of the text.

	Item 1 answers indicate:
2	Burroughs's purpose is to share his experience of nature and to consider his place in nature. At least two pieces of text evidence support the answer.
1	Burroughs's purpose is to share his experience of nature or to consider his place in nature. Supporting text evidence may be insufficient.
0	no understanding of the author's purpose and no supporting text evidence.

	Item 2 answers indicate:
2	the author uses language to express his sense of the sacredness of nature and his connection with it. At least two pieces of text evidence support the answer.
1	the author uses language to show that he loves nature. Supporting text evidence may be insufficient.
0	no understanding of the author's use of language and no supporting text evidence.

	Item 3 answers indicate:
2	an understanding of a central theme of the text. At least two pieces of text evidence support the answer.
1	an idea about a theme of the text that lacks clarity. Supporting text evidence is insufficient.
0	no understanding of the essay's theme and no supporting text evidence.

Return to the TEXT

Comprehension Check: The Halcyon in Canada

Answer the questions to demonstrate an understanding of what the text means.

1. What is the author's purpose in writing this text?
How does the text structure support that purpose?
Cite evidence from the text to support your answer.
Sample answer: Burroughs's purpose is to share his experience of solitude in nature and to understand something about his own place in nature. He starts by giving a picture of himself "slowly carried by the current" on the water and trying to catch "the spirit of the forest-bound lakes." At the beginning of paragraph 3, he explains that being in nature takes him out of himself—his "feelings and sympathies become external to him." Then he gives a long and detailed description of his surroundings. In the last paragraph, he describes an instance in which he becomes the thing observed, and he is a part of nature.

2. How does the author use language to reveal his feelings about nature?
Cite at least two examples from the text to support your answer.
Sample answer: The author uses language to show that he feels nature is alive and sacred. In paragraph 2, he uses "communion" to describe his connection with nature, and explains that when he "was alone with the spirit of the forest-bound lakes" he felt its "presence and magnetism." He also uses language to express his feelings of connection with nature. In paragraph 3, he explains that while floating on the lake, he can hear "if any creature had called in the forest for miles about" because the "lake is the ear as well as the eye of a forest" and while floating on it, he and the lake are connected.

3. What is one theme of this text?
Cite evidence from the text to support your response.
Sample answer: One theme is man's connection with nature. When we pay attention to how "the life of Nature ebbs and flows," and notice the way different elements interact with each other, we can anticipate Nature's reactions and act accordingly. In paragraph 3, Burroughs explains that when you are not aware of the relationship between the wind, water, and fish, "all pennants sink, your activity with your fly is ill-timed" and you won't catch a fish. But when you pay attention, you'll know when to cast your line, just as the birds know when to arrive, and you are more likely to catch a fish.

PROFESSIONAL DEVELOPMENT

Academic Language: Conversation

What Is It? Academic language is the language used in the classroom. It is more formal than casual, everyday conversation and may employ discipline-specific vocabulary and rhetorical conventions. It takes practice to become "fluent" in the use of academic language, particularly during classroom conversation where students may be tempted to slip into a more casual and informal way of communicating.

Why Is It Important? Using academic language in classroom discussion is essential for students to succeed in school. Students who use academic language in conversations with peers develop academic confidence, improve their communication skills, and encourage other students to

Read the text to learn why the author returns to the fields. You may want to read some sections more than once and make different annotations and Annotation Notes each time.
Sample annotations and notes appear throughout the text.

Returning to the Fields

by T'ao Chien

Dong Qichang (1555–1636)

T'ao Chien (365–427 CE) is one of the most influential pre-Tang Dynasty Chinese poets.

When I was young, I was out of tune with the herd:
My only love was for the hills and mountains.
? Unwitting I fell into the Web of the World's dust
And was not free until my thirtieth year.
The migrant bird longs for the old wood:
The fish in the tank thinks of its native pool.
I had rescued from wildness a patch of the Southern Moor
And, still rustic, I returned to field and garden.

ANNOTATION NOTES

1st Read:
The author loved nature and didn't fit in with other people, but he got caught up in the demands of life. At 30, he returned to the land.

What is "the Web of the World's dust"?

2nd Read:
"Unwitting"—the author didn't realize he was becoming imprisoned.

compares himself to a bird and fish that have migrated

3rd Read:
Life seemed to pull him away from his true self.

take what they say seriously. Using academic language sets a tone to indicate that it is time for a thoughtful discussion.

How Do I Use It? In conversation with students, respond to and rephrase students' ideas using academic language to demonstrate the practice. If students are not using academic language, point out academic words or phrases they could use to express their thoughts in a more precise way. For example, in a discussion of "Returning to the Fields," encourage students to use sequence words to express what the poem is about. It can be something like the following:

At first, the author ________. Then, he realizes ________.
As a result he ________.

Returning to the Fields

Tell students that they will read to learn why the author of the poem returns to the fields.

1st READ

Set a Purpose

Tell students they will be reading to find out what the poem is about.

Have students read "Returning to the Fields" independently, annotating the text as they read. Circulate and note students' markings, especially questions and confusions.

Text-Dependent Questions

1. What is this poem about? (Sample answer: The author of this poem loves nature but got caught up in everyday life. When he turned 30 he was able to return to nature and feel at peace.)

Think Aloud *I will reread the poem to see the changes in the author's life. In the first line, he describes himself when he was young. Then he falls into "the Web of the World's dust." I'm not sure what that means, but I know he's trapped in that life until his "thirtieth year." Then he describes the next phase of his life in the "field and garden."*

2. What is the setting of the last part of the poem? (Sample answer: The author is living on a patch of land that he "rescued from wildness." The land seems to be on the edge of a "half-deserted village.")

Partner Talk Have students discuss what happens in the poem.

Returning to the Fields

2nd READ

Set a Purpose

Tell students they will read to examine the author's use of language.

Text-Dependent Questions

1. What kind of language does the author use to describe the setting in lines 10 through 18? (Sample answer: The author uses simple language. The trees "cluster" and "grow." A "dog barks," and a "cock crows." To convey a sense of quiet serenity, he says there is "no murmur" of the outside world and there is a "deep stillness.")

2. Vocabulary: Figurative Language Discuss the author's use of figurative language.

Line 1: The author says he was "out of tune with the herd." What does he mean? (Sample answer: He is comparing other people to animals who don't think for themselves.)

Partner Talk Have students discuss how the author uses language to describe nature.

3rd READ

Set a Purpose

Tell students they will read to understand the poem's meaning.

Text-Dependent Question

1. What does the author of the poem value? How do you know? (Sample answer: He seems to value a life in which everything follows its true nature. Trees grow, smoke rises, and dogs bark. He also values quiet and serenity.)

Partner Talk Have students discuss contrasting images in the poem.

TEXT 3

ANNOTATION NOTES

1st Read:
The author now lives outside the "distant hamlets of men" and is happier that way.

2nd Read:
Image of "half-deserted village" and sounds of distant animals creates a solitary mood.

"bars of a cage"—old life was a trap

3rd Read:
Strong connection to Thoreau and Burroughs—quietness and solitude in nature is a kind of freedom.

My ground covers no more than ten acres:
My thatched cottage has eight or nine rooms.
Elms and willows cluster by the eaves:
Peach trees and plum trees grow before the hall.
Hazy, hazy the distant hamlets of men.
Steady the smoke of the half-deserted village,
A dog barks somewhere in the deep lanes,
A cock crows at the top of the mulberry tree.
At gate and courtyard—no murmur of the World's dust:
In the empty rooms—leisure and deep stillness.
Long I lived checked by the bars of a cage:
Now I have turned again to Nature and Freedom.

PROFESSIONAL DEVELOPMENT

Productive Conversation: Providing Appropriate Wait Time

What Is It? Wait time is the silence between comments or following a question during a group discussion. Providing an appropriate wait time is an important part of managing productive conversation.

Why Is It Important? It is during wait time that students are pushed to consider new perspectives, make connections between ideas, and/or come up with their own answers to questions. If wait time is too short, students will not have time to process information independently. As a teacher, providing appropriate wait time encourages students to do the same in group discussion and makes them better listeners.

Return to the TEXT

Comprehension Check: Returning to the Fields

Answer the questions to demonstrate an understanding of what the text means.

1. What does the author mean by the "Web of the World's dust"? Cite evidence from the text to support your answer.
   Sample answer: The "Web of the World's dust" refers to the concerns and demands of life detached from nature—dust is something useless and meaningless that is whirling around. In lines 1 and 2, the author says that when he was young and before he was caught in the "Web," his "only love was for the hills and mountains." Then in line 19, the "Web" becomes "the bars of a cage." In lines 17 and 18, he says that, now free, "no murmur of the World's dust" disturbs the "leisure and deep stillness" of his "empty rooms."

2. What are the "distant hamlets of men," and why are they "hazy, hazy"?
   Sample answer: The "distant hamlets of men" represent the life of men cut off from nature. They're "hazy, hazy" because the author has left that life behind, and because they are shrouded in the "Web of the World's dust."

3. What inferences can you make from the text about the author's view of freedom? Cite evidence from the text to support your answer.
   Sample answer: The author feels freedom is living in relation with nature. He begins the poem by saying that when he was young his "only love was for the hills and mountains." Later he wants to return to them as the migratory animals in lines 5 and 6 want to return to their true homes. Only after he returns "to field and garden" does he feel happy and free.

How Do I Use It? An appropriate amount of wait time varies by topic. Read students' facial expressions and body language to better understand what an appropriate wait time is for the current conversation. If students begin to look unengaged or to fidget, the wait time is too long.

Stop and Assess

Use the following rubrics to assess your students' understanding of the text.

	Item 1 answers indicate:
2	a clear understanding of the metaphor. At least two pieces of text evidence support the answer.
1	an understanding of the metaphor that lacks clarity. Text evidence may be insufficient.
0	no understanding of the metaphor and no supporting text evidence.

	Item 2 answers indicate:
2	a strong understanding of the metaphor. At least two pieces of text evidence support the answer.
1	an understanding of the metaphor that lacks clarity. Text evidence may be insufficient.
0	no understanding of the metaphor and no supporting text evidence.

	Item 3 answers indicate:
2	a sound inference supported by at least two pieces of text evidence.
1	a sound inference, but supporting text evidence is insufficient.
0	a poor inference or no inference, and no supporting text evidence.

ANALYZE and SYNTHESIZE ACROSS TEXTS

Return to the Focus Question

Explain to students that they will fill out a graphic organizer that helps them answer the Focus Question: How does nature benefit us?

CONNECT TEXTS Have small groups of students discuss how each text they read helps them answer the Focus Question.

Scaffolded Support You may provide the following sentence frames to support students in their use of academic language:

In the text ________, the author/artist makes the point that ________. He/she does this by ________.

Remind students to use their annotations and summaries to support their answers. They can also reread portions of the texts, if necessary.

Have students complete their graphic organizers individually.

REFLECT Remind students that each text provides different information about how nature benefits us. Ask, *How did reading all four texts give you a greater understanding of this topic?*

ANALYZE and SYNTHESIZE ACROSS TEXTS

Return to the Focus Question: How does nature benefit us?

Review your answers to questions about the texts as well as your annotations and Annotation Notes, and think about the discussions you've had about the texts. How does that information help you answer the Focus Question?

Use the graphic organizer to organize information about the texts.

1. In the appropriate box below, record the details that help you answer the Focus Question.
2. Make connections between those details to answer the Focus Question. Write your answer in the box provided.

Woman Kayaker (Visual Text)
Sample answer: People take pleasure in nature.

The Halcyon in Canada
Sample answer: We can experience ourselves as part of nature.

Solitude
Sample answer: The author lives alone but is never lonely for his companion is nature.

Returning to the Fields
Sample answer: The author feels free only after he "turned again to Nature."

How does nature benefit us?
Sample answer: Nature offers us companionship, comfort, and a sense of peace. It provides a setting in which we can reflect upon our thoughts and better understand ourselves. When we listen, we see that all of nature, including us, is connected.

REFLECT How did making connections between the four texts enable you to answer the Focus Question?

Sample answer: The four texts show that, in nature, we are more likely to be connected with our true selves. When we are disconnected from nature, we can feel lonely and trapped. Nature offers companionship and comfort and helps us feel true happiness and freedom.

PROFESSIONAL DEVELOPMENT

Differentiation: Graphic Organizers

What Is It? Graphic organizers are tools that assist students in recording their understandings of the texts they read. They include main idea charts, summary charts, Venn diagrams, and other visual resources.

Why Is It Important? Graphic organizers aid in comprehension of text ideas, assist in recognizing a text's structure, and help structure ideas for writing.

How Do I Use It? Use graphic organizers to assist students in analyzing and synthesizing information from one or more texts before writing about their conclusions. Summary organizers at the end of each unit provide space for students to answer

WRITE

Writing About the Focus Question

Now that you have answered the Focus Question using all four texts, expand on your thinking and communicate your ideas through your writing.

USE EVIDENCE

- Explain how nature benefits us. Use at least one piece of evidence from the Visual Text and at least two pieces of evidence from Texts 1, 2, and 3 to support your answer.
- If you need more room, use additional paper.

MONITOR

- Use the Writing Checklist as you write to make sure your writing meets all the necessary criteria.
- Use the rubric on page 84 when you have completed a first draft of your writing to help you evaluate, revise, and edit your work.

WRITING CHECKLIST ✓

Does my writing . . .

- ☐ answer the Focus Question?
- ☐ have a clear organizational structure?
- ☐ cite the correct amount of text evidence?
- ☐ correctly use language, spelling, and conventions?

the Focus Questions individually for each text, and then collectively. After students fill in the answers for each text, ask them to find commonalities between the four separate summaries. Encouraging students to fill out the organizers using sentence frames can help students make connections by using parallel language.

You can also ask students to add at least one or two specific supporting text details from each text into the graphic organizer. When students write their full summaries, ask them to choose one or two of the most relevant and clear details as support for their answer.

Writing About the Focus Question

USE EVIDENCE Remind students that they should use their graphic organizers as well as their annotations in the texts to write their responses.

Allow students to revisit the texts as frequently as they need to in order to support comprehension and to respond to the Focus Question.

MONITOR After students have completed their responses, have them review the Writing Checklist and revise their writing response.

DIFFERENTIATE AND EXTEND

In addition to or instead of the writing response, consider having students complete one of the following assignments:

Write Beyond Have students write a biographical essay about one of the writers represented in this unit.

Read Beyond Have students read a selection of poems by T'ao Chien. Stage an oral reading of some poems with student readers followed by discussion about the poems' common themes.

Research Have students research the American transcendentalist movement of the 1820s and 1830s. Then have them write about or discuss the role of nature in transcendentalist thought.

Create a Visual Text Have students storyboard an animated version of "Returning to the Fields."

SELF-ASSESS and REFLECT

SELF-ASSESS Have students use the Writing Rubric on page 84 to self-assess their writing response and write a final version. Tell them to assign themselves a score from 1–4 (with "4" being the highest) for each category in the first column.

Use the Writing Rubric on Student Worktext page 84 to assess each student's writing. Record points for each category in the first column of the rubric. Have students remove the page from their Student Worktexts and place it in their writing portfolios, along with the drafts and final versions of their responses.

SELF-ASSESS and REFLECT

Focus Question: How does nature benefit us?

This is the rubric that your teacher will use to assess your writing. Refer to it as you revise your work. After you have finished the final version of your response, assess your response and record your points for each category on the "Student" line in the first column.

	Accomplished (4 points)	Competent (3 points)	Developing (2 points)	Beginning (1 point)
RESPONSE Score: Student ____ Teacher ____	The response answers the question effectively and with insight.	The response answers the question effectively.	The response partially responds to the question but does not adequately address it.	The response addresses the texts but does not address the question.
ORGANIZATION Score: Student ____ Teacher ____	The main idea is convincingly stated. Ideas are organized in cohesive paragraphs that support the main idea.	The main idea is clearly stated. Ideas are organized in logical paragraphs.	The main idea is weak. Ideas are organized in a somewhat logical and cohesive way.	The main idea is missing. The organization of the paragraphs is not logical.
TEXT EVIDENCE Score: Student ____ Teacher ____	Response includes more than one piece of appropriate text evidence from each text. Evidence supports the main idea in a thorough way.	Response includes one piece of text evidence from each text. Evidence supports the main idea clearly.	Response does not include at least one piece of text evidence from each text. Text evidence does not adequately support the main idea.	Response does not contain relevant evidence.
LANGUAGE Score: Student ____ Teacher ____	Writing includes precise and sophisticated vocabulary related to the topic.	Writing includes appropriate vocabulary related to the topic.	Writing includes imprecise and inaccurate vocabulary.	Writing does not include vocabulary that appropriately reflects the topic of the response.
SPELLING AND CONVENTIONS Score: Student ____ Teacher ____	Response includes correct spelling, grammar, and punctuation consistently.	Response includes mostly correct spelling, grammar, and punctuation.	Response has many errors in spelling, grammar, and punctuation.	Response's errors in spelling, grammar, and punctuation make it extremely difficult to understand the response.

UNIT 5

Focus Question When was leisure time better—in the past or today?

Texts for Close Reading

GENRE STUDY

Discuss with students the genres of *Cassell's Book of In-door Amusements, Card Games, and Fireside Fun,* "Coney Island Souvenir Guide 1905," and "Leisure Activities in 2015."

Remind students that *genre* refers to the format and features of a text and typically falls into one of two categories—literature or informational text. Literature is a creative work that doesn't necessarily rely on facts, and informational text contains factual information. The texts in this unit are informational texts but with distinctly different purposes. With the class, list the features of procedural texts, guidebooks, and fact sheets. Have students identify how these three types of informational texts are alike and how they are different.

Focus Question

Have students read the Focus Question on Worktext page 85. Tell students that the texts they will read will help them answer the question.

Texts for Close Reading

Have students read to themselves the summaries about the texts in this unit.

There is no need to explain what students should expect to find in their close readings or to do any pre-teaching about the subject matter.

TEXT COMPLEXITY

Fun Park
- Style: figurative
- Knowledge demands: low
- Levels of meaning: literal

Cassell's Book of Fun

Quantitative: 1190L

Qualitative
- Structure: conventional
- Language: archaic
- Knowledge demands: medium
- Levels of meaning: literal

Coney Island Guide

Quantitative: 1200L

Qualitative
- Structure: conventional
- Language: academic
- Knowledge demands: medium
- Levels of meaning: literal

Leisure Activities in 2015

Quantitative: 1020L

Qualitative
- Structure: conventional
- Language: academic
- Knowledge demands: medium
- Levels of meaning: literal

Fun Park

Set a Purpose

Explain to students that they will look at the image on page 86 to think about activities people enjoy in their leisure time.

Visual Text Analysis

Remind students that an image can be analyzed as a text by looking at its details and making inferences. Direct students' attention to the image on Student Worktext page 86.

1. Have students record their immediate impressions after they look at the image. Lead them to discuss as a whole class, in small groups, or with a partner what they think is happening in the illustration.

2. Encourage students to make note of the details that support their observations in question 1. Have students explain as a whole class, in small groups, or with a partner what details they noted and what those details tell them about ways in which people spend their leisure time.

3. Tell students to discuss the impact of the image and the ideas it conveys. Small groups can compare the conclusions they drew.

Provide any additional information you feel is appropriate to enhance the discussion as necessary to support your students:

- Public parks have been a part of American towns and cities since the mid-1800s. Then, as today, parks were designed to provide open space for relaxation as well as sports fields and facilities.
- Amusement parks appeared at about the same time, while the modern theme park didn't appear for another 100 years.

VISUAL TEXT

Fun Park

Look at the Visual Text to answer the following questions. Review the image or parts of the image as many times as necessary.

1. What does this illustration show?
   Sample answer: The illustration shows a park with people engaged in many different activities.

2. What evidence in the illustration supports your first impression?
   Sample answer: There is a castle, a slide, a swing set, a soccer field, a swimming pool with a lifeguard, a ball pit, picnic tables, a miniature golf course, and lots of green space surrounded by trees. Children are playing and parents are standing by and watching.

3. What did the illustrator want to convey in this image?
   Sample answer: The artist wants to show that leisure takes many forms, including active, physical ones. This picture shows people having fun in a kind of idealized way.

86 • Unit 5

PROFESSIONAL DEVELOPMENT

Collaboration: Small Group

What Is It? Collaboration is constructive conversation between students during which they share questions about and understandings of a text to enhance comprehension. Collaboration can take place among a whole class, in small groups, or between pairs, but it is most effective when you predetermine which size group is best for a particular topic and proceed accordingly.

TEXT 1

✔ Self-Monitoring Strategies you used to help you check your understanding as you read.

☐ Visualize. ☐ Draw conclusions. ☐ Ask yourself questions. ☐ Reread to clarify.

Read the text to learn about some indoor games people played in the past. Make annotations in the text and write your notes in the Annotation Notes column.

Sample annotations and notes appear throughout the text.

Cassell's Book of In-door Amusements, Card Games, and Fireside Fun

This collection of entertainments was published in 1881.

Preface

1 The Editor hopes that this work may be the means of introducing many a new game to the young folk for whom it ? has been his happiness to cater. He will not tell them that all play and no work make Jack a stupid boy. That's because he has no doubt that his readers are just as fond of their lessons as they are of merry romps or quieter games.

The Feather

2 A small flossy feather with very little stem must be procured. The players then draw their chairs in a circle as closely together as possible. One of the party begins the game by throwing the feather into the air as high as possible above the center of the ring formed. The object of the game is to keep it from touching ? any one, as the player whom it touches must pay a forfeit. It is impossible to imagine the excitement that can be produced by each player preventing the feather from alighting upon him. Indeed, so absurd generally is the picture presented, that it is difficult to say whether the players or the watchers have the most fun.

Original Sketches

3 Each person must be supplied with paper and pencil. At the top of the paper a small sketch is then drawn by everyone. It should represent some historical incident, or any other subject chosen. The proper way is for the subject to be announced as

ANNOTATION NOTES

1st Read:
This is a collection of games young people could play at a party or just with friends at home.

2nd Read:
introduction followed by descriptions of four different games

"all play and no work"—author recognizes the importance of leisure time

3rd Read:
Blowing a feather produces excitement that is "impossible to imagine"—Would it do so today?

Why Is It Important? Choosing the properly sized group for a collaborative discussion is critical. Larger groups allow more students to hear one another's ideas, while smaller groups allow students to delve deeper into their understanding of a text. Collaborative discussion develops speaking and listening skills and encourages students to consider a text from more than one perspective.

How Do I Use It? Once students have studied the Visual Text on their own, divide them into small groups for collaboration. Instruct students to infer the message the author wants to convey in the image. Remind students to cite text evidence to support their inferences.

Cassell's Book of Fun

Tell students that they will read to learn about some indoor games people played in the past.

1st READ

Set a Purpose

Tell students they will be reading to find out what this text is about.

Have students read *Cassell's Book of In-door Amusements, Card Games, and Fireside Fun* independently, annotating as they read. Circulate and make notes of students' markings, questions, and confusions. Your notes can be used to inform instruction and as data for informal assessment.

Text-Dependent Questions

1. What is the text about? (The text provides instructions for playing several games that can be played at home in a group.)

Scaffolded Support Use the following scaffolded question and sentence frame as necessary to build comprehension.

Who is "the Editor"?

In 1881, people entertained themselves by ________.

2. Vocabulary: Words in Context Discuss the meanings of unfamiliar words in their contexts.

Paragraph 2: What does it mean to "pay a forfeit"? (In the game, The Feather, if the feather touches one of the players, he or she must pay a forfeit, that is, a fine or penalty. The object of the game is not to have to pay a forfeit.)

Partner Talk Have students discuss the particular challenge of each game and the skills they require.

Cassell's Book of Fun

2nd READ

Set a Purpose

Tell students that they will reread to understand how the author uses language to reveal meaning.

Text-Dependent Questions

1. Who is the author referring to when he writes "We must not forget to say" in paragraph 5? (The author is referring to himself in the plural.)

2. Who do the pronouns "he" and "him" refer to throughout the text? (The author is referring to a player when he uses these pronouns, even though he probably means both men and women.)

Think Aloud *When I read "preventing the feather from alighting on him," I was confused because I was not picturing only men and boys. I see that the author never uses "she" or "her." He does write about "the players" or "the Artists," and the plural pronouns do not have gender. I conclude that he wants to include both men and women in the "young folk" that are his audience even though his language names only men.*

3. Vocabulary: Idioms Discuss any idioms students may not understand.

Paragraph 3: What does the idiom "on no account" mean? (It means "for no reason," "under no circumstance," or "absolutely not.")

Partner Talk Have students discuss the effect of the contrast between the author's formal use of language and the subject matter.

ANNOTATION NOTES

1st Read:
Original Sketches is like a group version of today's popular picture game.

2nd Read:
scrutinized = inspected or examined closely

3rd Read:
Original Sketches assumes a common understanding or education about subjects like a "historical incident."

soon as the papers are delivered. However, if preferred, no restriction of any kind need be placed upon the Artists. All may draw whatever they like. We need not remark that the latter method renders the guessing business a much more difficult affair. On the sketches being completed, each player passes his paper to his left-hand neighbor, who, after closely examining it, writes down at the bottom of the paper what he imagines the drawing is meant to represent. The paper is then folded over so as to conceal the writing. It is passed on again to the left, every player examining each sketch as it reaches him, and putting down what he thinks it is intended for. However, on no account must any one look at what has already been written. As soon as ? the sketches have been scrutinized and pronounced upon by every player, they are collected, and the various opinions are read aloud.

Parlor games gave young men and women the chance to amuse themselves and share some laughs.

Shadow Buff

4 This game, if well played, may be productive of much merriment. A large white sheet is first hung securely on one side of the room, and on a table some distance behind a very bright lamp must be placed. All other lights being extinguished, one of the party takes a seat on a low stool between the lamp and the sheet, but nearer the latter than the former. One after

PROFESSIONAL DEVELOPMENT

Differentiation: Contingency Questions

What Is It? Some students may require additional scaffolded support beyond whole-class questions and discussion in order to access the meaning of the text. Small-group or individually targeted questions, called contingency questions, provide this support.

Why Is It Important? Contingency questions allow students of all learning abilities to practice text analysis and to gain deeper meaning from the text. They also allow more detailed ongoing assessment of why certain students may struggle.

TEXT 1

another the company pass behind him, their shadows of course falling upon the sheet as they pass. It is much more difficult than most people would imagine to guess the original from the shadow, especially as in this game it is allowable for the players to disguise themselves to some slight extent. Gestures of any kind may be practiced, masks may be worn, false noses, or anything else of the kind, to render the work of the guesser more difficult, for this always tends very considerably to add to the general fun.

The Stage Coach

5 Now for a really stirring game, provided that in the party a ! few energetic lively young people are to be found. Many a hearty laugh has been heard from big people, as well as little ones, while the stage coach has rattled along through the rain and snow and sunshine round the drawing-room table. The leader tells everyone to assume a name connected in some way with a stage coach. Any of the four wheels, the horses, the bridles, the whip, the windows, the cushions, any of the passengers, or numerous other things, may be chosen. The objects selected are generally written down on paper, linked with the name of each owner, unless it be that the leader can trust to his memory without any such assistance. He then begins his narrative, which must be as lively and ridiculous as possible, telling how the stage coach started, where from, where it was going, how many passengers there were, what they were like, and so on. The narrator will find that one thing suggests others to his mind; the difficulty will probably be to narrate every incident that occurred as the conveyance rolled along. We must not forget to say that the greatest part of the fun consists in the jumping up, twirling around, and changing seats, that have to be done while the narrative is proceeding. The names assumed by the company are mentioned as frequently as possible, each of whom must recognize the call by rising from his seat, turning round, and then sitting down again. When "the stage coach" itself is mentioned by any one all must change places, the person left without a seat being called upon for a forfeit.

ANNOTATION NOTES

1st Read:
Shadow Buff and The Stage Coach include role-playing.

2nd Read:
Language from 1881 sounds old-fashioned.

3rd Read:
The Stage Coach is "really stirring" because everyone is moving around, changing seats, while a funny story is told. An imaginative story-teller is the key to this game's success.

Cassell's Book of Fun

3rd READ

Set a Purpose

Tell students they will read to make inferences from the text.

Text-Dependent Questions

1. What inference can you draw from the Preface about the author? (The author says that the book is intended to introduce new games to young people "for whom it has been his happiness to cater." This suggests that this was not the first book he wrote for young people.)

2. What connections can you make between the four games? (All four games require a group of willing players and a few common props. All four require imagination. All four can be played by people of many ages and abilities.)

3. Vocabulary: Synonyms Discuss pairs of words that have similar meanings.

Paragraph 5: What words does the author use that have meanings similar to "stirring"? (lively, excitement, merry, absurd, fun, energetic)

Partner Talk Have students discuss the inferences they can draw from the text about people's social lives in the 1880s.

How Do I Use It? Contingency questions are so called because they are contingent on students' struggles with the main set of text-dependent and layered questions. Only when students continue to struggle after a complete set of scaffolded instruction should you need to intervene. One effective strategy is to chunk the text, analyzing a single section or paragraph. Group students who are having similar difficulties, and generate targeted additional questions for each. Use extensive Think Alouds and modeling. Work from simple, concrete, first-read questions toward greater understanding. For ELL students, consider providing first-language support.

Return to the TEXT

Respond to Reading

You may want to check students' understanding by having them complete pages 90–91 in the Student Worktext.

1. Remind students to review their annotations and recall discussions they have had in order to complete the summary chart. Remind students that only evidence from the text should be included in the summary chart.

As students complete their summary charts, circulate and note which students struggle to identify the correct text evidence. Some students may benefit from small-group instruction.

2. Remind students to include only the most important information in their summaries.

Have students work independently to complete page 90 of their Worktexts.

COLLABORATE When finished, have students exchange summaries with their partners and share their insights.

Return to the TEXT

Respond to Reading: Cassell's Book of In-door Amusements, Card Games, and Fireside Fun

Review your annotations and notes.
Think about how they can help you summarize the text.

1. Use this chart to help you summarize the text.

Summary Chart		
	Informational Text	
Who?	the people or subjects	games played by young people in the 1880s
What?	the topic or problem	Young people can have fun with a little imagination and a willingness to act silly.
Where?	the location or region events occur	indoors, probably in a living room
When?	the date, year, or time	during the 1880s
How?	the events, steps, or processes	The set of instructions for each game has its own steps for set-up and play. Each game is independent of the others.

2. Write a 2–3 sentence summary of the excerpt from *Cassell's Book of In-door Amusements, Card Games, and Fireside Fun.*

Sample summary: This excerpt describes four games meant for young people during the late 1800s. Each game requires very few materials and could be played indoors in someone's home. Together, the games show that people had fun by playing silly games, telling stories, making guesses, and acting out skits.

PROFESSIONAL DEVELOPMENT

Self-Monitoring Strategies: Ask Yourself Questions

What Is It? In self-monitoring, students keep track of their own progress as they read. Questions and answers are especially useful in helping students make inferences about what they read. The purpose of self-monitoring is to encourage and help students read independently outside the classroom.

Why Is It Important? Asking themselves questions and formulating answers keep students' attention on the text while removing the stress of being directly quizzed by the teacher. Self-monitoring builds confidence because it increases comprehension. Asking and answering self-formulated questions also help students prepare for class discussions, writing assignments, and assessments.

Return to the TEXT

3. What is the tone and the purpose of the first paragraph? Cite evidence in the text to support your answer.
   Sample answer: The tone is friendly and inviting. "The Editor" is writing in the third-person voice about himself. In paragraph 1, he engages readers by saying ironically that he knows he doesn't need to warn them against too much play because he knows they're "fond of their lessons." Then he tells readers that he will introduce "merry romps or quieter games."

4. Which game requires the most preparation beforehand? What does it require?
   Sample answer: Shadow Buff requires gathering a number of objects, including a sheet, a table, and a bright lamp. The players must assemble costumes and hang the sheet.

5. Which games are most likely to become loud and boisterous? Support your answer with evidence from the text.
   Sample answer: The Feather, paragraph 2, leads to "impossible to imagine" excitement, and possibly a lot of laughter and running around as players try to keep the feather in the air. The Stage Coach, paragraph 5, is a "really stirring game" that is known to provoke "many a hearty laugh." But all the games are meant to be amusing, and the level of boisterousness could depend on the players.

REFLECT What parts of the text did you have to visualize to make sure you understood?
Sample answer: I visualized the game described in paragraph 2, the Feather, because at first, I didn't understand how the players were to keep the feather in the air. The text doesn't say exactly, but I can imagine that people blow on the feather to keep it aloft.

Return to the TEXT

Encourage students to refer back to the text and their annotations and notes to help them answer the questions.

3. You can support students by reading the Preface aloud as they follow along.

4. Remind students that this question requires that they compare the four games and make an inference based on those comparisons.

5. Suggest that students review the text again, looking for words or phrases that suggest "loud and boisterous" behavior. If they do not know the word *boisterous*, explain that it means "rowdy, wild, and uncontrolled."

Have students work independently to complete page 91 of their Worktexts.

REFLECT Remind students that visualizing is a **Self-Monitoring Strategy** and that they have annotations and notes about descriptive language and verbal images in the text. Suggest that they review their annotations and think about any sections that they visualized to check their comprehension of the text.

How Do I Use It? Introduce and model the Self-Monitoring Strategy of asking and answering questions. Remind students of the strategy if they are confused by points in the text. For example, in paragraph 2 of *Cassell's Book of In-door Amusements,* the author calls for "a small flossy feather with very little stem." Asking yourself, *What does the author mean by* flossy? helps readers understand that the feather should be light enough that it will float in the air if a person blows on it. The word *alighting* helps readers imagine the feather moving slowly on an invisible breeze.

Return to the TEXT

Stop and Assess

Use the following to assess your students' understanding of the text.

Item 1 answers indicate:	
2	how the games might appeal to different kinds of people. Two pieces of text evidence support the answer.
1	how one game might appeal to a certain kind of person with one piece of evidence as support.
0	a lack of understanding of how the games might appeal to different people.

Item 2 answers indicate:	
2	three possible effects and one piece of text evidence to support each one.
1	two possible effects with text evidence to support each one.
0	only one or no possible effect(s) with no text evidence for support.

Item 3 answers indicate:	
2	a claim about the people who played these games, with at least two pieces of evidence to support it.
1	a claim about the people who played these games, with only one piece of evidence to support it.
0	no claim about people who played these games and no text evidence.

Option: If you choose not to work with Texts 2 and 3 and to conclude the unit here, use the Visual Text and the excerpt from *Cassell's Book of In-door Amusements, Card Games, and Fireside Fun* to answer the Focus Question: When was leisure time better —in the past or today?

Return to the TEXT

Comprehension Check: Cassell's Book of In-door Amusements, Card Games, and Fireside Fun

Answer the questions to demonstrate an understanding of what the text means.

1. How might the different games appeal to different people? Support your answer with evidence from the text.

Sample answer: The different games require different skills and personalities. For example, Original Sketches might appeal to quieter people who might feel shy around strangers since it is all done "with paper and pencil," and it's not until the end that "various opinions are read aloud." Shadow Buff might be more suited to groups who already know each other because it's about recognition.

2. What are three possible effects or consequences of these amusements? Cite examples from the text.

Sample answer: The author states one effect or consequence in paragraph 4: "This game, if well played, may be productive of much merriment." Another effect might be that a group of people who don't know each other will get acquainted by having fun together. A third effect is to produce something pleasurable such as the "stirring" narrative and "many a hearty laugh" in the Stage Coach.

3. What do readers learn about the people who played these games in the 1880s? Use examples from the text in your answer.

Sample answers: People were sociable, and they were willing to act silly to entertain themselves. The author claims it is "difficult to say whether the players or the watchers have the most fun." People must have liked a variety of games because some, like Original Sketches, are quiet and calm, while others, like the Feather and the Stage Coach could get very physical and even wild. These people depended on themselves, or just a few items like a sheet, for their amusement, and they must have appreciated free entertainment.

PROFESSIONAL DEVELOPMENT

Productive Conversation: Clear Up Confusions

What Is It? Productive Conversation about the confusing passages of a text can help students clarify their thinking.

Why Is It Important? A conversation with a goal, such as sequencing key events, gives students practice in using key words and expressing ideas and encourages further close reading. For the teacher, the same conversation is an opportunity to assess whether students understand key terms and concepts.

Read to find out about Coney Island in New York City. If you need to read any sections more than once, note the reason in the Annotation Notes column.

Sample annotations and notes appear throughout the text.

Coney Island Souvenir Guide 1905

by W. J. Ennisson

The New Coney Island

1 ! Booths and sheds of former days have now become the greatest popular resort in the world. It is now the daily recreation ground of the great population of the metropolis of New York. It has become the objective point of millions of visitors from every part of the country.

2 To attain this end, millions have been lavishly spent in the building and adornment of immense pleasure grounds. Inside these great amusement gardens are found theatres, ball rooms, restaurants and aerial railways. There are also roller coasters and elaborate amusements of almost every description. There are lakes and bridges, inviting nooks where tired pleasure seekers may rest undisturbed. There are balconies from which to watch the passing crowds and a thousand other refinements of detail which have their part in the making of a harmonious whole.

At the peak of its popularity, between 1880 and the end of World War II, several million people visited Coney Island every year.

The Transformation

3 As New York grew, it was inevitable that more breathing places be found for its teeming multitudes. It needed more places which, when the mercury went soaring, would furnish safety valves for the crowded city.

4 From the earlier Coney Island, there has developed the splendid Coney Island of today. It's now the home of magnificent palaces and stupendous amusement enterprises. It can be called the

ANNOTATION NOTES

1st Read: a guide that was likely handed out to attract visitors to the amusement park

2nd Read: "greatest popular resort in the world"—exaggerated claim

3rd Read: summer in the crowded city was unpleasant—people needed "more breathing places" and "safety valves"

How Do I Use It? As students read and annotate a text, notice where they place question marks or where they seem to skip to the next section without reading. Form small groups to talk about those skipped sections. Start the conversation by asking questions and asking for feedback. *I'm a bit confused about what the author meant by "the earlier Coney Island" in paragraph 4. If the one today is "splendid," "magnificent," and "stupendous," what did the earlier one look like? Was it just a town on the beach? When was the earlier one built and what happened to it? Maybe we can learn more about the history of Coney Island.*

Coney Island Guide

Tell students that they will read to find out about Coney Island in New York City.

1st READ

Set a Purpose

Tell students they will be reading to find out what "Coney Island Souvenir Guide 1905" is about.

Have students read "Coney Island Souvenir Guide 1905" independently, annotating the text as they read. Circulate and note students' markings, especially questions and confusions.

Text-Dependent Questions

1. What is this text about? (The text is a guidebook to the various entertainments at the "immense pleasure grounds" of Coney Island.)

Scaffolded Support Use the following scaffolded question and sentence frame as necessary to build comprehension.

How is the setting described in paragraph 2?

In paragraph 3, the author describes New York in the summer as ________.

2. Vocabulary: Figurative Language Discuss the literal and figurative meanings of phrases.

Paragraph 3: What are the literal and figurative meanings of "furnish safety valves"? (Literally, a safety valve is a device that prevents pressure from building too high in a machine. Figuratively, it is something that people do to relieve stress.)

Partner Talk Have students discuss the purposes Coney Island served as described in the text.

Coney Island Guide

2nd READ

Set a Purpose

Tell students that they will read to determine how the author uses language and text structure to reveal the message.

Text-Dependent Questions

1. Why does the author use the word *transformation* in the second subheading? (The author uses this word to stress that "Coney Island of the present" is so much bigger, better, and brighter than "the Coney Island of the past." It's a more powerful word than *change* or *growth*.)

2. What does the list in paragraph 11 suggest about Steeplechase Park? (The amusements were made to appeal to a wide variety of people. Some will make people laugh (Funny Stairway, Funny Art Gallery); others sound frightening (Cabaret de la Mort, Dante's Inferno); still others seem mysterious (Cave of the Winds, Bottomless Pit).

3. Vocabulary: Idioms Discuss any idioms with which students may be unfamiliar.

Paragraph 5: What does "run riot" mean in this context? (It means that the "charming architecture and lavish decorations" are completely unrestrained. It suggests that the designers had unlimited budgets and went a little wild.)

Partner Talk Have students discuss the author's use of persuasive language used in the text.

TEXT 2

ANNOTATION NOTES

1st Read:
Author continues to describe Coney Island in extravagant terms.

Who were the "shrewd capitalists"?

2nd Read:
focus shifts to different features

fairylands = unreal or pretend

pièce de résistance = French for "a thing's most remarkable feature"

3rd Read:
Airship Tower is the *pièce de résistance*. Super tall structure covered in lights is awe-inspiring.

paradise of the pleasure seeking New Yorker. Visitors to New York take in Coney Island as a matter of course.

5 The Coney Island of the present has been wrought from the Coney Island of the past by shrewd capitalists. They saw a chance to transform the place into a clean and wholesome pleasure resort. As a result, we now have Luna Park, Dreamland and Steeplechase Park. They're fairylands of the twentieth century. Here charming architecture and lavish ? decorations run riot, and at night thousands upon thousands of blazing electric lights dazzle the eye on every side.

Luna Park, Coney Island, 1905

6 One can scarcely be surprised, in view of all the advantages Coney Island possesses over all its neighbors on the Long Island and New Jersey shore, that it is the most popular and famous pleasure resort on the Eastern coast. One should not be surprised that every day, every hour is opening up newer and still brighter prospects for this fair daughter of the sea. One sees this dazzling and ever-varied charm, this concentration of all the wholesome fun and harmless merriment in the world. It is the Coney Island of today.

Steeplechase Park

7 Time was only three short years ago when Steeplechase was Coney's biggest attraction. Today, it still shines forth this Summer with a radiance fairly equaling Luna Park and Dreamland.

8 The most striking of the novelties at Steeplechase and the two which are most likely to prove the sensations of the season now will be the "Airship Tower" and "Atlantis Under the Sea." The *pièce de résistance*, so to speak, of Steeplechase Park is the Airship Tower.

9 The Tower, which stands in the very center of the park, stretches into the air nearly 300 feet. With its 15,000 electric lights of alternating crimson and white, it serves as a fitting landmark for this great pleasure garden.

PROFESSIONAL DEVELOPMENT

Think-Aloud Modeling: Annotating

What Is It? Think-Aloud modeling of annotating requires a personal demonstration of marking up a text to note important or confusing information.

Why Is It Important? Ongoing Think-Aloud modeling helps ensure that students are annotating key ideas and points of confusion in order to focus rereading.

How Do I Use It? As you annotate sections of the text, use Think-Aloud modeling. When demonstrating how to annotate language, say, *The author creates a powerful impression of the park that tries to create an emotional reaction. I'm going to look at the words that create this impression. For example,*

10 There are many other changes and new ideas throughout Steeplechase, among them being a magnificent tiled swimming pool 80 by 300 feet, which is supplied with heated sea water. A new trolley device runs 1,700 feet out over the ocean. It operates a large car especially constructed by the Pullman Car Company, at a cost of $10,000. Then there is a new four-story funny stairway, and a platform floor, near the entrance, where the beams and timbers all move and work different ways. There are six bands of music in the park. They consist of 115 musicians. There is continuous music in both dance halls, as each has a double orchestra. The Steeplechase Hotel is this year under the management of the International Hotel Company, of St. Louis World's Fair fame. There have been over 11,000 rose bushes placed in the center of the park, which makes a very handsome and attractive floral display.

Steeplechase Park, Coney Island's longest lasting park, was destroyed by fire in 1907, but reopened in 1909.

11 Steeplechase Park comprises: an extensive Ball Room, Diamond Electric Plant, Funny Stairway, Earthquake and Shaking Floor, Cave of the Winds, Region of the Third Degree, Electric Spring Fountain, Emperor's Seat, Magic Mirrors, ? Menagerie, House of Too Much Trouble, Razzle Dazzle, Haunted Swing, Dew Drops, Grand Canal, Ferris Wheel, Giant See-Saw, Upside Down House, Magnificent Satin Theater, Gypsy Cave, Barrel of Love, Cottage of Foxy Grand Pa, Cabaret de la Mort, Bottomless Pit, Dante's Inferno, Ocean Bathing Pavilion, Swimming Pool, A French Voyage, Ocean Pier, Hotel and Restaurant, Air Ship Tower, Atlantis, Funny Art Gallery.

ANNOTATION NOTES

1st Read:
More details about Steeplechase Park; paragraph 10 gives interesting facts; paragraph 11 lists park features.

2nd Read:
menagerie = a collection of wild animals kept in captivity for exhibition

opinion words:
magnificent, handsome, attractive, extensive

3rd Read:
It seems old-fashioned, but it served the same purpose as today's theme parks.

the image of "thousands upon thousands of blazing electric lights" must have been especially dramatic in 1905 when many people didn't have electricity in their homes. I'm going to circle that. Those lights "dazzle the eye." The author uses the word dazzling in the next paragraph, too. I'll circle it there since the repetition seems important. It's a strong word that seems like it describes the whole park, not just the lights.

Coney Island Guide

3rd READ

Set a Purpose

Tell students they will read to make inferences about the text.

Text-Dependent Questions

1. Why does the author consider the Airship Tower "a fitting landmark" for Steeplechase Park?
(It is "fitting" because it is very tall and covered with lights that blink red and white. It could probably be seen for miles around. Its flashing must have seemed modern.)

2. What conclusion can you draw about why Coney Island was so popular with New Yorkers?
(People in New York City wanted to escape the noise, the crowds, and the summer heat. They wanted amusement and sought "wholesome fun and harmless merriment.")

3. What connections does the author make between Coney Island and the five senses?
(Its lights "dazzled the eye." So many rose bushes must have smelled wonderful. Restaurants offered tastes and flavors. Orchestras played music. The swimming pool contained "heated sea water.")

Think Aloud *The author wants readers to understand that everything at Coney Island was done on a big scale and provides lots of details to support that idea. When I visualize 11,000 rose bushes, I really get a sense of how extravagant it must have been.*

Partner Talk Have students discuss the author's message and how it is conveyed in the text.

Return to the TEXT

Stop and Assess

Use the following to assess your students' understanding of the text.

	Item 1 answers indicate:
2	what the builders set out to accomplish, with at least two pieces of supporting text evidence.
1	what the builders set out to accomplish, but the text evidence is insufficient.
0	no understanding of what the builders set out to accomplish.

	Item 2 answers indicate:
2	the effect of the author's word choices, with at least two pieces of relevant evidence as support.
1	the effect of the author's word choices, with only one piece of relevant evidence as support.
0	a lack of understanding about the author's word choices.

	Item 3 answers indicate:
2	the author's predictions for the future of Coney Island, with at least two pieces of evidence as support.
1	the author's predictions for the future of Coney Island, with only one piece of evidence as support.
0	no understanding of the author's predictions for the future of Coney Island.

Return to the TEXT

Comprehension Check: Coney Island Souvenir Guide 1905

Answer the questions to demonstrate an understanding of what the text means.

1. What did Coney Island's builders set out to accomplish? Use evidence from the text to support your answer.
   Sample answer: The builders wanted to build "immense pleasure grounds" that combined "refinements of detail" into a "harmonious whole." They spent millions of dollars creating rides, theaters, ballrooms, restaurants, etc. to give pleasure and, as the author says in paragraph 3, to provide "safety valves for the crowded city." These "shrewd capitalists" wanted Coney Island to be the "most popular and famous pleasure resort on the Eastern coast," to draw big crowds, and to make money.

2. What is the effect of the words and phrases the author uses to describe Coney Island? Cite several examples.
   Sample answer: Because the text is meant to attract visitors, the author uses many flattering terms, including "greatest popular resort in the world," "splendid," "magnificent," "stupendous," and "the paradise of the pleasure seeking New Yorker." In paragraph 5, he says that the developer wanted to create a "clean and wholesome" park, probably to appeal to families with children. In paragraph 6, the author cites Coney Island's "dazzling and ever-varied charm" and calls it a "concentration of ... harmless merriment."

3. What future did the author predict or imagine for Coney Island? Cite specific details from the text.
   Sample answer: In paragraph 6, the author says, "every day, every hour is opening up newer and still brighter prospects for this fair daughter of the sea." This suggests that the resort will keep growing. The details in paragraphs 10 and 11 show the recently built attractions, with an implication of more to come: more rides, more hotels, more towers, more entertainments, and more gardens.

PROFESSIONAL DEVELOPMENT

Productive Conversation: Revoicing and Restating

What Is It? Productive Conversation strategies are ways to encourage student interactions while discussing a text, to clear up confusion, and to model academic language. Revoicing and restating involve either repeating a student's contributions in your own words, or asking another student to repeat and explain what a classmate said.

Why Is It Important? Teacher-restating can help students clarify ideas and use academic language if they are having trouble articulating their thoughts. It can also clarify a student's statement for his or her classmates in order to extend discussion. Student revoicing can prompt reluctant participants to speak

TEXT 3

Read to find out how Americans spent their leisure time in 2015. You may want to read some sections more than once and make different annotations and Annotation Notes each time.
Sample annotations and notes appear throughout the text.

Leisure Activities in 2015

1 On an average day, nearly everyone aged 15 and over is engaged in some sort of leisure activity. This may include watching TV, socializing, or exercising. Of those who engaged in leisure activities, men spent more time in these activities (5.8 hours) than did women (5.1 hours).

2 Watching TV was the leisure activity that occupied the most time (2.8 hours per day). It accounted for more than half of leisure time, on average, for those age 15 and over. Socializing, such as visiting with friends or attending or hosting social events, was the next most common leisure activity. It accounted for 41 minutes per day.

3 Men were more likely than women to participate in sports, exercise, or recreation on a given day, 23 percent compared with 18 percent. When men participated, they spent more time in these activities than did women. This was 1.7 hours compared with 1.2 hours.

Leisure is time free from obligations, work, or tasks needed for survival.

ANNOTATION NOTES

1st Read:
list of statistics about how people spent their leisure activity in 2015, including particular groups

2nd Read:
first point talks about types of people, then reports on particular activities

3rd Read:
The statements are data-driven and measured.

Unit 5 • 97

without feeling that they must contribute novel ideas. It can also help students analyze their classmates' thinking for strengths and/or weaknesses. It can also reinforce and validate students' abilities to contribute to a conversation.

How Do I Use It? Revoicing and restating can help students who need more support, either by clarifying their own statements, or directing them to a classmate who has greater understanding. If student-thinking seems unclear, say, *So let me see if I understand your thinking. You said ________, is that right?* To guide students toward a classmate's understanding, call on a new student and ask, *What do you think ________ is saying? Do you agree with him/her?*

Leisure Activities in 2015

Tell students that they will read to find out how Americans spent their leisure time in 2015.

1st READ

Set a Purpose

Explain to students that they will read to understand what the text is about. Have students read "Leisure Activities in 2015" independently, annotating the text.

Text-Dependent Questions

1. What do the statistics in the fact sheet reflect? (The statistics reflect the ways in which people spend time when they are free to choose what to do.)

2. What are some of the leisure activities included in this report? (The activities include watching TV, socializing, playing video games, using a computer, playing sports, and exercising.)

3. How does the author define "socializing"? (In paragraph 2, the author gives two examples: "visiting with friends" and "attending or hosting social events.")

4. According to the report, who has the most leisure time and how do they spend it? (In paragraph 4, the text states, "adults age 75 and over spent 7.8 hours engaged in leisure activities"—more than other age groups. They watch television, play games, use a computer, and do some reading.)

Partner Talk Have students discuss the statistics that surprised them the most.

Leisure Activities in 2015

2nd READ

Set a Purpose

Tell students they will read to examine how the text's structure supports its message.

Text-Dependent Questions

1. What is the purpose of the first paragraph? (Paragraph 1 includes general facts about who the study includes and what kinds of activities it covers.)

2. In general, how are the paragraphs ordered? (The focus of the paragraphs alternates between specific activities and specific groups.)

Partner Talk Have students discuss the text structure and its impact on their understanding.

3rd READ

Set a Purpose

Tell students they will read to make inferences from the statistics presented in the text.

Text-Dependent Questions

1. Which of the leisure activities described here were available to people in 1881 (Cassell's Book) or 1905 (Coney Island Guide)? Which were not? (People in 1881 and 1905 socialized, exercised, and played games in their homes or at amusement parks. They did not watch TV or use computers.)

2. What inference can you draw from the text about how raising young children affects adults' leisure time? (Raising children takes away from the parents' leisure time.)

Partner Talk Have students compare the uses of leisure time across the three texts.

TEXT 3

ANNOTATION NOTES

1st Read:
statistics about different age groups, households with and without children and how much time they spend reading, playing games, or using a computer

2nd Read:
"adults age 75 and over," "Individuals age 15 to 19," "employed adults"—study groups people by factual information

3rd Read:
Young people spend less time reading and more time on computers than older people. Did young people spend more time reading before computers?

4 On an average day, adults age 75 and over spent 7.8 hours engaged in leisure activities. This is more than any other age group. Thirty-five to forty-four-year-olds spent 4.0 hours engaged in leisure and sports activities. This was less than other age groups.

5 Time spent reading for personal interest and playing games or using a computer for leisure varied greatly by age. Individuals age 75 and over averaged 1.1 hours of reading per weekend day. They spent 20 minutes playing games or using a computer for leisure. Individuals age 15 to 19 read ! for an average of 8 minutes per weekend day. They spent 1.3 hours playing games or using a computer for leisure.

6 Employed adults living in households with no children under age 18 engaged in leisure activities for 4.5 hours per day. That was 1.1 hours more than employed adults living with a child under age 6.

98 • Unit 5

PROFESSIONAL DEVELOPMENT

Intertextual Analysis: Evidence from Multiple Texts

What is It? Students analyze a concept or explore a topic and cite evidence from more than one text to support their ideas. Citations can include quoting directly, paraphrasing, and summarizing.

Why Is It Important? Using more than one source for support adds to the force of an argument or the reliability of a claim. Citing multiple sources also indicates that the writer has researched the topic in a balanced manner.

Return to the TEXT

Comprehension Check: Leisure Activities in 2015

Answer the questions to demonstrate an understanding of what the text means.

1. What comparisons can you make between how men and women spend their leisure time? Cite evidence to support your answer.
   Sample answer: According to the text, men took more leisure time than women and their leisure activities were more likely to be physical. Paragraph 1 states that men spent more time than women daily in leisure activities (5.8 hours to women's 5.1 hours). Paragraph 3 states that men were more likely to "participate in sports, exercise, or recreation" on a given day and when they did, they spent more time doing it.

2. Which leisure activity was the most popular across all ages in the study? Cite text evidence to support your answer.
   Sample answer: According to the text, the most popular leisure activity in 2015 was watching television. Paragraph 2 states that watching television "occupied the most time (2.8 hours per day)" and accounted for "more than half of leisure time . . . for those 15 and over." This is more than double the amount of time spent on the second most popular leisure activity, socializing (41 minutes).

3. What does the report tell us about Americans' priorities regarding leisure time? Give text evidence for your response.
   Sample answer: It tells us that Americans preferred leisure activities that weren't very active. Watching TV came in first at 2.8 hours a day. Teenagers also spent "1.3 hours playing games or using a computer for leisure." This means that teenagers' total average screen time (4.1 hours) nearly exceeds the time average "employed adults" spent in total leisure activities each day.

How Do I Use It? As students work with the texts in this unit, remind them that they will need to support, with text evidence, any statements they make about the content. When they search the texts to answer questions, suggest that they use a specific color or type of highlighting to set apart sections they might want to quote directly. In the margin, have them note what the quotation explains or what inferences can be drawn from it. Remind students that quotations require attributions to identify the text from which they are drawn.

Return to the TEXT

Stop and Assess

Use the following to assess your students' understanding of the text.

Item 1 answers indicate:	
2	a comparison between how men and women spend their time based on at least two pieces of text evidence.
1	a comparison between how men and women spend their time based on only one piece of text evidence.
0	a lack of understanding of how men and women spend their time differently.

Item 2 answers indicate:	
2	that watching television is the most popular, with at least two pieces of supporting evidence.
1	that watching television is the most popular, with only one piece of supporting evidence.
0	no understanding of which activity is the most popular.

Item 3 answers indicate:	
2	a claim about Americans' priorities, with at least two pieces of supporting evidence.
1	a claim about Americans' priorities, with only one piece of supporting evidence.
0	no understanding of Americans' priorities regarding leisure time.

ANALYZE and SYNTHESIZE ACROSS TEXTS

Return to the Focus Question

Explain to students that they will fill out a graphic organizer that helps them answer the Focus Question: When was leisure time better—in the past or today?

CONNECT TEXTS Have small groups of students discuss how each text they read helps them answer the Focus Question.

Scaffolded Support You may provide the following sentence frames to support students in their use of academic language:

> In the text ________ ,
> the author/artist makes
> the point that ________ .
> He/she does this
> by ________ .

Remind students to use their annotations and summaries to support their answers. They can also reread portions of the texts, if necessary.

Have students complete their graphic organizers individually.

REFLECT Remind students that each text provides different information about how people spend their leisure time. Ask, *how did reading all four texts give you a greater understanding of whether leisure time was better spent today or in the past?*

ANALYZE and SYNTHESIZE ACROSS TEXTS

Return to the Focus Question: When was leisure time better—in the past or today?

Review your answers to questions about the texts as well as your annotations and Annotation Notes, and think about the discussions you've had about the texts. How does that information help you answer the Focus Question?

Use the graphic organizer to organize information about the texts.

1. In the appropriate box, record the details that help you answer the Focus Question.
2. Make connections between those details to answer the Focus Question. Write your answer in the box provided.

Fun Park (Visual Text)
Sample answer: A modern park offers a variety of activities for children and adults.

Coney Island Souvenir Guide
Sample answer: In 1905, Coney Island was filled with attractions for millions of visitors.

Cassell's Book of In-door Fun
Sample answer: In the 1880s, small groups of people played simple games at home.

Leisure Activities in 2015
Sample answer: Today, people spend most of their leisure time in front of screens.

When was leisure time better—in the past or today?
Sample answer: I believe leisure time was better in the past because people got together to play games in their homes or visited places filled with attractions, like Coney Island. Leisure was more interactive, creative, and likely less expensive. Today, people spend most of their leisure time in front of screens.

REFLECT How did making connections between the four texts enable you to answer the Focus Question?
Sample answer: The texts provided examples of leisure time in 1881, 1905, and 2015. The Visual Text provided imagery of family fun at a modern park. Together, I can compare and contrast what people did for leisure time in different historical periods.

PROFESSIONAL DEVELOPMENT

Intertextual Analysis: Analyzing Across Genres

What Is It? Students compare two or more texts of different genres in terms of purpose, point of view, or other specific aspects. The more specific the comparison being made, and the greater the variety of texts, the more useful it is for helping students develop reading and writing skills. Comparisons may be made across genres, as in comparing a photo to a written text, or across media, as in comparing a graph to a bulleted list.

WRITE

Writing About the Focus Question

Now that you have answered the Focus Question using all four texts, expand on your thinking and communicate your ideas through your writing.

USE EVIDENCE

- Explain what you have learned about leisure time in the past and in the present and which is "better." Use at least one piece of evidence from the Visual Text and at least two pieces of evidence from Texts 1, 2, and 3 to support your answer.
- If you need more room, use additional paper.

MONITOR

- Use the Writing Checklist as you write to make sure your writing meets all the necessary criteria.
- Use the rubric on page 102 when you have completed a first draft of your writing to help you evaluate, revise, and edit your work.

WRITING CHECKLIST ✔

Does my writing . . .

- ☐ answer the Focus Question?
- ☐ have a clear organizational structure?
- ☐ cite the correct amount of text evidence?
- ☐ correctly use language, spelling, and conventions?

Why Is It Important? Being able to approach a topic from multiple vantage points is an important higher-order thinking skill. Comparing texts of different genres helps students learn to distinguish between facts and opinions, analyze how authors use facts, and find details to support their own ideas.

How Do I Use It? Comparing multiple texts is an excellent way to take advantage of your students' strengths. For example, a visual or mathematical learner could help other students find and interpret the statistics on a complex chart. A verbal learner could explain thematic connections between written texts.

Writing About the Focus Question

USE EVIDENCE Remind students that they should use their graphic organizers as well as their annotations in the texts to write their responses.

Allow students to revisit the texts as frequently as they need to in order to support comprehension and to respond to the Focus Question.

MONITOR After students have completed their responses, have them review the Writing Checklist and revise their writing responses.

DIFFERENTIATE AND EXTEND

In addition to or instead of the writing response, consider having students complete one of the following assignments:

Write Beyond Have students take on the role of a travel writer. Have them write a descriptive article to attract people their age to Coney Island.

Create a Timeline Have students keep track of their use of leisure time over a period of a month. Invite individuals to report to the class on what they learned about themselves.

Debate an Issue Have students debate whether leisure time is better in the past or today.

Research Invite students to research the history of parlor games. Research might focus on a single culture or compare parlor games across cultures.

SELF-ASSESS and REFLECT

SELF-ASSESS Have students use the Writing Rubric on page 102 to self-assess their writing response and write a final version. Tell them to assign themselves a score from 1–4 (with "4" being the highest) for each category in the first column.

Use the Writing Rubric on Student Worktext page 102 to assess each student's writing. Record points for each category in the first column of the rubric. Have students remove the page from their Student Worktexts and place it in their writing portfolios, along with the drafts and final versions of their responses.

SELF-ASSESS and REFLECT

Focus Question: When was leisure time better—in the past or today?

This is the rubric that your teacher will use to assess your writing. Refer to it as you revise your work. After you have finished the final version of your response, assess your response and record your points for each category on the "Student" line in the first column.

	Accomplished (4 points)	Competent (3 points)	Developing (2 points)	Beginning (1 point)
RESPONSE Score: Student ____ Teacher ____	The response answers the question effectively and with insight.	The response answers the question effectively.	The response partially responds to the question but does not adequately address it.	The response addresses the texts but does not address the question.
ORGANIZATION Score: Student ____ Teacher ____	The main idea is convincingly stated. Ideas are organized in cohesive paragraphs that support the main idea.	The main idea is clearly stated. Ideas are organized in logical paragraphs.	The main idea is weak. Ideas are organized in a somewhat logical and cohesive way.	The main idea is missing. The organization of the paragraphs is not logical.
TEXT EVIDENCE Score: Student ____ Teacher ____	Response includes more than one piece of appropriate text evidence from each text. Evidence supports the main idea in a thorough way.	Response includes one piece of text evidence from each text. Evidence supports the main idea clearly.	Response does not include at least one piece of text evidence from each text. Text evidence does not adequately support the main idea.	Response does not contain relevant evidence.
LANGUAGE Score: Student ____ Teacher ____	Writing includes precise and sophisticated vocabulary related to the topic.	Writing includes appropriate vocabulary related to the topic.	Writing includes imprecise and inaccurate vocabulary.	Writing does not include vocabulary that appropriately reflects the topic of the response.
SPELLING AND CONVENTIONS Score: Student ____ Teacher ____	Response includes correct spelling, grammar, and punctuation consistently.	Response includes mostly correct spelling, grammar, and punctuation.	Response has many errors in spelling, grammar, and punctuation.	Response's errors in spelling, grammar, and punctuation make it extremely difficult to understand the response.

UNIT 6

Focus Question What purpose does volunteering serve?

Texts for Close Reading

GENRE STUDY

Discuss with students the genres of "Inaugural Address," "About CNCS," and "AmeriCorps State and National FAQs."

Remind students that *genre* refers to the format and features of a text and typically falls into one of two categories—literature or informational text. Literature is a creative work that doesn't necessarily rely on facts, and informational text contains factual information. All of the texts in this unit are informational texts, but Kennedy's speech uses some of the same language techniques as poetry, while the explanatory text and FAQ have more conventional fact-based structures. With the class, list the features of speeches, explanatory texts, and FAQs. Have students identify the shared characteristics of explanatory texts and FAQs.

Focus Question

Have students read the Focus Question on Worktext page 103. Tell students that the texts they will read will help them answer the question.

Texts for Close Reading

Have students read to themselves the summaries about the texts in this unit.

There is no need to explain what students should expect to find in their close readings or to do any pre-teaching about the subject matter.

TEXT COMPLEXITY

Ripples
- Style: documentary
- Knowledge demands: low
- Levels of meaning: inferential

Inaugural Address

Quantitative: 1140L

Qualitative
- Structure: conventional
- Language: academic
- Knowledge demands: high
- Levels of meaning: literal

About CNCS

Quantitative: 1140L

Qualitative
- Structure: conventional
- Language: familiar
- Knowledge demands: low
- Levels of meaning: literal

AmeriCorps FAQs

Quantitative: 1020L

Qualitative
- Structure: unconventional
- Language: familiar
- Knowledge demands: low
- Levels of meaning: literal

Ripples

Set a Purpose

Explain to students that they will look at the image on page 104 to gain a deeper understanding of how the effects of actions can spread.

Visual Text Analysis

Remind students that an image can be analyzed as a text by looking at its details and making inferences. Direct students' attention to the image on Student Worktext page 104.

1. Have students record their impressions after they look at the image. Lead them to discuss as a whole class, in small groups, or with a partner what they think happened just before the moment in the photo.

2. Encourage students to make note of the details that support their observations in question 1. Have students explain as a whole class, in small groups, or with a partner what details they noted and what the image might symbolize.

Provide any additional information you feel is appropriate to enhance the discussion as necessary to support your students:

- Symbolism is when one object or word stands for another object or idea.
- Symbolism can be a literary device, but it is also often used in visual art.
- Ripples are a common symbol of cause-and-effect relationships.

VISUAL TEXT

Ripples

Look at the Visual Text to answer the following questions. Review the image or parts of the image as many times as necessary.

1. What is happening in this image?
   Sample answer: Drops of water are falling into a blue pool of water and ripples are spreading out in a circle.

2. What details in the image support your answer to the previous question?
   Sample answer: The ripples, circular waves, are spreading out from the middle. A ripple is created when a drop splashes into the water. Where the drop falls is the middle of the circle. As more drops fall, more ripples are created.

3. When you think about this image, what ideas and feelings come to mind?
   Sample answer: The image is soothing because of the blue color and the gentle movement of the water. The image also shows that the drop of water causes the ripple to occur, which suggests that one action is dependent on another.

104 • Unit 6

PROFESSIONAL DEVELOPMENT

Teacher Observation: Student Annotations

What Is It? Circulating as students independently annotate a text provides you an opportunity to observe and take notes while recording key ideas students highlight, misunderstandings that arise, places where background information is lacking, and points of confusion.

Why Is It Important? While text-dependent questions and suggestions are provided, the most successful close-reading questions will arise from the comprehension needs of your students. Circulating and observing while students annotate texts can provide you with this valuable information and give you insight into how your students are thinking about what they read.

TEXT 1

✔ Self-Monitoring Strategies you used to help you check your understanding as you read.

☐ Visualize. ☐ Draw conclusions. ☐ Ask yourself questions. ☐ Reread to clarify.

Read the text to learn the message in President John F. Kennedy's January 20, 1961, inaugural speech, delivered in Washington, D.C. Make annotations in the text and write your notes in the Annotation Notes column.

Sample annotations and notes appear throughout the text.

Inaugural Address

by President John F. Kennedy

1 We observe today not a victory of party but a celebration of freedom—symbolizing an end as well as a beginning—signifying renewal as well as change. For I have sworn before you and Almighty God the same solemn oath our forebears prescribed nearly a century and three-quarters ago.

2 ? The world is very different now. For man holds the power to abolish all forms of human poverty and all forms of human life. And yet the same revolutionary beliefs for which our forebears fought are still at issue around the globe. We dare not forget today that we are the heirs of that first revolution. Let the word go forth that the torch has been passed to a new generation of Americans born in this century, tempered by war, disciplined by a hard and bitter peace, and proud of our ancient heritage. They are unwilling to witness or permit the slow undoing of those human rights to which this nation has always been committed today and around the world.

3 Let every nation know that we shall pay any price, bear any burden and meet any hardship. We will support any friend and oppose any foe to assure the success of liberty.

4 To those old allies whose cultural and spiritual origins we share, we pledge the loyalty of faithful friends. United there is little we cannot do in a host of cooperative ventures. Divided there is little we can do for we dare not meet a powerful challenge at odds and split asunder.

5 ? To those new states whom we welcome to the ranks of the free, we pledge our word that one form of colonial control shall not have passed away merely to be replaced by a far greater tyranny. We shall not always expect to find them supporting

ANNOTATION NOTES

1st Read:
Kennedy makes a speech in which he promises both change and a reaffirmation of the ideas America was founded on.

2nd Read:
lots of words referencing history: "forebears," "revolutionary," "heirs," "generation"

3rd Read:
The President's "victory" is not just a political change, it is a generational change.

How Do I Use It? You can create a simple three-column note-taking form. Use the headings "Preplanned Text-Dependent Questions"; "Observations of Students: Name/Misunderstanding"; and "New Text-Dependent Questions." Use your notes to create text-dependent questions, identify places in the text to model strategies, and modify your plans for upcoming close readings of the text. Use your observations and insights from student annotations to develop scaffolded text-dependent questions or probe the meaning of the annotations. You might probe the sample annotation on page 105, paragraph 2, by asking, *Why do you think Kennedy makes so many references to the American Revolution? What feelings do you think these references evoked in his audience?*

Inaugural Address

Tell students that they will read to learn the message in President John F. Kennedy's inaugural speech.

1st READ

Set a Purpose

Tell students they will be reading to find out what is happening in the text.

Have students read "Inaugural Address" independently, annotating as they read. Circulate and make notes of students' markings, questions, and confusions. Your notes can be used to inform instruction and as data for informal assessment.

Text-Dependent Questions

1. What is happening in this excerpt? (John F. Kennedy is giving a speech on the day he is sworn into office as President of the United States.)

2. What ideas does Kennedy include in the address? (Kennedy says that if people work together, they can bring about peace and prosperity around the world. While he doesn't call on people to volunteer for specific projects, he says that all Americans and people around the world need to pitch in to achieve this goal.)

3. Vocabulary: Idioms Discuss idiomatic use of language.

Paragraph 2: What does the phrase "the torch has been passed" mean here? (The phrase means that power or leadership is being transferred. The idiom comes from relay races in which runners take turns carrying an object.)

Partner Talk Have students discuss the main ideas of Kennedy's speech.

Inaugural Address

2nd READ

Set a Purpose

Tell students that they will be rereading parts of "Inaugural Address" to analyze Kennedy's word choices.

Text-Dependent Questions

1. Does Kennedy talk mostly about the past, the present, or the future? **(Kennedy talks about the past and present at first, but mostly he talks about the future.)**

Scaffolded Support Use this scaffolded question and sentence frame as necessary to build comprehension.

What verb tense do you see most often in the speech?

Kennedy talks mostly about ________ . I know this because ________ .

2. Vocabulary: Figurative Language Discuss how figurative language creates images or describes things.

Paragraphs 6 and 7: What image does Kennedy evoke by using the phrases "bonds of misery" and "chains of poverty"? **(He creates an image of poverty holding back people who might otherwise succeed.)**

Think Aloud *I'm not sure what "strengthen its shield of the new and the weak" means in paragraph 8. When I reread, I notice that Kennedy previously addressed new and poor countries and the United Nations. I can visualize the UN expanding like a shield to include new countries and "enlarge the area" it was protecting.*

Partner Talk Have students discuss the effects of Kennedy's frequent use of figurative language.

ANNOTATION NOTES

1st Read:
Kennedy has messages for allies, neighbors, and enemies.

2nd Read:
Paragraphs identify an issue and say how it will be resolved.

language: does not name people directly = "new states," "sister republics south of our border," "our adversary"

3rd Read:
Kennedy's message to each nation ends up nearly the same: we want to help you achieve freedom and prosperity.

our view. But we shall always hope to find them strongly supporting their own freedom.

6 To those people struggling to break the bonds of misery, we pledge our best efforts to help them help themselves, for whatever period is required. If a free society cannot help the many who are poor, it cannot save the few who are rich.

7 To our sister republics south of our border, we offer a special pledge—to convert our good words into good deeds to assist in casting off the chains of poverty. But this peaceful revolution cannot become the prey of hostile powers. Let all our neighbors know that we shall join with them to oppose aggression or subversion, and let every other power know that this Hemisphere intends to remain the master of its own house.

8 To that world assembly of sovereign nations, the United Nations, our last best hope in an age where the instruments of war have far outpaced the instruments of peace, we renew our pledge of support to strengthen its shield of the new and ? the weak—and to enlarge the area in which its writ may run.

9 Finally, to those nations who would make themselves our adversary, we offer not a pledge but a request. We ask that both sides begin anew the quest for peace.

10 We dare not tempt them with weakness. For only when our arms are sufficient beyond doubt can we be certain that they will never be employed. But neither can two great and powerful groups of nations take comfort from our present course. Both sides are overburdened by the cost of modern weapons, both rightly alarmed by the steady spread of the deadly atom, yet both are racing to alter that uncertain balance that stays the hand of mankind's final war.

11 So let us begin anew—remembering both sides that civility is not a sign of weakness, and sincerity is always subject to proof. Let us never negotiate out of fear. But let us never fear to negotiate.

12 Let both sides explore what problems unite us instead of belaboring those problems which divide us.

13 Let both sides, for the first time, formulate serious and precise proposals for the inspection and control of arms—and bring the ? absolute power to destroy other nations under the absolute control of all nations.

PROFESSIONAL DEVELOPMENT

Academic Language: Language Frames

What Is It? Academic Language is sometimes known as the "language of school." It differs from everyday spoken language, which is primarily social in nature. Academic Language includes those more sophisticated and specific words used in books, in students' more formal writing, and the language of instruction during lessons and classroom discussions.

Why Is It Important? Academic Language is necessary for school success. It involves the words and sentence structures used by educated adults and the language expected in college and in the workplace.

14 Let both sides seek to invoke the wonders of science instead of its terrors. Together let us explore the stars, conquer the deserts and eradicate disease. We can tap the ocean depths and encourage the arts and commerce.

15 Let both sides unite to "undo the heavy burdens and let the oppressed go free."

16 All this will not be finished in the first one hundred days. Nor will it be finished in the first one thousand days, nor in the life of this Administration; nor even perhaps in our lifetime on this planet. But let us begin. In your hands, my fellow citizens, more than mine, will rest the final success or failure of our course. Since this country was founded, each generation of Americans has been summoned to give testimony to its national loyalty. The graves of young Americans who answered the call to service surround the globe.

17 Now the trumpet summons us again—not as a call to bear arms, though arms we need—not as a call to battle, though embattled we are. It is a call to bear the burden of a long twilight struggle, year in and year out, "rejoicing in hope, patience in tribulation"—a struggle against the common enemies of man: ! tyranny, poverty, disease and war itself. Can we forge against these enemies a grand and global alliance, North and South, East and West, that can assure a more fruitful life for all of mankind?

18 In the long history of the world, only a few generations have been granted the role of defending freedom in its hour of maximum danger. I do not shrink from this responsibility, I welcome it. I do not believe that any of us would exchange places with any other people or any other generation. The energy, the faith, the devotion which we bring to this endeavor will light our country and all who serve it—and the glow from that fire can truly light the world.

19 And so, my fellow Americans: ask not what your country ! can do for you—ask what you can do for your country.

20 My fellow citizens of the world: ask not what America will do for you, but what together we can do for the freedom of man.

ANNOTATION NOTES

1st Read:
Plan for peace and prosperity involves many years of hard work.

2nd Read:
Who are "both sides"?

look up source of quotations in paragraphs 15 and 17

3rd Read:
Speech is an appeal to ordinary people to join the work to improve the world.

How Do I Use It? Focus on teaching words and phrases that may appear in rigorous texts but that students may be unfamiliar with or may not use in their everyday language. Examples in this text include *forebears* (paragraph 1), *sister republics* (paragraph 7), and *adversary* (paragraph 9).

Scaffolded Support Using discussion frames is an ideal way to assist students in using Academic Language (e.g., *The main idea of "Inaugural Address" is* ________, or *Based on my reading, I conclude that* ________.)

Inaugural Address

3rd READ

Set a Purpose

Tell students that their purpose for this reading is to understand Kennedy's central message.

Text-Dependent Questions

1. What problems does Kennedy address in his speech? (Kennedy mainly addresses the problems of poverty and war or arms.)

Scaffolded Support Use the following scaffolded sentence frame and question as necessary to build comprehension.

Kennedy promises poorer nations that he will ________.

What does Kennedy promise the enemies of the United States?

2. How does Kennedy propose that the American people can address these problems? (Kennedy proposes his "fellow Americans" should step forward to volunteer and work together for peace and prosperity.)

3. What does the quote in paragraph 19, "Ask not what your country can do for you…" show in terms of volunteering? (It means that people should not focus on the services that government provides them. Instead they should think about what they can do to support the country's goals.)

Partner Talk Have students discuss how Kennedy's message relates to volunteering.

Return to the TEXT

Respond to Reading

You may want to check students' understanding by having them complete pages 108–109 in the Student Worktext.

1. Remind students to review their annotations and recall discussions they've had in order to complete the summary chart. Remind students that only evidence from the text should be included in the summary chart.

As students complete their summary charts, circulate and note which students struggle to identify the correct text evidence. Some students may benefit from small group instruction.

2. Remind students to include only the most important information in their summaries.

Have students work independently to complete page 108 of their Worktexts.

COLLABORATE When finished, have students exchange summaries with their partners and share their insights.

Return to the TEXT

Respond to Reading: Inaugural Address

Review your annotations and notes.
Think about how they can help you summarize the text.

1. Use this chart to help you summarize the text.

Summary Chart		
	Informational Text	
Who?	the people or subjects	President John F. Kennedy, the citizens of the United States
What?	the topic or problem	the future of the United States and the world
Where?	the location or region events occur	Washington, D.C.
When?	the date, year, or time	January 20, 1961
How?	the events, steps, or processes	In his inaugural address, Kennedy calls on people around the world to work together to end poverty and war.

2. Write a 2–3 sentence summary of "Inaugural Address."

Sample summary: In his inaugural address, Kennedy says that a new generation is carrying forward the ideas of the American Revolution. This generation must support its allies, help new and struggling nations, and work toward peace with its enemies. The people, rather than the government, must fight to put an end to wars and poverty.

PROFESSIONAL DEVELOPMENT

Self-Monitoring Strategies: Draw Conclusions

What Is It? Drawing conclusions involves pulling together several ideas in order to generate an explanation, generalization, or a next logical step. Students must draw conclusions that are not directly stated in the text.

Why Is It Important? Drawing conclusions requires deeper understanding of a text's meaning. Drawing conclusions overlaps with making inferences, generalizations, and predictions.

Return to the TEXT

3. What is the basic structure of the speech?
Provide support for your answer with details from the text.
Sample answer: Kennedy starts with a general introduction that describes the early years of the U.S. Then, in paragraphs 4 through 8, he addresses different groups of nations, including "old allies," "new states," and "our sister republics." In pararaph 9 he shifts focus to "nations who would make themselves our adversary," and requests that they, along with people around the world, work toward peace. He addresses friends and rivals, and then unites them with a common request.

4. What are the characteristics of Kennedy's language in the speech?
Provide examples from the text to support your answer.
Sample answer: Kennedy's language is poetic, symbolic, and indirect. He does not name specific nations, but indirectly speaks to "those people struggling to break the bonds of misery," or "those nations who would make themselves our adversary." He refers to the atomic bomb as "the deadly atom" and "terrors" of science. He describes the call to work for peace as "the trumpet summons." The overall effect of this poetic language is a deep sense of seriousness.

5. What does Kennedy ask of his audience?
Support your answer with text evidence.
Sample answer: Kennedy asks ordinary people all over the world to work together toward a common goal of peace and prosperity. He makes it known that every person can make a difference when he says it is "in your hands, my fellow citizens, more than mine." Also, he calls on nations to fight against "tyranny, poverty, disease, and war" instead of fighting each other. He is encouraging everyone to fully participate in public life and to help each other.

REFLECT What questions did you ask yourself to make sure you understood the text?
Sample answer: After reading paragraphs 11 through 15, I asked myself who Kennedy was referring to when he said "both sides." I went back and reread above that, and found the answer in paragraphs 9 and 10. "Both sides" are the United States and its enemies.

Return to the TEXT

Encourage students to refer back to the text and their annotations and notes to help them answer the questions.

3. You can support students by directing them to certain sections of the speech and having them analyze connections between sections.

4. Guide students to note Kennedy's use of verbs and adjectives. Ask students how the atmosphere would be different if Kennedy had used different language.

5. Suggest that students review paragraphs 11 through 17 again, looking for words or phrases that describe what Kennedy is asking people to do.

Have students work independently to complete page 109 of their Worktexts.

REFLECT Remind students that asking yourself questions is a **Self-Monitoring Strategy** and that they made annotations and notes about confusions they may have had. Suggest that they review their annotations and think about any words, phrases, or sections that they asked themselves about to check their comprehension of the text.

How Do I Use It? When students analyze text in order to draw conclusions, use scaffolded questions to focus their attention on relevant details that can be synthesized in order to arrive at a conclusion. For example, direct students' attention to paragraphs 16 and 19 of Kennedy's speech and his statements about who will bear the burden of fulfilling his promises in order to help students draw conclusions about volunteering. If a student has drawn a conclusion independently, provide an opportunity for peer modeling by having him or her explain the conclusion and supporting evidence to a partner.

Return to the TEXT

Stop and Assess

Use the following to assess your students' understanding of the text.

Item 1 answers indicate:	
2	a general inference about tense conditions between the United States and its enemies and the threat of atomic warfare, with two supporting text details.
1	an awareness of tension, with few specifics and some text evidence.
0	no relevant inference or text evidence.

Item 2 answers indicate:	
2	that Kennedy speaks to different groups and makes promises to his audience, with at least two specific examples from the text.
1	an understanding that Kennedy is speaking to an audience, but no connections to specific groups. Insufficient evidence supports the answer.
0	no sense of the audience, and no relevant text evidence.

Item 3 answers indicate:	
2	Kennedy believes all are called to volunteer and it is a positive act, with at least two cited text details.
1	a generalized positive attitude about volunteering, with insufficient text details.
0	no connection to volunteering, and no text evidence.

Option: If you choose not to work with Texts 2 and 3 and to conclude the unit here, use the Visual Text and "Inaugural Address" to answer the Focus Question: What purpose does volunteering serve?

Return to the TEXT

Comprehension Check: Inaugural Address

Answer the questions to demonstrate an understanding of what the text means.

1. What inferences can you make about the historical and political situation at the time of Kennedy's speech? Cite evidence from the text to support your answer.

Sample answer: I can infer that there was great tension at that time. The United States and its enemies have built up lots of weapons that could cause great destruction. Kennedy mentions in paragraph 10 that "both sides are overburdened by the cost of modern weapons, both rightly alarmed by the steady spread of the deadly atom." In paragraph 12, he wants to "explore what problems unite us instead of...divide us." Kennedy references weapons again in paragraph 13 when he calls for "serious and precise proposals for the inspection and control of arms."

2. How does Kennedy make an appeal to his audience? Give specific examples from the text to support your idea.

Sample answer: Kennedy addresses different groups of his audience and makes great promises to help them. He uses *we* and *our* so that his audience knows that they are in this together and positive terms such as "pledge," "welcome," and "offer." He addresses the next generation of Americans as "proud of our ancient heritage" and willing to "support any friend and oppose any foe." He also makes people feel they can take action for the country's success when he says "[I]n your hands, my fellow citizens, more than mine, will rest the final success or failure of our course."

3. How does Kennedy address the idea of volunteering? Cite text details to support your answer.

Sample answer: Kennedy says that ordinary men and women must work to help make peace and prosperity happen. He believes volunteering is a calling "to bear the burden of a long twilight struggle" and says "the energy, the faith, the devotion...will...truly light the world." Finally he asks American citizens to "ask not what your country can do for you—ask what you can do for your country," which is a direct appeal for people to volunteer to help their government and each other.

PROFESSIONAL DEVELOPMENT

Intertextual Analysis: Compare and Contrast Authors' Use of Language and Text Structure

What Is It? When students compare texts on similar topics, they compare not only events and ideas, but how different authors present those events and ideas.

Why Is It Important? Language and text structure reveal different authors' purposes and points of view. Students analyze authors' use of language and text structure to draw larger inferences, connections, and conclusions.

TEXT 2

Read to find out about the work of an organization that supports volunteers. If you need to read any sections more than once, note the reason in the Annotation Notes column.

Sample annotations and notes appear throughout the text.

About CNCS

1 We are the Corporation for National and Community Service. CNCS is a federal agency that helps millions of Americans improve the lives of their fellow citizens through service. Working hand in hand with local partners, we tap the ingenuity and can-do spirit of the American people. Together we tackle some of the most pressing challenges facing our nation.

2 We invest in thousands of nonprofit and faith-based groups that are making a difference across the country. We are AmeriCorps, Senior Corps, the Social Innovation Fund, ? the Volunteer Generation Fund, and more. We serve, we build, and we make an impact that changes lives and communities.

We Serve Your Community

3 ! Serving at more than 50,000 locations across the country, we deliver result-driven service where it's needed most.

4 • We strengthen education from pre-school on up. Our Foster Grandparents spark a love of learning in kids and our AmeriCorps members keep students on track to graduate and succeed.

Classroom volunteers can serve as everything from chaperones to expert guests to full-time teachers.

ANNOTATION NOTES

1st Read:
CNCS is a government agency that supports and helps volunteer organizations.

2nd Read:
Not sure who AmeriCorps, Senior Corps, Social Innovation Fund, etc. are. Look up?

3rd Read:
CNCS is not a single volunteer organization; it assists a wide range of other helping organizations.

How Do I Use It? To focus comparison on language and structure, compare similar ideas or events from different texts. For example, President Kennedy and the authors of the article "About CNCS" both describe how citizens can improve their communities and the nation. Ask, *How are their approaches and purposes alike, and how are they different? How is the language of a speech different from that of an article, and why?* Once students have read both texts, have them compare purposes and intended audiences, using specific language from the texts as evidence.

About CNCS

Tell students that they will read to find out about the work of an organization that supports volunteers.

1st READ

Set a Purpose

Tell students they will be reading to find out what "About CNCS" is about.

Have students read "About CNCS" independently, annotating the text as they read. Circulate and note students' markings, especially questions and confusions.

Text-Dependent Questions

1. What is CNCS and what does it do? (CNCS stands for Corporation for National and Community Service. It is a federal agency that provides services to help improve communities, both local and national.)

Scaffolded Support Use the following scaffolded question and sentence frame as necessary to build comprehension.

What does the acronym CNCS stand for?

CNCS provides services to ________.

2. Vocabulary: Multiple-Meaning Words Discuss contextual meanings of familiar words and phrases.

Paragraph 2: What does *invest* mean in this context? (It may mean "providing money to support a business." It also could mean providing workers or supplies.)

Partner Talk Have students discuss the jobs CNCS volunteers do.

About CNCS

2nd READ

Set a Purpose

Tell students they will read to analyze the text's organization.

Text-Dependent Questions

1. How do the subheadings help organize the text? **(The subheadings tell what information can be found in that section.)**

2. What is the purpose of the bulleted list? **(The bulleted list organizes a range of facts into an easy-to-read format.)**

Scaffolded Support Use the sentence frames as necessary to build comprehension.

Each bullet point addresses ________ .

The bullet points help to ________ .

Think Aloud *When I think about the text structure of "About CNCS," I ask myself: What is the purpose of the bullets? On a reread of the text, I see that the bullets give specific details about what CNCS does. Instead of giving this information in one long paragraph, it is easier for me to read and understand what this volunteer organization does. By using bullets, the writer makes all the facts that are listed in the article more manageable.*

Partner Talk Have students discuss the text structure of the sections "We Serve Your Community" and "We Impact Our Nation."

ANNOTATION NOTES

1st Read:
CNCS helps people live healthy, independent lives and channels volunteer efforts where they are needed most.

2nd Read:
Bulleted lists emphasize the great number and wide range of projects.

3rd Read:
common themes in helping organizations: education, jobs, health

Veteran services are usually a combination of official military or government organizations and dedicated volunteers. CNCS organizes and coordinates these team efforts.

- We help communities recover and rebuild from natural disasters. We lead efforts to preserve our nation's natural resources in our parks and public lands.
- We stand behind our veterans and military families by supporting families during deployment. We also provide assistance to help our soldiers transition into the workforce or get an education after they come home.
- We improve health by supporting independent living for seniors, reducing childhood obesity, preventing disease, and helping families gain access to health care.
- We build economic opportunity for individuals and communities by helping more Americans graduate, pursue higher education, gain career skills, and find employment.

We Impact Our Nation

5 • Our nation's strength comes from our people. America has always been at its best when citizens work together, joined in common purpose. We help focus this energy on local challenges to make a difference in the lives of millions of Americans every day.

- We support high-impact service to meet pressing needs. These range from illiteracy and homelessness to hunger

PROFESSIONAL DEVELOPMENT

Think-Aloud Modeling: Using Different Strategies

What Is It? One of the goals of close reading is to develop real reader behaviors in your students, that is, to provide students with opportunities to approach text the way a skilled, proficient reader would, taking full advantage of the repertoire of **Self-Monitoring Strategies** these readers use. To do this, it is important to model the strategies skilled readers use when confronted with text challenges. These include asking yourself questions, drawing conclusions, visualizing, and rereading to clarify.

Why Is It Important? Modeling strategies using Think Alouds demonstrates your thinking to students and allows them repeated opportunities to see how skilled readers approach and disasters. More than 980,000 Americans have given more than 1.4 billion hours of service through AmeriCorps, helping millions of our most-vulnerable citizens.

- We create economic opportunity by working in schools to improve graduation rates and providing services that develop job skills that lead to new careers.
- We lead AmeriCorps VISTA, which has been on the front lines fighting poverty since 1965, helping improve the lives of low-income individuals and communities across the country.
- We increase educational opportunity through Segal AmeriCorps Education Awards. They have provided more than $3.3 billion to more than 980,000 Americans to lessen college costs.
- We lead Days of Service on Martin Luther King Day and September 11th that encourage millions of citizens to volunteer in their communities.

6 Volunteering and national service are vital and cost-effective solutions to our nation's most-difficult challenges. The Corporation for National and Community Service stands ready to help Americans tackle these challenges and build a better future for our people, neighborhoods, and nation.

Volunteers often coordinate with government organizations, such as the National Guard, during natural disasters and other crises.

ANNOTATION NOTES

1st Read:
Volunteer work helps the local community but also the nation as a whole.

2nd Read:
several mentions of AmeriCorps—important?

language is a bit vague: "create," "helping"

3rd Read:
Text strongly promotes the organization and its work.

comprehension difficulties. With repeated exposures, students will begin to internalize and use these strategies while reading on their own.

How Do I Use It? Use the Think Alouds provided in the lessons. In addition, model strategies to address comprehension issues your students face or to emphasize strategies your students need to use more frequently. Some students will focus on one or two favorite strategies and need support in trying other strategies that might be more effective in specific reading situations. Modeling these strategies will expand their strategy repertoire.

About CNCS

3rd READ

Set a Purpose

Tell students that they will read to make inferences from the text.

Text-Dependent Questions

1. How does CNCS make a difference in the United States? (CNCS provides a range of services, including helping to improve the education and health of U.S. citizens and supporting military families. In paragraph 6, the writer says providing these services are "vital and cost-effective solutions to our nation's most-difficult challenges.")

Scaffolded Support Use the following scaffolded question and sentence frame as necessary to build comprehension.

In what areas does CNCS work?

Providing these services is important because ________ .

2. What links does the text make between CNCS's work and the U.S. economy? (CNCS helps with job training and education, which helps people contribute to the economy. Paragraph 5, bullet 3 says it "create[s] economic opportunity...and [provides] services that develop job skills that lead to new careers.")

3. Vocabulary: Context Clues Discuss the use of vocabulary strategies to understand word meanings.

Paragraph 4, bullet 3: What clues help you know what *deployment* means? (*Deployment* is contrasted with "after they come home," so I can infer that it means "serving overseas.")

Partner Talk Have students discuss the impact of CNCS's work on our nation.

Return to the TEXT

Stop and Assess

Use the following to assess your students' understanding of the text.

	Item 1 answers indicate:
2	the text provides information to an audience of people specifically seeking it and explains how the information is presented, with two pieces of text evidence.
1	the text informs the audience, but evidence is insufficient to support the answer.
0	no sense of the audience, and no text support.

	Item 2 answers indicate:
2	the text structure organizes a large amount of information to make it accessible, with at least two specific examples cited.
1	the text structure keeps the information organized, with some text examples.
0	no understanding of the organization, and no cited evidence.

	Item 3 answers indicate:
2	the organization's positive view of volunteering, with specific and relevant text evidence.
1	the organization's positive view of volunteering, with insufficient text evidence.
0	no analysis of the organization's view on volunteering, and no relevant evidence.

Return to the TEXT

Comprehension Check: About CNCS

Answer the questions to demonstrate an understanding of what the text means.

1. Who is the audience for "About CNCS," and how does the text present information about the organization? Cite examples from the text to support your answer.
   Sample answer: The audience is people who want to learn more about CNCS and what the organization does. The title "About CNCS" suggests that this text acts as an introduction for people who aren't familiar with the organization. The text provides a list of facts to describe the organization's work. It describes CNCS as "a federal agency that helps millions of Americans" by "working hand in hand with local partners."

2. What is the text structure of "About CNCS"? Explain your answer using evidence from the text.
   Sample answer: The subheadings and bulleted lists help organize the very wide range of CNCS's work into an easy-to-read list. The first paragraphs serve as an introduction. Each bullet describes a type of work the organization does, including "strengthen education," "help communities recover and rebuild from natural disasters," and supporting military members and families. The focus goes from the service they provide to the community to nationwide.

3. What are the views of "About CNCS" on volunteering? Cite evidence from the text to support your answer.
   Sample answer: According to the text, CNCS believes that volunteering is one of the most important and best ways to tackle problems. The introduction states that "we tackle some of the most pressing challenges facing our nation." The conclusion states that "volunteering and national service are vital and cost-effective solutions to our nation's most difficult challenges."

PROFESSIONAL DEVELOPMENT

Intertextual Analysis: Analyzing Multiple Accounts of the Same Event or Topic

What Is It? A similar aspect can be compared across different texts. Many students are familiar with comparing and contrasting opposing viewpoints. They can build on this type of analysis by comparing subtle differences in genre, perspective, purpose, audience, structure, and language across multiple accounts of the same event or topic.

Why Is It Important? Analyzing similar texts may be critical during research to determine reliability or to gain multiple perspectives on the same topic.

Read to find out about the work of one volunteer organization. You may want to read some sections more than once and make different annotations and Annotation Notes each time.
Sample annotations and notes appear throughout the text.

AmeriCorps State and National FAQs

This FAQ, or "Frequently Asked Questions," article describes the AmeriCorps organization.

! Explain to me the different types of AmeriCorps programs.

1 There are several different programs. AmeriCorps State and National supports a broad range of local service programs that engage thousands of Americans in intensive service to meet critical community needs.

AmeriCorps volunteers do a wide variety of work, including serving low-income communities.

2 AmeriCorps VISTA provides full-time members to community organizations and public agencies. These members create and expand programs that build capacity and ultimately bring low-income individuals and communities out of poverty.

3 The AmeriCorps National Civilian Community Corps is a full-time residential program for men and women, ages 18–24. It strengthens communities while developing leaders through direct, team-based national and community service.

? I'm confused. There are different programs, with different names, but they're all AmeriCorps?

4 Yes, basically. AmeriCorps is a national network of hundreds of programs across the nation. Two of these programs are managed nationally: AmeriCorps VISTA and AmeriCorps NCCC. The other program under the general heading of AmeriCorps State and National, also referred to simply as AmeriCorps, funds local and national organizations throughout the United States to

ANNOTATION NOTES

1st Read:
AmeriCorps is an organization that supports service programs and volunteers. It sends people to help communities.

2nd Read:
Not sure who is asking questions. Who is "I"?

3rd Read:
This information will help me better understand Text 2 and its references to AmeriCorps.

How Do I Use It? Graphic organizers can be a powerful tool for analyzing multiple accounts of the same event or topic. An interactive organizer can expand or contract to allow a visual representation of topic overlap. A Venn diagram for "About CNCS" and "AmeriCorps State and National FAQs" would include information about coordinating volunteers and describing the work they do in the overlapping area. The nonoverlapping areas would include specific areas of work ("About CNCS") and information about the volunteers themselves ("AmeriCorps FAQ"). These distinctions help students grasp the different purposes of the two texts.

AmeriCorps FAQs

Tell students that they will read to find out about the work of one volunteer organization.

1st READ

Set a Purpose

Explain to students that they will read to find out about AmeriCorps. Have students read "AmeriCorps State and National FAQs" independently, annotating the text.

Text-Dependent Questions

1. Where do AmeriCorps volunteers work? (They work in low-income areas of the United States.)

2. What are the requirements to volunteer with AmeriCorp? (Volunteers must be at least 17 years old or an out-of-school 16-year-old who hasn't left school to join the organization. For some programs you may need a college degree or a few years of experience.)

3. **Vocabulary: Context Clues** Discuss the use of context clues to figure out word meanings.

Paragraph 3: What does the word *civilian* mean here? (*Civilian* means "not a member of the military." Although the word *corp* is in the title, and I think of the military when I hear that word, the phrase "residential program" suggests a nonmilitary situation.)

Partner Talk Have students discuss the types of jobs AmeriCorps volunteers might do.

AmeriCorps FAQ

2nd READ

Set a Purpose

Tell students that they will read to analyze the text's structure and its message.

Text-Dependent Questions

1. Who asks the questions in an FAQ? (The questions are ones that an organization is repeatedly asked or questions that the writer anticipates readers will ask.)

2. Why did the writer use *I* and *you* in the FAQ? (The questions use the word *I* to indicate a reader, and the answers use the word *you* to indicate someone at AmeriCorps answering. The FAQ is written in a conversational style to address questions anyone would have and to keep the interest of the reader.)

Partner Talk Have students discuss the structure of an FAQ.

3rd READ

Set a Purpose

Tell students they will read to make inferences about the text.

Text-Dependent Questions

1. What is the difference between CNCS (Text 2) and AmeriCorps? (CNCS supports a wide range of volunteer organizations. AmeriCorps is an individual volunteer organization that CNCS might support.)

Partner Talk Have students discuss how the work of AmeriCorps compares to that of other volunteer organizations.

TEXT 3

ANNOTATION NOTES

1st Read: AmeriCorps helps young people volunteer full time.

2nd Read: The "I" seems to be a person interested in volunteering.

3rd Read: The questions and answers suggest that joining AmeriCorps is a big commitment.

recruit AmeriCorps members. Depending upon your interests and availability, we can help you determine which program might be best for you.

What skills do I need to have?

5 Some programs have specific skill requests in certain areas, and others look for a bachelor's degree or a few years of related volunteer/job experience. For others, your motivation and commitment may be the primary requirement.

AmeriCorps volunteers may serve for as long as a full year.

Is there an age requirement?

6 To be eligible, an AmeriCorps participant must be at least 17 years of age or be an out-of-school youth 16 years of age who has not left school to join AmeriCorps.

Is AmeriCorps like the Peace Corps?

7 Yes. AmeriCorps is often referred to as "the domestic Peace Corps." Both agencies are committed to service, and both offer challenging and rewarding full-time opportunities. Peace Corps assignments are all overseas, and AmeriCorps members serve only in the United States. While Peace Corps volunteers serve ! for two years, a stint in AmeriCorps usually lasts 10 months to one year. (Some AmeriCorps projects also offer part-time opportunities, and some AmeriCorps members serve more than one term of service.)

PROFESSIONAL DEVELOPMENT

Annotations: Connections

What Is It? As they annotate multiple texts, students circle or otherwise highlight key terms or ideas that the texts share, and they add information gleaned from other texts. They use graphic organizers and other strategies to combine this information and achieve a global view of the topic.

Why Is It Important? Multiple texts can present the same information from different viewpoints or with different emphases. Noting the key ideas in common also helps students notice areas of differences. Viewing a topic from different angles helps readers comprehend the whole picture.

Return to the TEXT

Comprehension Check: AmeriCorps State and National FAQs

Answer the questions to demonstrate an understanding of what the text means.

1. What is the purpose of this text?
   Support your answer with relevant evidence.
   Sample answer: The purpose is to give facts that answer "frequently asked questions" about AmeriCorps, specifically for people who might be interested in volunteering. The text addresses specific questions that have been asked frequently. Each paragraph includes answers with supporting facts about what skills are needed, what are the age requirements, and what the differences between the programs are.

2. How does the question-and-answer structure help the text describe the AmeriCorps program? Cite evidence from the text to support your answer.
   Sample answer: The question-and-answer structure is a conversational format, which is helpful for people because it is easy to understand. It is also organized based on exactly what the reader might want to know. For example, after the first question describing the different types of AmeriCorps programs, there is a follow-up question that begins, "I'm confused," which is followed by more clarification about the different programs—"AmeriCorps is a national network of hundreds of programs."

3. What is Americorps's perspective on volunteering?
   Cite evidence from the text to support your answer.
   Sample answer: AmeriCorps believes that volunteering is a great way to improve people's lives. Paragraphs 1 and 2 state that AmeriCorps helps "meet critical community needs" and "ultimately bring low-income individuals and communities out of poverty." Paragraph 7 states that the organization offers "challenging and rewarding...opportunities," so the organization believes that the work that they do is appealing.

How Do I Use It? As students annotate the texts and talk with partners, draw attention to words and phrases that they have already encountered, not only repetitions of words such as *volunteer* and *community,* but also synonyms, such as *workers* and *members, neighborhood* and *society*. You might create small discussion groups and have students create graphic organizers, one column per text, to compare words and phrases side by side. Then have them compose sentences that compare or contrast at least two texts, using the shared words.

Return to the TEXT

Stop and Assess

Use the following to assess your students' understanding of the text.

	Item 1 answers indicate:
2	a purpose of informing potential volunteers, with two pieces of text evidence.
1	a purpose of informing potential volunteers, but evidence is insufficient to support the answer.
0	no understanding of the text's purpose, and no support cited.

	Item 2 answers indicate:
2	how the FAQ is structured and that it anticipates readers' needs, with at least two relevant examples.
1	the FAQ structure is convenient, with some text support.
0	no understanding of the contribution of the structure, and no supporting evidence.

	Item 3 answers indicate:
2	the writer of the FAQ believes volunteerism improves both volunteers and communities, with two pieces of text evidence.
1	the writer feels positively about volunteering, with some text evidence.
0	no undersanding of the writer's perspective, and no cited evidence.

ANALYZE and SYNTHESIZE ACROSS TEXTS

Return to the Focus Question

Explain to students that they will fill out a graphic organizer that helps them answer the Focus Question: What purpose does volunteering serve?

CONNECT TEXTS Have small groups of students discuss how each text they read helps them answer the Focus Question.

Scaffolded Support You may provide the following sentence frames to support students in their use of academic language:

> In the text ________, the author/photographer makes the point that ________. He/she does this by ________.

Remind students to use their annotations and summaries to support their answers. They can also reread portions of the texts, if necessary.

Have students complete their graphic organizers individually.

REFLECT Remind students that each text provides different information about the purpose of volunteering. Ask, *how did reading all four texts give you a greater understanding of what purpose volunteering serves?*

ANALYZE and SYNTHESIZE ACROSS TEXTS

Return to the Focus Question: What purpose does volunteering serve?

Review your answers to questions about the texts as well as your annotations and Annotation Notes, and think about the discussions you've had about the texts. How does that information help you answer the Focus Question?

Use the graphic organizer to organize information about the texts.

1. In the appropriate box below, record the details that help you answer the Focus Question.
2. Make connections between those details to answer the Focus Question. Write your answer in the box provided.

Ripples (Visual Text)
Sample answer: A single drop of water creates ripples that spread outward.

About CNCS
Sample answer: CNCS supports organizations who help fellow citizens through service.

Inaugural Address
Sample answer: Kennedy calls on others to work toward peace and prosperity.

AmeriCorps FAQs
Sample answer: National network of service programs and volunteers provides community service.

What purpose does volunteering serve?
Sample answer: Volunteers can join organizations that have a common goal to serve others, helping local communities to meet needs that aren't met otherwise. This can lead to improving conditions that impact their area, their country, and the world.

REFLECT How did making connections between the four texts enable you to answer the Focus Question?

Sample answer: The different texts showed that one action can impact another. The ripple that moved outward was created from a single drop of water, just as the work of community volunteers can impact not only their local area but the nation and the world.

PROFESSIONAL DEVELOPMENT

Differentiation: Scaffolding with Graphic Organizers

What Is It? Graphic organizers are visual organizational tools that assist students in recording their understandings of texts they are reading. They include main idea charts, Venn diagrams to compare and contrast information, word webs, thinking maps, and many other visual resources. You can present graphic organizers as scaffolding in the course of whole-class and small-group discussion or have students make and complete simple graphic organizers of their own.

Why Is It Important? Graphic organizers represent a concise, visual, preformatted guide to analyzing ideas and relationships. They can provide a significant scaffold for students who are having difficulty, especially with abstract ideas.

Writing About the Focus Question

Now that you have answered the Focus Question using all four texts, expand on your thinking and communicate your ideas through your writing.

USE EVIDENCE

- Explain what you have learned about the purpose of volunteering. Use at least one piece of evidence from the Visual Text and at least two pieces of text evidence from Texts 1, 2, and 3 to support your answer.
- If you need more room, use additional paper.

MONITOR

- Use the Writing Checklist as you write to make sure your writing meets all the necessary criteria.
- Use the rubric on page 120 when you have completed a first draft of your writing to help you evaluate, revise, and edit your work.

WRITING CHECKLIST ✔

Does my writing . . .

- ☐ answer the Focus Question?
- ☐ have a clear organizational structure?
- ☐ cite the correct amount of text evidence?
- ☐ correctly use language, spelling, and conventions?

How Do I Use It? The graphic organizer on page 118 is intended to help students simplify and connect ideas from different texts in order to give a short answer to the Focus Question. You can provide additional graphic organizers to assist students in fleshing out their ideas. For example, a supporting details graphic organizer can help students find text support for each of the ideas they propose in their answer. A flow chart can help students organize and make logical connections between paragraphs. A blank idea web can help with brainstorming.

Writing About the Focus Question

USE EVIDENCE Remind students that they should use their graphic organizers as well as their annotations in the texts to write their responses.

Allow students to revisit the texts as frequently as they need to in order to support comprehension and to respond to the Focus Question.

MONITOR After students have completed their responses, have them review the Writing Checklist and revise their writing responses.

DIFFERENTIATE AND EXTEND

In addition to or instead of the writing response, consider having students complete one of the following assignments:

Write Beyond Have students write a blog or journal from the point of view of a volunteer serving a tour in AmeriCorps VISTA or another long-term volunteer organization.

Research Have students research the volunteer organizations in their neighborhood or community. Have students summarize what the organizations do in short oral presentations.

Make a Plan Have students plan or take part in a volunteer event, either individually or as a whole class. Have students develop a presentation about their experiences.

Interview an Expert
Have students conduct a video, audio, or text interview with a volunteer or nonprofit employee about his or her work.

SELF-ASSESS and REFLECT

SELF-ASSESS Have students use the Writing Rubric on page 120 to self-assess their writing response and write a final version. Tell them to assign themselves a score from 1–4 (with "4" being the highest) for each category in the first column.

Use the Writing Rubric on Student Worktext page 120 to assess each student's writing. Record points for each category in the first column of the rubric. Have students remove the page from their Student Worktexts and place it in their writing portfolios, along with the drafts and final versions of their responses.

SELF-ASSESS and REFLECT

Focus Question: What purpose does volunteering serve?

This is the rubric that your teacher will use to assess your writing. Refer to it as you revise your work. After you have finished the final version of your response, assess your response and record your points for each category on the "Student" line in the first column.

	Accomplished (4 points)	Competent (3 points)	Developing (2 points)	Beginning (1 point)
RESPONSE Score: Student ____ Teacher ____	The response answers the question effectively and with insight.	The response answers the question effectively.	The response partially responds to the question but does not adequately address it.	The response addresses the texts but does not address the question.
ORGANIZATION Score: Student ____ Teacher ____	The main idea is convincingly stated. Ideas are organized in cohesive paragraphs that support the main idea.	The main idea is clearly stated. Ideas are organized in logical paragraphs.	The main idea is weak. Ideas are organized in a somewhat logical and cohesive way.	The main idea is missing. The organization of the paragraphs is not logical.
TEXT EVIDENCE Score: Student ____ Teacher ____	Response includes more than one piece of appropriate text evidence from each text. Evidence supports the main idea in a thorough way.	Response includes one piece of text evidence from each text. Evidence supports the main idea clearly.	Response does not include at least one piece of text evidence from each text. Text evidence does not adequately support the main idea.	Response does not contain relevant evidence.
LANGUAGE Score: Student ____ Teacher ____	Writing includes precise and sophisticated vocabulary related to the topic.	Writing includes appropriate vocabulary related to the topic.	Writing includes imprecise and inaccurate vocabulary.	Writing does not include vocabulary that appropriately reflects the topic of the response.
SPELLING AND CONVENTIONS Score: Student ____ Teacher ____	Response includes correct speling, grammar, and punctuation consistently.	Response includes mostly correct spelling, grammar, and punctuation.	Response has many errors in spelling, grammar, and punctuation.	Response's errors in spelling, grammar, and punctuation make it extremely difficult to understand the response.

INTRODUCE THE UNIT

UNIT 7

Focus Question What can we learn from close study of ice and snow?

Texts for Close Reading

GENRE STUDY

Discuss with students the genres of "Snow Beauties," "Climate at the Core," and "Sizing Up the Earth's Glaciers."

Remind students that *genre* refers to the format and features of a text and typically falls into one of two categories—literature or informational text. Literature is a creative work that doesn't necessarily rely on facts, and informational text includes factual information.

Each text in this unit is informational. With the class, list the features of articles, such as bylines, subheads, and graphics that support the text. Discuss ways in which the publishing medium can affect the written and visual content, such as the difference in space available online and in print.

Focus Question

Have students read the Focus Question on Worktext page 121. Tell students that the texts they will read will help them answer the question.

Texts for Close Reading

Have students read to themselves the summaries about the texts in this unit.

There is no need to explain what students should expect to find in their close readings or to do any pre-teaching about the subject matter.

TEXT COMPLEXITY

Summer in Antarctica

- Style: documentary
- Knowledge demands: medium
- Levels of meaning: literal

Snow Beauties

Quantitative: 1060L

Qualitative

- Structure: conventional
- Language: academic
- Knowledge demands: high
- Levels of meaning: literal/inferential

Climate at the Core

Quantitative: 1100L

Qualitative

- Structure: conventional
- Language: academic
- Knowledge demands: medium
- Levels of meaning: literal

Sizing Up the Earth's Glaciers

Quantitative: 1110L

Qualitative

- Structure: conventional
- Language: academic
- Knowledge demands: medium
- Levels of meaning: literal

Summer in Antarctica

Set a Purpose

Explain to students that they will look at the image on page 122 to see what they can learn from the landscape.

Visual Text Analysis

Remind students that an image can be analyzed as a text by looking at its details and making inferences. Direct students' attention to the image on Student Worktext page 122.

1. Have students look at both the image and the caption to get information.

2. Have students identify details in the photograph that are unique to this place.

3. Have students respond with their thoughts about the conditions shown in the photograph.

Optional: Provide any additional information you feel is appropriate to enhance the discussion:

- Antarctica is in the Southern Hemisphere, where it is summer in December and January.
- Average summer high temperatures for the Antarctic coast are still below freezing: about –3°C (26.6° F).
- Despite cold temperatures, Antarctic waters contain lots of nutrients and support productive ecosystems.

VISUAL TEXT

Summer in Antarctica

Look at the Visual Text to answer the following questions. Review the image or parts of the image as many times as necessary.

1. What is shown in this image?
   Sample answer: The image shows chunks of ice and icebergs floating in the water and the coast of Antarctica in the background.

2. What details support your answer to the previous question?
   Sample answer: I see snow on the land and bare rocks on a mountain that is bare of plants. The caption identifies the location as Antarctica.The photo shows land and ocean, so I think it must be a coastline.

3. When you look again, what are you thinking and feeling?
   Sample answer: The caption says it is summer. It looks very cold for summer even with the sun shining brightly. I think it must be a difficult place for any plants or animals to live in, but it is very beautiful.

122 • Unit 7

PROFESSIONAL DEVELOPMENT

Productive Conversation: Revoicing Students' Responses

What Is It? Productive Conversation moves are ways to encourage student interaction while discussing a text, to clear up confusion, and to model academic language. These moves include revoicing, restating, adding on, reasoning, extending, giving examples, and providing appropriate wait time. For example, after a student answers a question you might say, *So let me see if I understand your thinking. You said* ________. *Is that right?* In revoicing the student's response, you use more academic language to express his or her ideas.

Why Is It Important? Productive Conversation moves are beneficial for all students but are especially important for

✔ Self-Monitoring Strategies you used to help you check your understanding as you read.

☐ Visualize. ☐ Draw conclusions. ☐ Ask yourself questions. ☐ Reread to clarify.

Read the text to find out what one person learned by studying snow. Make annotations in the text and write your notes in the Annotation Notes column.

Sample annotations and notes appear throughout the text.

Snow Beauties

by Wilson A. Bentley

1 What magic is there in the rule of six that makes the snowflake conform so rigidly to its laws? Here is a gem of nature possessing the charm of mystery and the unknown. For something over a quarter of a century I have been studying it, and the work has proved to be wonderfully fascinating. Each snowfall, during all these years, has brought things that were new and beautiful to my hand. I have never yet found a time when I could entertain an idea of letting this work go. During the time ! that I have carried on the work, I have made sixteen hundred photo-micrographs of snow crystals alone. No two are alike. Doubtless these pictures serve to represent with some fairness almost every type and variety of snow that occurs in nature. But they show scarcely a small fraction of the individual variation of form and design among the crystals that make up each type.

2 Clouds, and the tiny liquid particles of water and dust of which they consist, do not play a part in true snow crystal formation. The true crystals, forming the bulk of the snowfall, are formed directly. They are made from the almost infinitely small and invisible molecules of water within the air.

3 Snow crystals exhibit such a bewildering diversity and beauty. They form within a very thin gaseous solvent, the air. This allows the molecules of water an unexampled freedom of motion and adjustment while arranging themselves in crystal form. The fact doubtless explains why snow crystals far exceed other crystals in complexity and symmetry. Snow crystals, like all crystals of water, develop under the hexagonal system and divide into six. Nothing absolutely certain is known as to why they grow thus.

4 Crystals that grow rapidly, or within relatively warm low clouds, usually build upon this plan. In the case of the

ANNOTATION NOTES

1st Read:

Bentley photographed snowflakes for years, and found that no two were alike.

2nd Read:

language is very formal

What does he mean by "formed directly"? —reread paragraph 2

3rd Read:

Bentley is making a scientific study, but he is also captured by the beauty of his subject.

English learners as they provide guided opportunities and support in expressing ideas about the text. They also provide students with rich, structured conversation opportunities and time to develop collaborative conversation behaviors (for example, listening and responding to or building on the responses of others).

How Do I Use It? Instead of responding in generic ways to student responses during discussions ("Great," "That's right," "And what else?"), use students' answers as opportunities to develop language and deepen comprehension by selecting one or two accountable talk moves to focus on during each discussion (e.g., "Can anyone add to what ________ said?").

Snow Beauties

Tell students that they will read to find out what one person learned by studying snow.

1st READ

Set a Purpose

Tell students they will be reading to find out about William Bentley's work.

Have students read "Snow Beauties" independently, annotating as they read. Circulate and make notes of students' markings, questions, and confusions. Your notes can be used to inform instruction and as data for informal assessment.

Text-Dependent Questions

1. What is this text about? (A man who studied snow crystals and how they form.)

2. What did Bentley learn through his study? (He learned about the conditions in which snowflakes form.)

Think Aloud *I had trouble understanding the language in paragraph, 2, so I'll reread and use a graphic organizer to clarify. Bentley contrasts two ideas, which I can put in a T chart. The first idea is that liquid particles do not form snowflakes. Instead, Bentley says, crystals form directly from molecules of water in the air. Now I think I understand. The water goes from a gas straight to ice crystals without ever being liquid.*

Partner Talk Have students discuss the gist of this text.

Snow Beauties

2nd READ

Set a Purpose

Tell students they will read to analyze the author's language.

Text-Dependent Questions

1. What tone does the author's use of words create? (Sample answer: Sometimes the tone is scientific, and Bentley uses words such as "gaseous solvent" and "nucleus." When Bentley describes the beauty of snowflakes, the tone of the text becomes more enthusiastic and imaginative and he uses words like "magic" and "charm.")

Scaffolded Support Use the following sentence frame as necessary to build comprehension.

> Bentley uses words such as ________ to describe snowflakes, which creates a tone of ________.

2. Vocabulary: Multiple-Meaning Words Discuss the use of words in context.

Paragraph 7: What is the meaning of *sense* as it is used in paragraph 7? (Sample answer: Here, it means *meaning*. I know this because the author is describing snow crystals as works of art.)

3. How does the organization of the text help you understand its meaning? (Sample answer: The author organizes the text by main ideas. First he describes how he studies snowflakes, then how they form, and then why they are important.)

Partner Talk Have students discuss how Bentley's language reveals his point of view.

ANNOTATION NOTES

1st Read:
Reread paragraph 5 about how snowflakes form.

2nd Read:
look up: concentric, symmetry, hasten, alternate

keeps returning to amazement: "wonder," "marvelous and mysterious"

3rd Read:
Bentley must have observed the types of clouds and conditions his flakes came from.

concentric or layer habit, growth tends to arrange itself around the nucleus to produce the close, solid flakes.

5 The growth, habits and conditions under which the crystals form therefore are commonly unstable. Different conditions tend to hasten or to retard their rate of development or modify their forms and cause them to be increasingly complex as they grow. In those special cases where the crystals form and grow wholly within a single relatively thin and uniform cloud, they are likely to follow from start to finish. The frail branching snow crystals, falling during snow flurries, are often like this.

Bentley's collection of snowflake photographs supplied science museums for decades.

6 It is all most marvelous and mysterious, these changing habits of growth, and this momentary shifting about of the points of maximum development. Growth often occurs in alternate order. First at the corners of the hexagon, and then at the sides. In some cases, this pendulum-like swing of growth may continue from beginning to end. The form is always ? balanced. This is a fascinating mystery as to why crystals assume such a marvelous diversity of form. They do so even ? though forced by the crystallographic law to assume always

PROFESSIONAL DEVELOPMENT

Self-Monitoring Strategies: Reread to Clarify

What Is It? Rereading to clarify is one of the **Self-Monitoring Strategies** students can employ to ensure comprehension while reading.

Why Is It Important? When students return to a confusing portion of a text to reread it, they are setting a goal—to make sense of something unclear. This sharpens their focus and hones their thinking process. Rereading to clarify develops critical thinking and independent learning and builds students' literacy confidence.

TEXT 1

the hexagonal form. Six rays or parts, there always are. Yet what an amazing variety these parts exhibit. Individual crystals of the open, branching variety, differ one from another in the shape, size or thickness of their primary rays. These rays in turn, vary in the number, size or shape, of the secondary branches that they possess. In countless cases the crystals assume, at ? some one or more stages of growth, identical forms and outlines.

7 The snow crystals are, in the truest sense, exquisite works of art in themselves. They charmingly adapt themselves to a great variety of uses in the industrial arts, and in various other ways. These uses are steadily broadening, though they and their artistic possibilities have hardly been discovered or realized by artisans in general. Metal workers and wall paper manufacturers are, however, beginning to realize their value. There should be a great field of usefulness for them in these lines. They also seem well adapted for use in designing patterns for porcelain, china, glassware and many other things. Silk manufacturers are beginning to see their adaptability as patterns. Their value as models in the realm of pure art is also being demonstrated. Their uses as models in art schools and in craft shops are steadily increasing. Only recently Dr. Denman W. Ross, lecturer at Harvard on the theory of pure design, has adopted a large number for classroom use. Professor John Ward Stimson used them to illustrate the 'beauty of nature's art,' in his book *The Gate Beautiful*.

8 Perhaps their greatest field of usefulness, however, is along other lines. Think of them also as objects for nature study, and for illustrating the forms of water. They should be invaluable to the scientist. They show the forms and habits of growth of crystals in a most charming way. Certain it is that schools and museums are finding them most useful in an educational way. One university alone—Wisconsin—has over one thousand ? lantern slides of snowflakes. Indeed, it seems likely that these wonderful bits of pure beauty will soon come into their own. Soon they'll receive the full appreciation and study to which their exquisite loveliness and great scientific interest entitle them.

ANNOTATION NOTES

1st Read:
Snowflakes are valuable to art and science.

2nd Read:
more language describing the beauty of snowflakes, even in the context of science

lantern slide?

3rd Read:
Bentley seems to want to spread his passion about snowflakes.

How Do I Use It? Model rereading using a portion of "Snow Beauties" to clarify for students how it works. *The end of paragraph 5 is confusing. I'm not sure what the author means by "they are likely to follow from start to finish." I'll read the paragraph again. The first part is about the changing conditions where snowflakes form. Just before the confusing sentence, the author talks about "special cases" where crystals form "within a single. . . uniform cloud." Now I get it—Bentley is comparing and contrasting a crystal that grows "from start to finish" in one cloud versus those that form as they move from cloud to cloud.*

Snow Beauties

3rd READ

Set a Purpose

Tell students they will read to understand the author's perspective and intentions.

Text-Dependent Questions

1. What is the author's opinion of snowflakes? (Sample answer: The author thinks snowflakes are impressive, beautiful, and useful.)

2. How does the author support this opinion? (Sample answer: The author supports this opinion of how snowflakes are beautiful by comparing them to a work of art. He describes what he learned about them, and describes their many uses.)

Scaffolded Support Use the following scaffolded question and sentence frame as necessary to build comprehension.

How do the paragraphs about snowflake formation support the author's perspective?

The author ends the essay by saying ________.

3. According to the author, what can be gained by studying snowflakes? What evidence supports your answer? (Sample answer: The author thinks that the most important reason is to gain scientific knowledge. He calls science the "greatest field of usefulness" and devotes much of the text to the scientific ideas he learned.)

Partner Talk Have students discuss how Bentley's work reflected his perspective on the value of studying snowflakes.

Respond to Reading

You may want to check students' understanding by having them complete pages 126–127 in the Student Worktext.

1. Remind students to review their annotations and recall discussions they've had in order to complete the summary charts. Remind students that only evidence from the text should be included in the summary chart.

As students complete their summary charts, circulate and note which students struggle to identify the correct text evidence. Some students may benefit from small group instruction.

2. Remind students to include only the most important information in their summaries.

Have students work independently to complete page 126 of their Worktexts.

COLLABORATE When finished, have students exchange summaries with their partners and share their insights.

Return to the TEXT

Respond to Reading: Snow Beauties

Review your annotations and notes.
Think about how they can help you summarize the text.

1. Use this chart to help you summarize the text.

Summary Chart		
	Informational Text	
Who?	the people or subjects	Wilson A. Bentley, snowflake photographer
What?	the topic or problem	Bentley shares what he has learned studying snowflakes through his photography.
Where?	the location or region events occur	?
When?	the era, year, or time	?
How?	the events, steps, or processes	Bentley develops a theory of how snow crystals form by studying their shapes and their formation conditions.

2. Write a 2–3 sentence summary of the article "Snow Beauties."

Sample summary: After years of photographing snowflakes, Bentley is able to understand how they form. They all have six sides, but because each one forms under different conditions, they are all different. Their beautiful forms may be valuable to art and science.

PROFESSIONAL DEVELOPMENT

Collaboration: Partner Talk

What Is It? Partner talk is a brief, planned conversation between pairs of students on a specific topic. Partner talk can be a response to either a question or a prompt.

Why Is It Important? Partner talk allows for short-term sharing in a setting that can be less stressful than whole-class or small-group speaking. It also allows for targeted peer interaction in which partners who have a more complete understanding explain to partners who have a less advanced comprehension. It provides an opportunity for collaboration between partners with different levels of language or thinking skills.

Return to the TEXT

3. What is Bentley's explanation for why every snowflake is different? Support your answer with evidence from the text.
Sample answer: Bentley believes every snowflake is different because each one grows under slightly different conditions. Air "allows the molecules of water . . . freedom of motion . . . while arranging themselves." He notes that "different conditions tend to hasten or to retard their rate of development or modify their forms."

4. Why does Bentley consider his work important? Use text evidence to support your answer.
Sample answer: Bentley believes that snowflake shapes can be used in art, and that crystal formation could be important to science. In paragraph 7, he notes that "metal workers and wall paper manufacturers" are using snowflake shapes. He also suggests that they may be useful for designing "patterns for porcelain, china, glassware and many other things." Bentley argues that snowflakes "show the forms and habits of growth of crystals."

5. What words and phrases reveal Bentley's point of view about snowflakes? Cite text evidence to support your answer.
Sample answer: Bentley's language consistently expresses delight with snowflakes. His first sentence describes the "magic" of their formation. He uses the words "charm," "beauty," "marvelous," and "exquisite" to describe the snowflakes themselves. He says that his photography work "has proved to be wonderfully fascinating."

REFLECT What conclusions did you draw to help you understand the text?
Sample answer: Bentley talked about how different snowflakes formed in different types of clouds. I drew the conclusion that he must have observed the clouds as well as the snowflakes.

How Do I Use It? Pair partners with varied skill levels. Allow time for students to finish their summaries of "Snow Beauties." Then, have students take turns explaining their ideas, each allowing the other time to share their thoughts. Circulate to ensure that students are taking proper turns and contributing fairly. You can observe partner talk as ongoing informal assessment.

Return to the TEXT

Encourage students to refer back to the text and their annotations and notes to help them answer the questions.

3. Refer students to paragraphs 3 and 5. Encourage students to call out any difficult vocabulary that may be hindering their understanding.

4. Students can reread paragraphs 7 and 8 and list the various uses of information gained from snowflakes that Bentley mentions.

5. Have students review the annotations they made about language and tone during their 2nd read.

Have students work independently to complete page 127 of their Worktexts.

REFLECT Remind students that drawing conclusions is a **Self-Monitoring Strategy** and that they made annotations and notes about connections they made. Suggest that students refer to their annotations and review places where they made connections or drew conclusions to check their comprehension of the text.

Return to the TEXT

Stop and Assess

Use the following to assess your students' understanding of the text.

Item 1 answers indicate:	
2	author's purpose of informing and persuading about the value of snowflakes, with at least two pieces of text evidence.
1	author's purpose of either informing or persuading, with insufficient text evidence.
0	no understanding of author's purpose, and no supporting evidence.

Item 2 answers indicate:	
2	the inference that Bentley studied atmospheric conditions as well as snowflakes, with two examples of text evidence.
1	the description of Bentley studying snowflakes, with insufficient text support.
0	no understanding of Bentley's methods, and no text evidence.

Item 3 answers indicate:	
2	snowflakes are important in the arts and science, with specific text examples.
1	snowflakes are important in either arts or science, with some text evidence.
0	no understanding of snowflakes' importance, and no supporting evidence.

Option: If you choose not to work with Texts 2 and 3 and to conclude the unit here, use the Visual Text and "Snow Beauties" to answer the Focus Question: What can we learn from close study of ice and snow?

Return to the TEXT

Comprehension Check: Snow Beauties

Answer the questions to demonstrate an understanding of what the text means.

1. Why did Bentley write this text?
Cite evidence from the text to support your answer.
Sample answer: Bentley wrote this text to explain what he had learned about snowflakes and to encourage others to study them. Bentley first describes how much effort he has put into his work by stating that he's made "sixteen hundred photo-micrographs" over "a quarter of a century." He tries to explain the "marvelous and mysterious" way that all snowflakes grow differently. In paragraphs 7 and 8, he lists the industries and institutions that value snowflakes, and says that he hopes "these wonderful bits of pure beauty will soon come into their own."

2. What inferences can you make about how Bentley studied snowflakes and their formation? Provide the text you used as a basis for your inferences.
Sample answer: Bentley's main method was to look very carefully at the tiny structures of snowflakes, and try to link them to the conditions in the clouds where they formed. Bentley notes that every snowflake has six sides, but that they differ "in the shape, size or thickness of their primary rays" and "[t]hese rays in turn, vary in the number, size or shape, of the secondary branches." Bentley also observed the conditions from which the flakes fell, noting that some flakes form "within relatively warm low clouds," while others fall during "snow flurries." I can infer that Bentley must have noted the clouds and conditions of the snowfall before photographing the flakes.

3. Summarize Bentley's perspective on the importance of snowflakes.
Cite text evidence to support your ideas.
Sample answer: Bentley believes that snowflakes are or will become important to the arts, industry, and science. He notes that many types of decorative artists, including "wall paper manufacturers" and "silk manufacturers" have begun using snowflake patterns. Scientists are also studying snowflakes to understand "the forms and habits of growth of crystals."

PROFESSIONAL DEVELOPMENT

Layered Questions: Scaffolding

What Is It? Layered questions are a series of text-dependent questions related to the same topic that are designed to guide a student into a deeper level of comprehension. The first layered question requires a surface understanding. Each subsequent layered question tunnels deeper into a text's meaning, guiding the student step-by-step to a more complete understanding.

Why Is It Important? Text-dependent layered questions provide a scaffold for students to answer questions about the text that they can't answer on their own. Layered questions model how to think through a difficult question by breaking up a complex idea

Read the text to find out what climate information scientists learn from ice. If you need to read any sections more than once, note the reason in the Annotation Notes column.
Sample annotations and notes appear throughout the text.

Climate at the Core

by Amy Dusto

This article was published by the National Oceanic and Atmospheric Administration (NOAA). The NOAA studies Earth's weather, climate, and atmosphere.

1 Like a prehistoric fly trapped in amber, airborne relics of Earth's earlier climate can end up trapped in glacial ice for eons. These relics include dust, air bubbles, sea salts, volcanic ash, and soot from forest fires. To climate scientists, these relics tell a story about how our planet's climate and atmosphere have changed over thousands of years.

2 What they find out could have an impact on worldwide civilization within a few generations. This is especially true in coastal regions. Ice cores may reveal whether Antarctica's western ice sheet melted fully the last time Earth's climate warmed to the temperatures the planet is predicted to reach in the next two centuries. If it did, it's likely to again. That would raise sea levels enough to threaten many seaside cities.

Like the concentric circles of tree rings, the layers of an ice core represent one year of the ice sheet's growth via snowfall.

ANNOTATION NOTES

1st Read: Information about Earth's past is trapped in glaciers.

2nd Read: The first paragraphs describe the importance of the research.

3rd Read: How can scientists know whether an ice sheet melted just from studying cores?

into smaller, easier-to-manage chunks. This process strengthens independent thinking and literacy confidence.

How Do I Use It? When you note students are unable to answer a question about the text, ask several layered questions related to the question. Begin with a question that calls for a recall of information provided explicitly in the text. For example, when constructing scaffolding for question 2 on page 128, ask, *What parts of the snowflake did Bentley look at? What were the conclusions he drew?* Each subsequent question should dig a little deeper. Now ask, *What other information would Bentley need to construct a story about how a snowflake forms?* Continue until the student arrives at an answer for the original text-dependent question.

Climate at the Core

Tell students that they will read to find out what information scientists learn from ice.

1st READ

Set a Purpose

Tell students they will be reading to find out what can be found in ice.

Have students read "Climate at the Core" independently, annotating the text as they read. Circulate and note students' markings, especially questions and confusions.

Text-Dependent Questions

1. What is this text about? (Sample answer: It is about the study of ice cores, which are tubes of ice that scientists drill out from within ice sheets or glaciers.)

2. What are scientists studying in the ice cores? (Sample answer: Scientists study sea salt, pollution, and air trapped in the cores.)

3. Vocabulary: Figurative Language Discuss the use of figurative language in a scientific text.

Paragraphs 1 and 4: What is the effect of the author's use of figurative language such as "Like a prehistoric fly trapped in amber" and "coffee-can-wide"? (Sample answer: The figurative language helps readers visualize and understand an unfamiliar topic or object by comparing it to something familiar.)

Partner Talk Have students discuss what scientists learn by studying ice cores.

Climate at the Core

2nd READ

Set a Purpose

Tell students they will read to examine the text's structure.

Text-Dependent Questions

1. How does the author organize information about the process scientists use to study ice cores? (Sample answer: The author follows the ice cores from the glacier to the lab, step by step.)

Scaffolded Support Use the following sentence frame as necessary to build comprehension.

The event that is described first is ________.

Think Aloud *I'll reread for transition words to figure out how the author presents information. The words "first" and "then" in paragraph 8 tell me the text is describing a procedure.*

2. What is the effect of the description of the melting ice sheet at the beginning of the article? (The author builds tension by describing the dramatic melting of the ice sheet before explaining what the research scientists are doing.)

3. Vocabulary: Multiple-Meaning Words Discuss a word with multiple definitions.

Paragraph 8: What is the meaning of *composition* in this context? (Here it refers to the make-up of something, in this case, the atmosphere.)

Partner Talk Have students discuss how the structure of the article helps reveal the author's purpose.

TEXT 2

ANNOTATION NOTES

1st Read:
Scientists take apart the ice cores and study their contents in the lab.

2nd Read:
Second section describes how scientists get info from cores.

"Look for patterns" suggests they have to check many samples before they understand it.

3rd Read:
Scientists put a lot of effort into ice cores—the information must be important.

Formation of Ice

Under pressure, the weight of accumulated snowflakes squeezes out the air, and the flakes become denser. Lower temperatures cause melted crystals on the surface to refreeze and stick together, and they are transformed into ice. This metamorphosis takes place over many years (up to 3,500 in Antarctica).

3 "We have some evidence that may have happened, but we aren't sure," says Erich Osterberg, who studies ice cores in the Department of Earth Science at Dartmouth College.

4 To unlock the information inside an ice core, researchers in the lab may melt or crush the sample bit by bit. Each deeper layer represents a slightly earlier time in the Earth's climate history. The ice arrives in small strips, about 1-by-1 inch apiece. These are smaller slices of the roughly three-foot-long, coffee-can-wide pieces a drill pulls out of a glacier.

5 Sometimes researchers are studying actual bubbles of the early atmosphere, trapped in the ice as it formed. To collect them, they crush the sample under a vacuum hood. This keeps other air out while they pull the newly released air into vials.

6 Scientists run melted samples through various instruments. They are looking for tiny pieces of pollution, like sulfates, traces of metals, or radioactive fallout, or natural aerosols like dust or volcanic ash.

7 Because every clue in the ice is miniscule, measurements must be incredibly precise. This holds true whether it's a grain of sea salt or an air bubble. Any analysis must be done in a "clean room" setting. The researchers wear body suits and multiple layers of gloves. The room must have ultraclean filters and vents to keep the air pure. "Even a fingerprint from a scientist holding the core can ruin the sample," Osterberg says.

8 Researchers first analyze many ice core slices. These may each represent anywhere from a week to a year of time. Then they look for patterns to track changes in the atmosphere's composition and temperature, and what activity on Earth shaped it.

130 • Unit 7

PROFESSIONAL DEVELOPMENT

Intertextual Analysis: Analyzing vs. Summarizing

What Is It? Analysis involves making inferences and drawing conclusions in order to understand the most important meanings, themes, and messages of a text. Analysis draws from what the text says but goes beyond what is directly stated.

Why Is It Important? Text analysis represents a higher-order thinking skill that is essential to school, citizenship, and work. Additionally, the ability to be metacognitively aware of one's own inferences and conclusions and the evidence that does or does not support those thoughts is important to build students' judgment.

9 The ratio of "light" oxygen to "heavy" oxygen in a sample, ? for instance, reveals a great deal. It tells scientists the global temperature when the ice formed. It takes colder temperatures for water vapor containing the lighter oxygen to turn into precipitation. Examining the gasses trapped in ice cores is how scientists first learned something extraordinary. They discovered that the amount of carbon dioxide and the global temperature have ! been linked for at least the last million years of Earth's history.

10 Osterberg even thinks ice cores will help figure out whether Antarctica's western ice sheet melted 125,000 years ago. That's the last time Earth's climate warmed to the temperatures the planet is predicted to reach in the next two centuries.

11 Scientists hope to collect a new ice core from the eastern side of the Trans-Antarctic Mountains. Today, they separate the East and West Antarctic Ice Sheets. Much of the land under the West Antarctic Ice Sheet is below sea level. If the ice sheet did disintegrate, then the proposed ice core drilling location would have been coastal real estate 125,000 years ago.

12 "We would see much warmer temperatures and higher levels of sea salt reflected in the ice core chemistry if this location was ! hundreds of miles closer to the ocean in the past," Osterberg said.

13 Before the climate fossils can tell their stories, however, ? they must be retrieved. Rugged researchers may spend multiple summers scoping never-before-explored areas on glaciers before trekking out to collect a core.

Scientists drill out ice cores using hand or power tools, depending on the depth and hardness of the ice.

ANNOTATION NOTES

1st Read:
Scientists can tell the temperature and location of oceans from ice cores.

Scientists might be able to tell if the ice sheet melted.

2nd Read:
Third section explains exactly what helps scientists learn more about the climate.

Trans-Antarctic Mountains—check map

3rd Read:
Reread pararaphs 11–12: what info do researchers connect to tell if land was closer to the ocean?

Climate at the Core

3rd READ

Set a Purpose

Tell students they will read to make connections in the text.

Text-Dependent Questions

1. How will scientists' work with ice cores affect their understanding of today's climate? (Sample answer: Cores provide a record of climate patterns that can be used to compare to and make predictions about today's climate.)

Scaffolded Support Use the following scaffolded question and sentence frame as necessary to build comprehension.

What information do ice cores provide a record of?

Scientists use the information from ice cores to ________.

2. What would evidence that the ice sheet melted indicate? (Sample answer: It would indicate the temperature and atmospheric conditions that would cause the sheet to melt again.)

Think Aloud *The text says the scientists will be looking for higher levels of sea-salt ice in the core from the Trans-Antarctic Mountains. I can conclude that the presence of sea salt would prove that what is now dry land was once under or close to the ocean.*

Partner Talk Have students discuss how making connections helped them understand the text.

How Do I Use It? Students may experience two common problems with analyzing versus summarizing. Some students may be able to retell or recall without being able to make connections or inferences in order to more deeply analyze the text. Scaffolded questions can lead to greater understanding. *What do these two things have in common? Why do you think the author wrote this?* More sophisticated students may make inferences without realizing it, and draw conclusions that are not supported by text evidence. For these students, asking them to cite evidence and explain thinking is essential. *I understand what you're thinking. Can you show me where it says that in the text?*

Return to the TEXT

Stop and Assess

Use the following to assess your students' understanding of the text.

	Item 1 answers indicate:
2	an understanding that the structure and language inform average readers, with specific supporting text examples.
1	an identification of the structure, with one or two text examples.
0	no understanding of the structure, and no text evidence.

	Item 2 answers indicate:
2	an accurate and complete account of the process, with text citations to support each step.
1	an accurate if incomplete account of the process, with text citations for some steps.
0	an inaccurate or missing account, and no text support.

	Item 3 answers indicate:
2	scientists study ice cores to learn about past and future climate changes, with sufficient text support.
1	scientists study ice cores to learn about past climates, with insufficient text support.
0	no understanding of why scientists study cores, and no text support.

Return to the TEXT

Comprehension Check: Climate at the Core

Answer the questions to demonstrate an understanding of what the text means.

1. How do the structure and language of the article contribute to the author's purpose? Use evidence from the text to support your answer.
   Sample answer: The structure and language of the text are both engaging and casual, which helps draw readers into a technical subject. The article begins with a familiar image of a fly trapped in amber, and an emphasis on the importance of the research, which "could have an impact on worldwide civilization." The text then describes the technical details of how scientists study ice cores before revealing what the scientists learned. The language uses familiar comparisons and concrete details, like "coffee-can-wide" and "even a fingerprint from a scientist . . . can ruin the sample."

2. Create a numbered list that summarizes the journey of a bubble of ancient air from the atmosphere to a scientist's lab. Include text evidence or cite the visual source in your summary.
   Sample answer: 1. The air bubble gets trapped by falling snow, as shown in the diagram. 2. The air bubble gets squeezed and trapped as the snow is crushed into ice, as shown in the diagram. 3. Scientists drill into the ice and bring the air bubble to the surface, as shown in the photo of the ice driller. 4. Scientists "in the lab may melt or crush the sample bit by bit" and collect the air bubble "under a vacuum hood."

3. Why do scientists study ice cores? Support your answer with evidence from the text.
   Sample answer: Scientists study ice cores to reconstruct Earth's ancient climate and use it to predict future climate changes and their effects. Paragraph 1 states that "these relics tell a story about how our planet's climate and atmosphere have changed over thousands of years." Scientists want to compare the data to "temperatures the planet is predicted to reach in the next two centuries." This comparison will help them predict the behavior of Antarctica's ice sheet, which, if it melts, could "threaten many seaside cities."

PROFESSIONAL DEVELOPMENT

Intertextual Analysis: Making Thematic Connections

What Is It? A theme may be present across texts with either very similar or very different topics and structures. Thematic connections draw lines between the deeper meanings or generalized applications of different texts.

Why Is It Important? Making thematic connections across texts is one of the highest order skills in close reading. Students must not only find the meaning of individual complex texts, but must also connect, compare, and contrast those meanings across multiple texts.

Read the text to find out what scientists learn by studying mountain glaciers. You may want to read some sections more than once and make different annotations and Annotation Notes each time.

Sample annotations and notes appear throughout the text.

Sizing Up the Earth's Glaciers

by Evelyne Yohe

This web article comes from the National Snow and Ice Data Center at NASA.

1 Visit the world's high mountain ranges and you'll probably see less ice and snow today than a few decades ago. More than 110 glaciers have disappeared from Montana's Glacier National Park over the past 150 years. And researchers estimate that the ! park's remaining 37 glaciers may be gone in another 25 years. Half a world away, the snows of Africa's Kilimanjaro are steadily melting. They could completely disappear in the next 20 years. And in the Alps, glaciers are retreating and disappearing every year. This is happening much to the dismay of mountain climbers, tourist agencies, and environmental researchers.

2 "Receding and wasting glaciers are a sign of global climate change," said Jeff Kargel, head of the Global Land Ice Measurements from Space Coordination Center at the United States Geological Survey. Kargel is part of a research team that's developing an inventory of the world's glaciers. The team is combining current information on size and movement with historical data, maps, and photos.

Many glaciers around the world have shrunk dramatically in the past century.

3 In response to climate fluctuations, glaciers grow and shrink in length, width, and depth. Glaciers are sensitive to temperature and precipitation changes. Therefore, the rate of their growth or decline can serve as an indicator of regional and global climate

ANNOTATION NOTES

1st Read:
Scientists are trying to keep track of all Earth's glaciers to measure how they react to climate change.

2nd Read:
"receding," "wasting," "decline"—negative language gives a serious tone to the article

3rd Read:
Text gives impression that glaciers are disappearing around the world.

How Do I Use It? The focus questions in this book are designed to elicit thematic connections between the texts in a unit. Each text will have some information to answer the focus question, or part of it, in its own way. In this unit, each text tackles the theme of scientific study of ice and snow, and each views this topic from a different perspective. Have students summarize the purpose and results of each research project. Then have them write a short summary explaining the deeper understandings each project has gained or hopes to gain. Summarizing in a graphic organizer can help students compare and contrast.

Sizing Up Earth's Glaciers

Tell students that they will read to find out what scientists learn by studying mountain glaciers.

1st READ

Set a Purpose

Tell students they will be reading to find out what is happening in the article.

Have students read "Sizing Up Glaciers" independently, annotating the text as they read. Circulate and note students' markings, especially questions and confusions.

Text-Dependent Questions

1. What is this text about? (A team of scientists is building a full inventory of the world's glaciers to study how they are changing.)

2. What reason does the article give for this project? (Glaciers are a good indicator for how the climate has changed.)

3. What process is the team using to achieve their goal? (They are combining satellite information with old data.)

Think Aloud *I'm going to reread this article and use a graphic organizer to help me understand what's going on. There are lots of cause-and-effect relationships here, so I can use a flowchart. If the temperatures rise, glaciers will melt, which will eliminate some water sources. That helps me understand why the work is important.*

Partner Talk Have students discuss what the the team of scientists is doing.

Sizing Up Earth's Glaciers

2nd READ

Set a Purpose

Tell students they will read to analyze the text's language.

Text-Dependent Questions

1. How does the author's word choice contribute to your understanding of what is happening to glaciers over time? (Sample answer: The author's use of negative words such as "receding," "wasting," and "decline" convey the idea that glaciers are disappearing.)

2. What does the author mean when she says glaciers are "sensitive to temperature and precipitation changes"? (Sample answer: She means that they physically respond, by growing or shrinking, to temperature and precipitation.)

Partner Talk Have students discuss the author's word choices.

3rd READ

Set a Purpose

Tell students they will read to understand the importance of the scientists' work.

Text-Dependent Questions

1. What will this project help scientists understand? (Sample answer: It will help scientists track the rate of climate change and learn how to protect glaciers.)

Partner Talk Have students discuss the point of view of the article's author.

TEXT 3

ANNOTATION NOTES

1st Read:
Glaciers store fresh water.

2nd Read:
Paragraph 4 includes lists of things that depend on glaciers, which underscore the importance of tracking glacial melt.

3rd Read:
connection between disappearing glaciers and a lack of drinking water

Scientists compare satellite photographs taken by NASA to historical data.

change. Tracking and comparing recent and past changes in the world's glaciers can help researchers understand global warming and its causes. Glacial changes can also have a more immediate impact on communities that rely on glaciers for their water supply. They can also impact regions susceptible to floods, avalanches, or landslides triggered by abrupt glacial melt.

4 About three-quarters of the Earth's fresh water is held in ice sheets and mountain glaciers. For this reason, recognizing glacial changes is crucial to monitoring water supplies. "Glaciers serve as a natural regulator of regional water supplies," said Kargel. During periods of warm weather and intense sunlight during dry seasons and droughts, glaciers melt quickly. As a result, they provide a water source for the surrounding ecosystems and communities. However, during cold, rainy seasons, glaciers produce less meltwater. "Glacier changes, especially recent melting, can affect agriculture, drinking water supplies and hydroelectric power. It can even affect transportation, tourism, coastlines, and ecological habitats," he added.

5 While current melting trends can't be slowed or reversed, the information collected through this project is critical. It will enable researchers to better understand the relationship between climate and glaciers, and to better predict areas of future glacier changes.

PROFESSIONAL DEVELOPMENT

Annotations: Avoiding Over-Annotating

What Is It? Annotations are intended to help readers identify the most important parts of the text. Over-annotating happens when readers mark up so much of the text that the most important ideas are no longer the focus.

Why Is It Important? Over-annotation can cause two main obstacles to understanding the text. First, students may overlook important ideas, because they do not stand out from inessential text. Second, students may spend too much time and energy attempting to find meaning in inessential text that has been unnecessarily annotated.

Return to the TEXT

Comprehension Check: Sizing Up Earth's Glaciers

Answer the questions to demonstrate an understanding of what the text means.

1. What is the goal of the Global Land Ice Measurements from Space team, and how are they pursuing it? Cite details from the text to support your answer.
   Sample answer: The organization's goal is to develop a database that tracks all the world's glaciers and how they change. The text describes it as "an inventory of the world's glaciers." The team is "combining current information on size and movement with historical data, maps, and photos." From the words "from Space" in the organization's name, I can infer that they use photos taken from satellites.

2. What can you infer might happen if glaciers around the world disappear? Cite the evidence from the text you used to make your inference.
   Sample answer: If glaciers around the world disappear, regional water supplies could be threatened, and disasters could increase. The text notes that there are "communities that rely on glaciers for their water supply," and that glaciers "provide a water source for the surrounding ecosystems and communities." In paragraph 4, the scientist quoted in the article says that recent melting "can affect agriculture, drinking water supplies, and hydroelectric power." Since people rely on glaciers for water, I can infer that if glaciers disappear, drinking water will, too.

3. What is the tone of the text, and what language does the author use to achieve it? Cite specific examples from the text to support your answer.
   Sample answers: The tone of the text is a bit worried, but still scientific. In paragraph 1, the author includes surprising statistics about how fast the world's ice is disappearing and says it is to the "dismay" of many people. The scientist and the author use vivid and negative words such as "wasting" and "decline" to describe what is happening to the glaciers. The author emphasizes the importance of the research by describing it as "critical."

How Do I Use It? It can be difficult to find a balance between over- and under-annotation. Often, the best strategy is to instruct students in small groups or individually based on your observation of their annotations. For students who over-annotate, provide small sticky-note tabs and have them annotate the text twice. First, they can mark the text as they normally would with sticky notes. Then, they should review their notes and remove all but the five or so most important, which they can mark on the page.

Return to the TEXT

Stop and Assess

Use the following to assess your students' understanding of the text.

Item 1 answers indicate:	
2	a goal of creating an inventory of the world's glaciers, with specific text citations.
1	a goal of studying the world's glaciers, with some text support.
0	no understanding of the goal, with no text citations.

Item 2 answers indicate:	
2	the disappearance of water sources, with at least two relevant text citations.
1	the disappearance of water sources, with insufficient text support.
0	no relevant answer, and no text support.

Item 3 answers indicate:	
2	a tone that is both warning and scientific, with sufficient text support for each.
1	a tone that is worried, with some text support.
0	no identification of tone, and no text support.

Return to the Focus Question

Explain to students that they will fill out a graphic organizer that helps them answer the Focus Question: What can we learn from close study of ice and snow?

CONNECT TEXTS Have small groups of students discuss how each text they read helps them answer the Focus Question.

Scaffolded Support You may provide the following sentence frames to support students in their use of academic language:

> In the text ________, the author/photographer makes the point that ________. He/she does this by ________.

Remind students to use their annotations and summaries to support their answers. They can also reread portions of the texts, if necessary.

Have students complete their graphic organizers individually.

REFLECT Remind students that each text provides different facts about the information found in ice and snow. Ask, *How did reading all four texts give you a greater understanding of what we can learn from studying ice and snow?*

ANALYZE and SYNTHESIZE ACROSS TEXTS

Return to the Focus Question: What can we learn from close study of ice and snow?

Review your answers to questions about the texts as well as your annotations and Annotation Notes, and think about the discussions you've had about the texts. How does that information help you answer the Focus Question?

Use the graphic organizer to organize information about the texts.

1. In the appropriate box, record the details that help you answer the Focus Question.
2. Make connections between those details to answer the Focus Question. Write your answer in the box provided.

Summer in Antarctica (Visual Text)
Sample answer: Antarctica has snow and ice even in summer.

Climate at the Core
Sample answer: Ice cores provide climate history data.

Snow Beauties
Sample answer: The formation of snowflakes is complex and fascinating.

Sizing Up the Earth's Glaciers
Sample answer: A world glacier inventory helps scientists track climate change.

What can we learn from close study of ice and snow?
Sample answer: Ice and snow contain information about the climate in which they formed. Snowflake structures reveal "the growth, habits, and conditions under which the crystals form," and ice cores "tell a story about how our planet's climate and atmosphere have changed." Glacial melt is "a sign of global climate change."

REFLECT How did making connections between the four texts enable you to answer the Focus Question?

Sample answer: The texts described crystal structure and formation, core scientists learning about ancient climate conditions, and glacier scientists finding clues about Earth's current state. The visual text gave a good representation of what scientists are studying.

136 • Unit 7

PROFESSIONAL DEVELOPMENT

Differentiation: End-of-Unit Writing Assignment

What is It? An end-of-unit writing assignment is a form of differentiation that calls upon students to take what they have learned throughout the unit and expand upon it. The assignment, Write Beyond, invites students to write original material that either extends a storyline from the unit or rewrites a storyline from a different perspective.

Why Is It Important? Writing beyond a reading encourages creativity and develops writing skills. When writing beyond, the students apply their understanding of the text in creating new storylines. In the process, they reexamine the text and uncover deeper meaning.

WRITE

Writing About the Focus Question

Now that you have answered the Focus Question using all four texts, expand on your thinking and communicate your ideas through your writing.

USE EVIDENCE

- Explain what people learn from the close study of ice and snow. Use at least one piece of evidence from the Visual Text and at least two pieces of evidence from Texts 1, 2, and 3 to support your answer.
- If you need more room, use additional paper.

MONITOR

- Use the Writing Checklist as you write to make sure your writing meets all the necessary criteria.
- Use the rubric on page 138 when you have completed a first draft of your writing to help you evaluate, revise, and edit your work.

WRITING CHECKLIST ✔

Does my writing . . .

- ☐ answer the Focus Question?
- ☐ have a clear organizational structure?
- ☐ cite the correct amount of text evidence?
- ☐ correctly use language, spelling, and conventions?

How Do I Use It? Assign the Write Beyond, featured on page 137 of this guide. Have students review the text prior to writing. Remind students to use what they learned from the text to inform their writing.

Writing About the Focus Question

USE EVIDENCE Remind students that they should use their graphic organizers as well as their annotations in the texts to write their responses.

Allow students to revisit the texts as frequently as they need to in order to support comprehension and to respond to the Focus Question.

MONITOR After students have completed their responses, have them review the Writing Checklist and revise their writing response.

DIFFERENTIATE AND EXTEND

In addition to or instead of the writing response, consider having students complete one of the following assignments:

Write Beyond Have students write a journal from the point of view of a scientist drilling for ice cores.

Create a Visual Text Have students make paper "snowflakes" and a diagram explaining why their snowflake formed the way it did given what they learned about crystals and atmospheric conditions from "Snow Beauties."

Research As the climate changes, some glaciers are actually advancing. Have students research and analyze a text describing why.

Interview an Expert Have students write questions they would ask in an interview with a expert on glaciers.

SELF-ASSESS and REFLECT

SELF-ASSESS Have students use the Writing Rubric on page 138 to self-assess their writing response and write a final version. Tell them to assign themselves a score from 1–4 (with "4" being the highest) for each category in the first column.

Use the Writing Rubric on Student Worktext page 138 to assess each student's writing. Record points for each category in the first column of the rubric. Have students remove the page from their Student Worktexts and place it in their writing portfolios, along with the drafts and final versions of their responses.

SELF-ASSESS and REFLECT

Focus Question: What can we learn from close study of ice and snow?

This is the rubric that your teacher will use to assess your writing. Refer to it as you revise your work. After you have finished the final version of your response, assess your response and record your points for each category on the "Student" line in the first column.

	Accomplished (4 points)	Competent (3 points)	Developing (2 points)	Beginning (1 point)
RESPONSE Score: **Student** ______ **Teacher** ______	The response answers the question effectively and with insight.	The response answers the question effectively.	The response partially responds to the question but does not adequately address it.	The response addresses the texts but does not address the question.
ORGANIZATION Score: **Student** ______ **Teacher** ______	The main idea is convincingly stated. Ideas are organized in cohesive paragraphs that support the main idea.	The main idea is clearly stated. Ideas are organized in logical paragraphs.	The main idea is weak. Ideas are organized in a somewhat logical and cohesive way.	The main idea is missing. The organization of the paragraphs is not logical.
TEXT EVIDENCE Score: **Student** ______ **Teacher** ______	Response includes more than one piece of appropriate text evidence from each text. Evidence supports the main idea in a thorough way.	Response includes one piece of text evidence from each text. Evidence supports the main idea clearly.	Response does not include at least one piece of text evidence from each text. Text evidence does not adequately support the main idea.	Response does not contain relevant evidence.
LANGUAGE Score: **Student** ______ **Teacher** ______	Writing includes precise and sophisticated vocabulary related to the topic.	Writing includes appropriate vocabulary related to the topic.	Writing includes imprecise and inaccurate vocabulary.	Writing does not include vocabulary that appropriately reflects the topic of the response.
SPELLING AND CONVENTIONS Score: **Student** ______ **Teacher** ______	Response includes correct spelling, grammar, and punctuation consistently.	Response includes mostly correct spelling, grammar, and punctuation.	Response has many errors in spelling, grammar, and punctuation.	Response's errors in spelling, grammar, and punctuation make it extremely difficult to understand the response.

UNIT 8

Focus Question
How did cars and highways connect America?

Texts for Close Reading

GENRE STUDY

Discuss with students the genres of "The Automobile and Automobiling," "What the Dixie Highway Is," and "Brief History of Route 66."

Remind students that *genre* refers to the format and features of a text and typically falls into one of two categories—literature or informational text. Literature is creative work that doesn't necessarily rely on facts, while informational texts are based on factual information. The texts in this unit are all informational but have different purposes.

With the class, list the features of magazine articles and explanatory texts. Have students identify how these informational texts are alike and how they are different.

Focus Question

Have students read the Focus Question on Worktext page 139. Tell students that the texts they will read will help them answer the question.

Texts for Close Reading

Have students read to themselves the summaries about the texts in this unit.

There is no need to explain what students should expect to find in their close readings or to do any pre-teaching about the subject matter.

TEXT COMPLEXITY

Travel Concept
- Style: documentary
- Knowledge demands: medium
- Levels of meaning: literal/inferential

Automobile and Automobiling

Quantitative: 1100L

Qualitative
- Structure: conventional
- Language: archaic
- Knowledge demands: high
- Levels of meaning: literal/inferential

What the Dixie Highway Is

Quantitative: 1090L

Qualitative
- Structure: conventional
- Language: familiar
- Knowledge demands: medium
- Levels of meaning: literal

Brief History of Route 66

Quantitative: 1170L

Qualitative
- Structure: narrative
- Language: familiar
- Knowledge demands: medium
- Levels of meaning: literal

Travel Concept

Set a Purpose

Explain to students that they will look at the image on page 140 to think about America's cars and highways.

Visual Text Analysis

Remind students that an image can be analyzed as a text by looking at its details and making inferences. Direct students' attention to the image on Student Worktext page 140.

1. Have students look at the image. Lead them to discuss as a whole class, in small groups, or with a partner their first impressions of the photograph.

2. Have students make note of the details that support their observations in question 1. Have students explain as a whole class, in small groups, or with a partner what details they noted and what those details suggest about cars and highways in America.

3. Have students record their inferences about the intended meaning of the image. Have students present the evidence for their inferences.

Provide any additional information you feel is appropriate to enhance the discussion as necessary to support your students:

- U.S. highways are numbered based on their direction and location. Routes with odd numbers run north–south. Routes with even numbers run east–west. Beltways around major cities carry a three-digit number.
- The longest road in the country is U.S. route 20 at 3,365 miles. It runs from Boston, Massachusetts, to Newport, Oregon.

VISUAL TEXT

Travel Concept

Look at the Visual Text to answer the following questions. Review the image or parts of the image as many times as necessary.

1. What is your first impression of this image?
   Sample answer: Someone is planning a road trip that includes the area indicated by the red pushpin.

2. What details support your answer to the previous question?
   Sample answer: The photograph shows a section of a map of the U.S. highways with a pushpin above Kansas and a red toy car sitting above it. The pushpin could represent a destination or starting point of the trip. The sporty car suggests that it's a recreational trip.

3. What do you think the photographer's message is?
   Sample answer: The message could be that there are a lot of highways and places to see across America. Get out there and drive!

PROFESSIONAL DEVELOPMENT

Small-Group Discussion: Hearing Multiple Perspectives

What Is It? Groups of 3–6 students work independently to have informal discussions of the text or an assigned topic. The teacher circulates to monitor, motivate, and keep the discussion on topic.

Why Is It Important? Small-group discussions can help ease the pressure individuals may feel when speaking in front of an entire class but continue to give students practice in hearing multiple perspectives and negotiating group conversations.

TEXT 1

✔ Self-Monitoring Strategies you used to help you check your understanding as you read.

☐ Visualize. ☐ Draw conclusions. ☐ Ask yourself questions. ☐ Reread to clarify.

Read the text to learn about the early automobile in the United States. Make annotations in the text and write your notes in the Annotation Notes column.

Sample annotations and notes appear throughout the text.

The Automobile and Automobiling

by George Latham

An early American automoblie

1 Five years ago one might have counted the automobiles in the United States on one's fingers. In 1903 more of the machines will be made here than in any other country in the world. And the industry is yet in its infancy. E. E. Schwarzkopf, than whom there is no better authority on the subject, has compiled statistics that show its growth during the past three years. In 1900 there were about eight hundred machines built in America, the average price being a thousand dollars, or eight hundred thousand in all. This year it is estimated that at least twenty-eight thousand machines will be turned out.

Hostility to the Automobile

2 Automobilists are almost without exception enthusiasts. They are apt to be impatient with those who have not passed

ANNOTATION NOTES

1st Read:
In 1903, the demand for automobiles in the U.S. skyrocketed.

2nd Read:
"the machines"—shows that cars were still new

heading tells what section is about

3rd Read:
Just as the initial hostility toward the railway engine faded, so too will the hostility toward the automobile.

How Do I Use It? Small-group discussions work best when planned. Choose groups based on the purpose of the discussion. During discussion, note individual participation, including whether students are reluctant or domineering. Record data and use it for future groupings.

The Automobile and Automobiling

Tell students that they will read to learn about the early automobile in the United States.

1st READ

Set a Purpose

Tell students they will be reading to find out what this text is about.

Have students read "The Automobile and Automobiling" independently, annotating as they read. Circulate and make notes of students' markings, questions, and confusions. Your notes can be used to inform instruction and as data for informal assessment.

Text-Dependent Questions

1. What is this text about? (This text is about the first automobiles and automobilists in the early 1900s, and about how many people thought cars were just another fad.)

2. When was this article written? (The article was written in 1903. In paragraph 1, the author uses "1903" and later "This year" to refer to the same year.)

3. Vocabulary: Words in Context Discuss how readers can infer meanings of unfamiliar words from context.

Paragraph 2: What can you infer about the meaning of *imputation*? (It is used to mean "accusation." I know it has a negative meaning in this context because it names what drivers "chafe" about when people call them "dangerous.")

Partner Talk Have students discuss how people responded to the first cars.

The Automobile and Automobiling

2nd READ

Set a Purpose

Tell students they will read to understand how the author uses language to reveal meaning.

Text-Dependent Questions

1. What effect does using the phrase "unmitigated cranks" in paragraph 2 have on the text? (This phrase adds an element of humor to an otherwise serious text.)

Scaffolded Support Use the following scaffolded question as necessary to build comprehension.

What do you think of when you hear the word *crank*?

Think Aloud *In paragraph 5, I was confused by the author's use of the phrase "hard muscular exertion" when referring to riding a bicycle or roller-skating. I usually think of those as fun, leisurely activities. However, when I visualize trying to ride a bike or roller skate for as far as a car might go, I can see why the author would use this phrase.*

2. What effect does the author achieve with the use of words like *logical argument, assertion,* and *falsity of . . . reasoning*? (He establishes his own voice as the voice of reason and lends credibility to his own arguments.)

3. What is the effect of the repeated sentence structure in paragraph 8? (The author repeats "Where the horse. . . the automobile" four times to emphasize that the horse represents the past and the automobile represents the greatly improved future.)

Partner Talk Have students discuss the language of the text.

ANNOTATION NOTES

1st Read:
The author counters the argument that the automobile is a fad like roller skating and bicycling.

Automobiling won't go away as driving requires no physical exertion and cars are useful.

2nd Read:

chafe = to feel irritation

unmitigated cranks—language adds some humor

six day go-as-you-please contest?

3rd Read:
The reality confirms the author's argument—cars have not gone away.

through the exhilarating experience which comes with the successful handling of a steering wheel for the first time. They chafe under the imputation of being considered dangerous citizens, and look upon the promoters of anti-speed legislation as unmitigated cranks. They should have patience. The present generation is no more hostile to the automobile than its great-grandfathers were, less than a century ago, to the railway engine.

Is Automobiling a Fad?

3 "But it's a fad that will soon die out, like the bicycle," is the comment most frequently heard when one speaks of the great future of the automobile.

4 Against such a sweeping assertion it would seem almost useless to offer a logical argument. Still, where the assertion is made on what is believed to be reasonable ground, it may be well to show the falsity of such reasoning. The bicycle craze, or fad, as one may wish to call it, followed almost on the heels of another of its kind, the roller-skating mania. In both, the essence of the craze was the same, namely, the gratification of a desire for swift locomotion. The little wheel of the roller-skate was the precursor to the solid rubber tire of the early bicycle. Expert skaters developed into expert bicyclists. Since the disappearance of the roller-skate and the decadence of the bicycle, many expert cyclists have in turn become expert chauffeurs, and some bicycle manufacturers have become famous as automobile builders. Hence, argue those who predict a short life for the self-propelled vehicle, the third craze will go the way of its predecessors.

5 Fortunately for the automobile, the one feature which was primarily responsible for the decline of the roller-skate and the bicycle does not enter into the sport of automobiling. That is hard muscular exertion. Grant, for the purpose of argument, that there is a possibility of comparison, however absurd, between the roller-skate, the bicycle and the automobile—all being classed alike as fads. Let us carry out the comparison to ? a plain issue. Call it a six day go-as-you-please contest. At the end of a few hours, at most a day, the roller-skater is down and out. A second day finds the bicyclist, if he has lasted so long, a nervous wreck. But at the end of the week the automobilist is for all practical purposes as fresh as when he began. He has missed no sleep, has had his meals regularly, his machine

PROFESSIONAL DEVELOPMENT

Academic Language: Conversation

What Is It? Academic Language is the language used in the classroom. It is a more formal way of speaking than casual conversation and employs academic vocabulary. Students must practice using Academic Language to become "fluent." Use language frames to help students learn how to effectively use Academic Language. Language frames are sentences with intentional blank spaces that students complete.

Why Is It Important? Academic Language is frequently found in higher-education, workplace, and legal situations. Much of the formal vocabulary and sentence structures are essential tools in a writer's repertoire.

hums along as merrily as when it started, and is as fit as ever for another week's contest.

6 Compare the endurance of the three contestants, and you have the relative duration of the "fads."

The Utility of the Auto

7 There is still a stronger reason why the automobile has come to stay—its utility. We call the horse man's best friend because he relieves us of the trouble of walking and is useful in bearing our heaving burdens. Yet whatever the horse can do, the automobile can do a hundred times better.

8 Where the horse would drop from fatigue, the automobile knows no weariness. Where the horse would slip and flounder over the impassable roads, the automobile will carry its human burden safe and dry-shod. Where the horse may "eat its head off" in fodder, the automobile only feeds when it works. Where the horse may shy or bolt in spite of its horse sense, the automobile knows no terrors. Its fidelity is limited only by the intelligence of the man who guides it. It is the horse's best friend as well as man's. It relieves the horse of its burdens.

The Cost of Automobiles

9 A machine of from sixteen to twenty-four horse-power is all that any man requires for touring. With such a car he can go as far as he likes over ordinary roads, carrying a supply of gasoline that should last him for two days at least. Where the roads are clear, he may spin along as fast as the average man cares to travel, and certainly as fast as is consistent with the admiration of the scenery.

10 Of course there are many enthusiastic automobilists who delight in possessing cars of forty or even sixty horse-power. That is their privilege, and they can afford to pay for it. Just as some men choose to own fast horses for which they pay enormous sums.

11 On the other hand, where the automobile is not intended for touring, but rather as a substitute for the old-fashioned horse and buggy, a little six to ten horse-power runabout will amply answer the purpose. And such a machine in constant use for city work, or in making short trips to the country, is cheaper in the long run even than a horse and buggy. Such an automobile is no fad.

ANNOTATION NOTES

1st Read:
compares cars
favorably to horses

different automobiles
to suit different needs

2nd Read:
"drop from fatigue,"
"slip and flounder" create
visual of horse vs. auto

"knows no weariness,"
"automobile only feeds,"
"knows no terrors" give
animal-like qualities
to automobile

3rd Read:
Latham uses logic,
not emotion, to argue
why automobiles are
not a fad and are
better than horses.

How Do I Use It? Model the use of Academic Language by rephrasing and restating students' ideas. You can ask students to compare how the same idea sounds when expressed in informal vs. academic speech. Students can practice rephrasing a partner's statements using academic speech. Both partners can rephrase the same idea more than once to illustrate that Academic Language can still vary depending on the author. For example, for the Partner Talk on page 143, offer these sentence frames to encourage students to practice using Academic Language:

The author wrote this article to inform about ________.

I know this from the details ________, ________, and ________.

The Automobile and Automobiling

3rd READ

Set a Purpose

Tell students they will read to make inferences about early cars and drivers in the U.S.

Text-Dependent Questions

1. What inference can you draw about roads at the time the article was written? What evidence do you have for your answer? (The roads were used mainly for horse-drawn vehicles, and, therefore, most were probably not paved. The author notes in paragraph 9 that cars can spin along "[w]here the roads are clear," which suggests that roads were not consistently kept clear of obstructions as they are today. He also compares horses to automobiles several times.)

2. Why did the author write this magazine article? (He defends the automobile and predicts that it will dominate personal transportation in the future. He is responding to people who think that it may be "a fad that will soon die out.")

Scaffolded Support Use the following scaffolded sentence frames as necessary to build comprehension.

The author defends ________ .

The author predicts ________ .

3. Why does the author call these machines "the horse's best friend"? (Although they eventually replaced horses, automobiles saved horses a lot of work and "relieve[d] the horse of its burdens.")

Partner Talk Have students discuss the effect paved roads had on early cars and drivers in the U.S.

Return to the TEXT

Respond to Reading

You may want to check students' understanding by having them complete pages 144–145 in the Student Worktext.

1. Remind students to review their annotations and recall discussions they've had in order to complete the summary chart. Remind students that only evidence from the text should be included in the summary chart.

As students complete their summary charts, circulate and note which students struggle to identify the correct text evidence. Some students may benefit from small-group instruction.

2. Remind students to include only the most important information in their summaries.

Have students work independently to complete page 144 of their Worktexts.

COLLABORATE When finished, have students exchange summaries with their partners and share their insights.

Return to the TEXT

Respond to Reading: The Automobile and Automobiling

Review your annotations and notes.
Think about how they can help you summarize the text.

1. Use this chart to help you summarize the text.

Summary Chart		
	Informational Text	
Who?	the people or subjects	automobiles, automobilists
What?	the topic or problem	automobile numbers in U.S. increasing dramatically; they are better than horses for traveling
Where?	the location or region events occur	the U.S.
When?	the date, year, or time	1903
How?	the events, steps, or processes	The author favorably compares cars to horses and discusses the utility of cars.

2. Write a 2–3 sentence summary of "The Automobile and Automobiling."

Sample summary: In 1903, automobile production in the U.S. skyrockets. Many believe automobiling is a fad, but the author doesn't agree. He points out that automobiles can travel long distances, traverse difficult roads, and carry heavy loads, while horses fatigue, struggle on tough roads, and are unpredictable.

PROFESSIONAL DEVELOPMENT

Collaboration: Small Groups

What Is It? Collaboration is working in small groups, including pairs, toward a common goal. The small groups can be highly structured, with the teacher assigning individual roles within each group, or more loosely formed, with group members deciding how to assign roles and divide responsibilities. Students might work together on projects or engage in collaborative discussion.

Why Is It Important? Collaboration helps students develop speaking and listening skills. Reading out loud helps them develop command of formal spoken English, and listening for content helps them learn to integrate and evaluate information.

Return to the TEXT

3. How is automobiling similar to roller-skating and bicycling? How is it different? Cite evidence from the text to support your answer.
Sample answer: Latham states in paragraph 4 that automobiling, like roller-skating and bicycling, provides "gratification of a desire for swift locomotion." The main difference between the three activities, however, as expressed in paragraph 5, is "hard muscular exertion." Latham also points out in paragraph 5 that unlike a skater or cyclist, an "automobilist" could drive for hours and yet feel "as fresh as when he began."

4. Explain how the term "horse-power" relates to the automobile. Cite evidence from the text to support your answer.
Sample answer: The term "horse-power" relates to how fast and/or powerful the automobile is. In paragraph 11, Latham explains that "a little six to ten horse-power runabout" is perfect for a person who simply wants to replace their "horse and buggy," while in paragraph 9 he explains that a "machine of from sixteen to twenty-four horse-power" is appropriate for touring, or driving at slow to moderate speeds "over ordinary roads."

5. What is the main reason Latham believes automobiles are not going away? Cite evidence from the text to support your answer.
Sample answer: Latham believes the automobile is here to stay because of its utility. He notes that cars can be used for "touring" and for "city work" and says that "whatever the horse can do, the automobile can do a hundred times better." He also states that the automobile is better than the horse as transport, because horses tire, while autos don't; horses eat a lot, while cars need fuel; horses "slip and flounder" on difficult roads, while autos don't; and horses may "shy or bolt," but an automobile "knows no terrors."

REFLECT What words, phrases, or sections did you visualize to make sure you understood the text?
Sample answer: I visualized paragraph 8 to better understand why the automobile was better than the horse for traveling and carrying heavy loads.

Return to the TEXT

Encourage students to refer back to the text and their annotations and notes to help them answer the questions.

3. You can support students by directing them to paragraphs 4 and 5.

4. Remind students that they will be drawing an inference to answer this question since the text does not explicitly define "horse-power."

5. Suggest that students review the text again, looking for sentences in which the author states and restates his prediction about the automobile's future.

Have students work independently to complete page 145 of their Worktexts.

REFLECT Remind students that visualizing is a **Self-Monitoring Strategy** and that they made annotations and notes about imagery that seemed especially powerful or important. Suggest that they review their annotations and think about any words or phrases they needed to visualize to check their comprehension of the text.

For many students, small-group discussion is less stressful than speaking in front of the entire class.

How Do I Use It? Small-group collaboration can prompt close reading and assure that students do not overlook any important details in a text. One effective approach is to assign a category from the 5Ws to each member of a team. Have students find and list details in their assigned categories, share the details they find, and combine them to paraphrase or explain the text. You might also assign each team member a different "Who" from the text, have them find the other details about that person, and, again, share and combine what they have learned. By sharing and combining details, students review and discuss text content and extract more meaning.

Stop and Assess

Use the following to assess your students' understanding of the text.

	Item 1 answers indicate:
2	that if automobilists just wait, others will catch up to their enthusiam. Two pieces of text evidence support the claim.
1	that drivers should just wait but doesn't explain why. Text evidence is insufficient to explain.
0	a lack of understanding of why the author claims that drivers should have patience with no relevant evidence.

	Item 2 answers indicate:
2	that the tone is serious but also humorous with at least two examples from the text as support.
1	an idea about the tone being serious or humorous but with only one piece of supporting evidence.
0	no understanding about the author's tone and no evidence.

	Item 3 answers indicate:
2	that the author is a fan of the automobile and believes automobiliing has a long, bright future. Two pieces of text evidence support the claims.
1	that the author likes both but only provides one piece of text evidence as support.
0	a lack of understanding about the author's point of view and no supporting evidence.

Option: If you choose not to work with Texts 2 and 3 and to conclude the unit here, use the Visual Text and "The Automobile and Automobiling" to answer the Focus Question: How did cars and highways connect America?

Comprehension Check: The Automobile and Automobiling

Answer the questions to demonstrate an understanding of what the text means.

1. What does the author mean by "They should have patience" in paragraph 2? Cite evidence from the text to support your answer.
   Sample answer: Latham means that the automobilists who are impatient with those who do not find automobiling an "exhilarating experience" should wait—the "unmitigated cranks" will come around soon enough. He explains that the anti-automobile people are "no more hostile" to automobiles than their "great-grandfathers were, less than a century ago, to the railway engine." His readers don't need to be told that the railway engine had not gone away.

2. What is the tone of this text? Cite evidence from the text to support your answer.
   Sample answer: The tone of this text is serious, but has some wit. Latham constructs a convincing argument using facts, while words and phrases such as "they chafe under the imputation of being considered dangerous citizens" (paragraph 2), "call it a six day go-as-you-please contest" (paragraph 5), and "a nervous wreck" (paragraph 5) help create a humorous tone.

3. What can you infer about how the author feels about automobiles and automobiling? Cite at least two pieces of evidence from the text to support your answer.
   Sample answer: I can infer that the author both enjoys automobiling and believes in the practical value of the automobile. In paragraph 2, he uses the phrase "exhilarating experience" to describe "the successful handling of a steering wheel." In paragraph 7 he declares, "whatever the horse can do, the automobile can do a hundred times better."

PROFESSIONAL DEVELOPMENT

Annotations: Key Words and Phrases

What Is It? Annotations are marks that students make as they read the text, such as highlighting, underlining, and circling key words. Students add annotations in layers as they read and reread.

Why Is It Important? Making annotations helps keep the student's attention focused on specific words. Students can mark places of confusion, note questions to ask, or write their own reactions to text information. Marking up a page makes the reading experience personal.

Read to find out about the Dixie Highway. If you need to read any sections more than once, note the reason in the Annotation Notes column.

Sample annotations and notes appear throughout the text.

What the Dixie Highway Is

by John Chapman Hilder

This article was published in Harper's Weekly *in 1916.*

1 The Dixie Highway is conclusive evidence of a spirit of civic pride. Its outward manifestations have for so long taken the form of cannon balls piled in sentimental pyramids on our village greens. At last, it has awakened to a realization of its potential for lasting good.

2 Briefly stated, the purpose of the Dixie Highway is to join the north and the south by means of a concrete road of uniform excellence. It takes no clairvoyance to see what benefits will accrue from this plan. This is true not only to those states through which the Highway is to pass, but to the entire country. And the enthusiasm with which those states have seized upon the Dixie Highway idea is a healthy sign. It shows that their citizens have come to realize that cooperation is the engine not only of today's but tomorrow's success. A few years ago, the slogan was "Every state for itself. Let the nation survive as it may." Today we find groups of men making and selling the same kind of product, pooling their advertising monies for the good of the group. The states and counties through which the Dixie Highway will pass are doing the same thing. Instead of improving their own roads at random, they are cooperating with other states. They are making a great highway intended to unify an enormous section of the country. When the project is completed, they will undoubtedly receive far more money and influence through being part of the unit, than they would if they spent on their own.

3 Consider the fact that land values have already increased in sections which lie along the Dixie Highway route. Consider also the money that will be spent daily by each of the thousand or so motorists passing along the highway in regions, which, except for the highway, they would not be able to visit.

ANNOTATION NOTES

1st Read:

Dixie Highway will connect the north and south.

The highway idea got states to work together for the improvement for all, not "every state for itself."

2nd Read:

to-the-point and matter-of-fact language: "Briefly stated," "It takes no clairvoyance to see"

claim in first sentence supported in paragraph 2

3rd Read:

Now that the car has become a regular part of life, we move on to developing highways.

How Do I Use It? As you introduce Text 2, model how to annotate by underlining the first sentence and circling the phrase "civic pride." Then Think Aloud to demonstrate that annotations can be used to keep track of key facts and clear up confusions. *The author begins with a broad statement that makes me wonder "How can a highway show civic pride?" In the second paragraph, he writes about cooperation as "the engine . . . of tomorrow's success." That sounds like something to be proud of, and since many states are working together and the highway passes through so many cities and towns, it is certainly "civic." As I reread, I'll mark other words and phrases that recall and reflect "civic pride."*

What the Dixie Highway Is

Tell students that they will read to learn about the Dixie Highway.

1st READ

Set a Purpose

Tell students they will be reading to find out what the text is about.

Have students read "What the Dixie Highway Is" independently, annotating as they read. Circulate and note students' markings, especially questions and confusions.

Text-Dependent Questions

1. What does the author say will result from the completion of the Dixie Highway? **(It will "unify an enormous section of the country," promote cooperation among many states, and bring more money into the states.)**

Scaffolded Support Use the following scaffolded question and sentence frame as necessary to build comprehension.

What is the difference between how states thought of themselves before and after the Dixie Highway idea?

The states' motto was ________.

2. Vocabulary: Figurative Language Discuss the meaning of figures of speech in the text.

Paragraph 2: How can cooperation be an "engine of success"? **(This metaphor suggests that cooperation moves everyone forward as long as it has fuel, is maintained, and keeps working.)**

Partner Talk Have students discuss how the Dixie Highway changed from an idea into a reality.

What the Dixie Highway Is

2nd READ

Set a Purpose

Tell students they will read to examine the author's use of language and how he organized the information in the text.

Text-Dependent Questions

1. How does the author connect paragraphs 2 and 3? (He ends paragraph 2 by stating that participating states will "receive far more money and influence" and then begins paragraph 3 with the fact that "land values have already increased" along the highway, reinforcing what he had previously said.)

2. How do the verbs and the hourglass comparison in paragraph 4 reinforce the author's main idea? (The verbs—*follows, meet, run into, connecting, converge*—make the highway seem like an intregrated web. The hourglass comparison suggests both movement and progress.)

3. What is the overall tone of this text? (Although the language is somewhat formal, the overall tone is energetic and positive. The author is an enthusiastic booster of the highway project.)

4. Vocabulary: Multiple-Meaning Words Discuss words that have multiple meanings.

Paragraph 5: What does *afford* mean in the last sentence? What other, more common meaning does it have? (Here, *afford* means "to make available, to offer." It commonly means "to be able to pay for.")

Partner Talk Have students discuss the organization and language of the text.

TEXT 2

ANNOTATION NOTES

1st Read:
States along highway benefit more by working together, rather than only looking out for themselves.

Dixie Highway extends from Michigan and Illinois down to Florida.

2nd Read:
moves from selling the highway to detailed description of route

3rd Read:
Was there already a highway along the East Coast?

4 As it now stands, the route laid out for the Dixie Highway resembles in shape an hour glass. From Mackinac, Michigan, the Highway's most northerly point, the route follows the shores of Lake Michigan and Lake Huron. These two routes

In 1926, the Dixie Highway ceased to exist by that name when federal and state highway officials replaced named trails across America with numbered highways. Because the Dixie Highway was not a single highway, its various divisions became parts of the new U.S. numbered highway system, plus a variety of state-numbered highways.

PROFESSIONAL DEVELOPMENT

Intertextual Analysis: Comparing and Contrasting Big Ideas

What Is It? Students compare more than one visual or written text in terms of the overarching concepts they express. Through close reading of both the visual and verbal texts, students make comparisons that lead them toward larger concepts.

Why Is It Important? Comparing texts with similar big ideas helps students identify the overarching concepts the texts have in common. Even more critically, it helps students analyze what the texts do not share, which leads to higher-order thinking skills such as distinguishing the purposes, points of view, and relative reliability of texts.

TEXT 2

run practically parallel down through Kalamazoo and Detroit respectively. Further south, the routes run into Indiana and Ohio. The western road is met at Indianapolis by a branch which starts at Chicago. And from Indianapolis also runs a cross-road, connecting the western with the eastern route by a junction at Dayton. From Indiana and Ohio, the two routes run down into Kentucky and through that state into Tennessee, where they converge at Chattanooga, headquarters of the Highway's administration. From Chattanooga the road goes to Macon, Georgia, where it again splits in two. One branch goes southwest to Tallahassee, Florida, and thence inland to ? Arcadia and on to the coast, and Miami. The objective of the other branch has not yet been decided, both Savannah and Jacksonville being under consideration. The latter is on the Highway anyway, since a cross-road runs from Tallahassee to it and continues along the coast to meet the inland route of Miami.

5 I started this article by talking about civic pride and then switched into the subject of rewards. This may have seemed paradoxical and contradictory. But is it? The standard of road construction and maintenance set by the Dixie Highway should prove to be such that no state will rest easy until all its roads are equally good. Civic pride will play a part in that. And then the problem of beautifying the highway in places where nature and steam shovels may have chanced to be harsh will afford another opportunity for the exercise of civic pride.

6 In order that the residents of the various counties may have part in the work of the Dixie Highway Association, county councils are being organized in each county. Altogether the Association seems to be organized on an unusually sound efficient basis.

ANNOTATION NOTES

1st Read:
The highway inspires civic pride, and civic pride will help to keep the highway profitable.

2nd Read:
"civic pride" and "rewards"—why contradictory?

"But is it?"—author is having conversation with reader

3rd Read:
The highway system helped the economy grow and changed the way Americans live. Families spread out to towns and cities that are far apart, people commute long distances to work, and we drive long distances for pleasure.

How Do I Use It? Texts 1 and 2 in this unit reflect two aspects of the Focus Question. Once students have read both texts, have them collaborate in small groups to compare and contrast the big ideas that each text illuminates and supports. Encourage them to use Venn diagrams to explore both similarities and differences. This process will lead students to see how the big ideas of each text relate to each other and how comparing more than one text can lead a reader to understand big ideas more fully.

What the Dixie Highway Is

3rd READ

Set a Purpose

Tell students they will read to make inferences about the text.

Text-Dependent Questions

1. What can you infer about how the Dixie Highway changed people's lives? (I can infer that people in different states felt connected to one another. I can also infer that people were able to have more options in where to live because it was easier to get to work, and that it was easier to visit family who lived farther away.)

Think Aloud *At first, I didn't understand when the author suggested that pride and rewards are opposite, so I started asking myself questions. Is road construction a reward? Is seeing beautiful scenery a reward? Is making money a reward? I guess if you add up all these "rewards," people might be proud of their accomplishments. The author says they are not opposite at all when he asks, "But is it?" He believes that rewards create pride.*

2. What can you conclude about the author from this article? (The author firmly and passionately believes that highways are bridges between people, states, and the present and the future.)

Scaffolded Support Use the following scaffolded question and sentence frame as necessary to build comprehension.

What does the author care about?

Hilder praises ________ .

Partner Talk Have students discuss the author's ideas about the importance of the Dixie Highway.

Return to the TEXT

Stop and Assess

Use the following to assess your students' understanding of the text.

Item 1 answers indicate:	
2	that the author's purpose is to explain, describe, and promote, with at least two pieces of text evidence.
1	that the author's purpose is to inform and includes one piece of evidence as support.
0	a lack of understanding of author's purpose and no evidence from the text.

Item 2 answers indicate:	
2	how the map helped them understand the text, with at least two relevant supporting examples.
1	that the map was helpful with only one piece of supporting evidence.
0	no knowledge of how the map might support a reader's understanding with no evidence.

Item 3 answers indicate:	
2	one relevant and thoughtful theme with at least two pieces of evidence as support.
1	a possible theme with only one piece of text evidence as support.
0	no understanding of the theme of the text and no supporting evidence.

Return to the TEXT

Comprehension Check: What the Dixie Highway Is

Answer the questions to demonstrate an understanding of what the text means.

1. What is the author's purpose in writing this text?
Cite evidence from the text to support your answer.
Sample answer: The author's purpose is to give readers a complete understanding of the Dixie Highway and to promote the highway. He describes the highway's route in paragraph 4. Hilder explains in paragraph 2 that states are working together "to unify an enormous section of the country" and paragraph 5 states that it will take "civic pride" to ensure the highway is built "equally good" in all states. In paragraph 3, Hilder points out that "land values have already increased" along the highway.

2. How does the map of the Dixie Highway help you understand the text?
Sample answer: I didn't know exactly where all the cities are that Hilder mentions in his description of the highway, so the map helped me visualize its route. The map also shows very clearly how the highway connects points throughout an important strip of the country. In looking at the map, I also inferred that goods were getting to points on the Great Lakes by boat and then being trucked down the highway.

3. What is one theme of this text?
Cite evidence from the text to support your answer.
Sample answer: One theme of this text is that people benefit more when they work together. In paragraph 2, the author states that people realized "that cooperation is the engine not only of today's but tomorrow's success" and that states working together to build the highway "receive far more money and influence through being part of the unit, than they would if they spent on their own."

PROFESSIONAL DEVELOPMENT

Classroom Management: Discussions

What Is It? Effective teaching requires thoughtful planning and classroom management. In order for discussions to be fruitful, plan group sizes ahead. Broader topics covering main ideas are well suited for whole-class discussion. Topics that require personal reflection or connection are best suited for smaller groups. Pairs are most effective when students are asked to review each other's writing.

Why Is It Important? Class time spent in actual discussion is limited. Using an appropriately sized group for the day's topics/questions ensures students will have the best opportunity to

Read to find out about U.S. Highway 66. You may want to read some sections more than once and make different annotations and Annotation Notes each time.

Sample annotations and notes appear throughout the text.

Brief History of Route 66

1 U.S. Highway 66—popularly known as Route 66—holds a special place in American consciousness. Its name commonly evokes images of simpler times. Travelers on Highway 66 today can easily experience this past, as many of the motels, gas stations, cafés, parks, trading posts, bridges, and roadbeds remain along the thoroughfare. These historic resources are reminders of our past and evidence of the origins of our current automobile-influenced society.

Vintage signs along Route 66

ANNOTATION NOTES

1st Read:
Route 66 has historical value and is a reminder of simpler times.

2nd Read:
list of things travelers can see on Route 66 that remain unchanged and are now historic landmarks

3rd Read:
Original sites and structures along Route 66 show how cars influenced American culture.

Like the Dixie Highway, Route 66 benefitted people financially and culturally.

explore and comprehend the text. Reducing group size allows each individual maximum speaking time. Pairing students provides a degree of privacy and helps reserved students gain confidence.

How Do I Use It? Before students read "Brief History of Route 66," have them preview the text and make predictions about its content. Decide how it would be best discussed—whole class, small group, or pairs. Encourage students to look at the title, the illustration, and the first sentence and ask these questions to guide the discussion: *What do you think this text will be about? What do you think you will learn from it?*

Brief History of Route 66

Tell students that they will read to learn about U.S. Highway 66.

1st READ

Set a Purpose

Explain to students that they will read the text to find out what it is about. Have students read "Brief History of Route 66" independently, annotating the text.

Text-Dependent Questions

1. What is the main idea of this text? (Route 66 was an important highway that connected "the East and the West." Today it connects "the past and the present.")

2. How did Route 66 come into existence? (It was created by the Bureau of Public Roads as part of the federal highway system, and it was patched together from existing roads.)

3. **Vocabulary: Figurative Language** Discuss the author's use of figurative language and its impact.

Paragraph 2: To what does the author compare Route 66 in this paragraph? (He compares the highway to a knife that "slices across the continent.")

Partner Talk Have students discuss what they would see along Route 66.

Brief History of Route 66

2nd READ

Set a Purpose

Tell students they will read to examine the author's word choices.

Text-Dependent Questions

1. What is the effect of calling Route 66 "an artery of transportation"? (A body cannot live without its central artery, so the highway is essential to the country's health and vitality.)

2. What do words such as *symbol*, *heritage*, and *legacy* contribute to the author's purpose? (They point to the highway's significance in American history. They connect the road to major historic events and founding principles.)

Partner Talk Have students discuss the author's use of descriptive language.

3rd READ

Set a Purpose

Tell students they will read to infer the overall meaning of the text.

Text-Dependent Questions

1. What makes Route 66 so unusual? (It crosses almost two-thirds of the country and its importance was recognized by Congress.)

2. How does the author's perspective in Text 2 compare to the author's perspective in this text? (The author of Text 2 promotes a new highway. The author of Text 3 reflects on the history of an important highway. Both authors are strong proponents of "their" highways.)

Partner Talk Have students discuss why Congress designated Route 66 as a national symbol.

TEXT 3

ANNOTATION NOTES

1st Read:
Route 66 was created in 1926 by linking numerous existing roads.

represents a time in America when many traveled by car across the country in search of a better life

2nd Read:
"legacy," "spirit of Route 66," "remarkable journey"—inspire feelings of national pride and excitement

3rd Read:
What was traveling across the country like before Route 66 was created?

2 Route 66 embodies a complex, rich history that goes well beyond any chronicle of the road itself. An artery of transportation, an agent of social transformation, and a remnant of America's past, it stretches 2,400 miles across two-thirds of the continent. The highway winds from the shores of Lake Michigan across the agricultural fields of Illinois. It goes to the rolling hills of the Missouri Ozarks and through the mining towns of Kansas. It spans across Oklahoma where the woodlands of the East meet the open plains of the West. And travels to the open ranch lands of Texas; the enchanted mesa lands of New Mexico and Arizona; to the Mojave Desert; and finally to Los Angeles and the shores of the Pacific Ocean. Flanked by historic buildings and diverse cultural resources, Route 66 slices across the continent. This fabled highway's multiple alignments connect not only the East and the West, but also the past and the present.

3 Route 66 had its official beginnings in 1926 when the Bureau of Public Roads launched the nation's first federal highway system. Like other highways in the system, the path of Route 66 was a cobbling together of existing local, state, and national roads. The highway quickly became a popular route because of the active promotion of the U.S. 66 Highway Association. It advertised Route 66 as "the shortest, best and most scenic route" from Chicago through St. Louis to Los Angeles.

4 In 1990, the United States Congress passed Public Law 102-400, the Route 66 Study Act of 1990, recognizing that Route 66 had "become a symbol of the American people's heritage of travel and their legacy of seeking a better life." The spirit of Route 66 lives in the people and their stories, the views and buildings, and travelers' perceptions of the highway. Today's travelers can still experience a remarkable journey traveling through time on Route 66.

152 • Unit 8

PROFESSIONAL DEVELOPMENT

Intertextual Analysis: Comparing and Contrasting Authors' Perspectives

What Is It? An effective way to analyze more than one text is to focus on the authors' perspectives. A perspective, or point of view, is the author's way of looking at the world. We compare authors' perspectives by considering their life experiences and the times in which they lived and by analyzing language for the attitudes it reveals.

Why Is It Important? An author's perspective determines many aspects of a text, such as purpose, word choice, and arguments. Asking questions such as *What is the author's attitude? How does he or she feel about ________?* may help readers draw inferences from the author's statements to better understand the text.

Return to the TEXT

Comprehension Check: Brief History of Route 66

Answer the questions to demonstrate an understanding of what the text means.

1. What is the author's purpose for writing this text? Cite at least two pieces of evidence from the text to support your answer.
   Sample answer: The author wants to inform readers of the history and significance of Route 66. In paragraph 2, the author calls Route 66 "an agent of social transformation, and a remnant of America's past" and then describes the various states and landscapes Route 66 passes through. The author explains Route 66's "official beginnings" in paragraph 3 and adds in paragraph 4 that in 1990, Congress "passed Public Law 102-400" to recognize the highway's historical and cultural significance.

2. Why does the author include so much information about Route 66 in paragraph 2? Cite evidence from the text to support your answer.
   Sample answer: The author includes descriptive words and phrases such as "rolling hills," "woodlands," "open ranch lands," and "enchanted mesa lands" to help readers envision the different landscapes they would see if they were traveling along Route 66 toward California. This language paints a beautiful and intriguing picture of the highway.

3. What can you infer about the relationship between auto travel and Route 66? Cite evidence from the text to support your answer.
   Sample answer: I infer that as more people began traveling longer distances in cars, the need for a highway extending across the country became clear. In paragraph 3, the author explains that in 1926, numerous existing roads were cobbled together to create Route 66, and the highway became popular after it was promoted as "'the shortest, best and most scenic route.'" I also infer that as more people used Route 66, more businesses and sites were built, which drew even more people to the highway.

How Do I Use It? This unit contains two texts that describe two different highways. Draw students' attention to the similarities and differences between the two authors' perspectives. Use sentence frames such as these to prompt discussion:

Hilder uses words to ________, and the author of "Brief History" uses words to ________.

Hilder organizes details by ________, while the author of "Brief History" organizes details by ________.

Hilder focuses on ________, while the author of "Brief History" focuses on ________.

Hilder's perspective is ________, while the perspective of the author of "Brief History" is ________.

Return to the TEXT

Stop and Assess

Use the following to assess your students' understanding of the text.

Item 1 answers indicate:	
2	that the author's purpose is to inform and/or inspire, with at least two pieces of text evidence as support.
1	that the author's purpose is to inform, with only one piece of supporting evidence.
0	a lack of understanding of author's purpose and no evidence.

Item 2 answers indicate:	
2	that the author includes these details to reveal scenic beauty and variety, with at least two pieces of supporting evidence.
1	that the author includes these details to add meaning, with only one piece of evidence as support.
0	no understanding of why the author includes this information.

Item 3 answers indicate:	
2	a thoughtful inference about the relationship between travel and Route 66, with at least two pieces of supporting evidence.
1	an idea about the relationship between travel and Route 66, with only one piece of supporting evidence.
0	no understanding about the relationship between Route 66 and auto travel with no evidence.

ANALYZE and SYNTHESIZE ACROSS TEXTS

Return to the Focus Question

Explain to students that they will fill out a graphic organizer that helps them answer the Focus Question: How did cars and highways connect America?

CONNECT TEXTS Have small groups of students discuss how each text they read helps them answer the Focus Question.

Scaffolded Support You may provide the following sentence frames to support students in their use of academic language:

> In the text ________,
> the author/artist makes
> the point that ________.
> He/she does this by ________.

Remind students to use their annotations and summaries to support their answers. They can also reread portions of the texts, if necessary.

Have students complete their graphic organizers individually.

REFLECT Remind students that each text provides different information about how cars and highways connected America. Ask, *How did reading all four texts give you a greater understanding of this connection?*

ANALYZE and SYNTHESIZE ACROSS TEXTS

Return to the Focus Question: How did cars and highways connect America?

Review your answers to questions about the texts as well as your annotations and Annotation Notes, and think about the discussions you've had about the texts. How does that information help you answer the Focus Question?

Use the graphic organizer to organize information about the texts.

1. In the appropriate box below, record the details that help you answer the Focus Question.
2. Make connections between those details to answer the Focus Question. Write your answer in the box provided.

Travel Concept (Visual Text)
Sample answer: Highways make it fast and easy to travel from state to state by car.

What the Dixie Highway Is
Sample answer: Dixie Highway is the result of many states working together for the good of all.

Automobile and Automobiling
Sample answer: In 1903, automobile production skyrocketed; long-distance travel became easier.

Brief History of Route 66
Sample answer: In the 1920s, Route 66 made travel from Lake Michigan to California easy and fast.

How did cars and highways connect America?
Sample answer: Cars allowed people to travel longer distances, while highways provided fast and direct routes between states. Together they allowed commerce and cultural ideas to spread, and encouraged a sense of unity and civic pride across states.

REFLECT How did making connections between the four texts enable you to answer the Focus Question?

Sample answer: I was able to see how highways provided fast and easy routes for cars to travel, which enabled people to experience different cultures and search for a better life. The construction of highways also fostered a sense of unity among states.

PROFESSIONAL DEVELOPMENT

Collaboration: Whole-Class Collaboration

What Is It? Whole-class collaboration means working with the entire class toward a single goal, such as the planning and execution of a project. Collaborative projects can be quite complex—for example, creating an assembly presentation. Simpler, on-the-spot collaborations can be even more effective in close reading.

Why Is It Important? Having the whole class thinking and working together has many benefits for you as well as your students. You can regroup after small-group discussion or pause at intervals for a quick group activity that gets all the students "on the same page."

WRITE

Writing About the Focus Question

Now that you have answered the Focus Question using all four texts, expand on your thinking and communicate your ideas through your writing.

WRITING CHECKLIST ✔

Does my writing . . .

- ☐ answer the Focus Question?
- ☐ have a clear organizational structure?
- ☐ cite the correct amount of text evidence?
- ☐ correctly use language, spelling, and conventions?

USE EVIDENCE

- Explain what you have learned about how cars and highways connected America. Use at least one piece of evidence from the Visual Text and at least two pieces of evidence from Texts 1, 2, and 3 to support your answer.
- If you need more room, use additional paper.

MONITOR

- Use the Writing Checklist as you write to make sure your writing meets all the necessary criteria.
- Use the rubric on page 156 when you have completed a first draft of your writing to help you evaluate, revise, and edit your work.

How Do I Use It? Use on-the-spot projects to focus student attention, review vocabulary, or spark discussion. Use planned activities to deepen and extend learning. For example, the "Make a Plan" activity begins as a small-group activity but opens up to the whole class and provides an opportunity for students to examine attitudes toward cars and highways in earlier times.

Writing About the Focus Question

USE EVIDENCE Remind students that they should use their graphic organizers as well as their annotations in the texts to write their responses.

Allow students to revisit the texts as frequently as they need to in order to support comprehension and to respond to the Focus Question.

MONITOR After students have completed their responses, have them review the Writing Checklist and revise their writing responses.

DIFFERENTIATE AND EXTEND

In addition to or instead of the writing response, consider having students complete one of the following assignments:

Write Beyond Have students take the role of one of the first car salesmen and write a sales pitch.

Read Beyond Have students read *Motoring West: Volume 1: Automobile Pioneers, 1900–1909.*

Design a Brochure Have students design an informational travel brochure for a local highway.

Make a Plan Have students work in small groups to develop plans for a highway connecting your region to another part of the country. Then have them pitch their plans to the class in a "town meeting." Have classmates rate the plans based on a rubric.

SELF-ASSESS and REFLECT

SELF-ASSESS Have students use the Writing Rubric on page 156 to self-assess their writing response and write a final version. Tell them to assign themselves a score from 1–4 (with "4" being the highest) for each category in the first column.

Use the Writing Rubric on Student Worktext page 156 to assess each student's writing. Record points for each category in the first column of the rubric. Have students remove the page from their Student Worktexts and place it in their writing portfolios, along with the drafts and final versions of their responses.

SELF-ASSESS and REFLECT

Focus Question: How did cars and highways connect America?

This is the rubric that your teacher will use to assess your writing. Refer to it as you revise your work. After you have finished the final version of your response, assess your response and record your points for each category on the "Student" line in the first column.

	Accomplished (4 points)	Competent (3 points)	Developing (2 points)	Beginning (1 point)
RESPONSE Score: Student _____ Teacher _____	The response answers the question effectively and with insight.	The response answers the question effectively.	The response partially responds to the question but does not adequately address it.	The response addresses the texts but does not address the question.
ORGANIZATION Score: Student _____ Teacher _____	The main idea is convincingly stated. Ideas are organized in cohesive paragraphs that support the main idea.	The main idea is clearly stated. Ideas are organized in logical paragraphs.	The main idea is weak. Ideas are organized in a somewhat logical and cohesive way.	The main idea is missing. The organization of the paragraphs is not logical.
TEXT EVIDENCE Score: Student _____ Teacher _____	Response includes more than one piece of appropriate text evidence from each text. Evidence supports the main idea in a thorough way.	Response includes one piece of text evidence from each text. Evidence supports the main idea clearly.	Response does not include at least one piece of text evidence from each text. Text evidence does not adequately support the main idea.	Response does not contain relevant evidence.
LANGUAGE Score: Student _____ Teacher _____	Writing includes precise and sophisticated vocabulary related to the topic.	Writing includes appropriate vocabulary related to the topic.	Writing includes imprecise and inaccurate vocabulary.	Writing does not include vocabulary that appropriately reflects the topic of the response.
SPELLING AND CONVENTIONS Score: Student _____ Teacher _____	Response includes correct spelling, grammar, and punctuation consistently.	Response includes mostly correct spelling, grammar, and punctuation.	Response has many errors in spelling, grammar, and punctuation.	Response's errors in spelling, grammar, and punctuation make it extremely difficult to understand the response.

UNIT 9

Focus Question What are the challenges and rewards of renewable energy?

Texts for Close Reading

GENRE STUDY

Discuss with students the genres of "Some of the Problems Awaiting Solution," "Wave of Discovery," and "Solar Basics."

Remind students that *genre* refers to the format and features of a text and typically falls into one of two categories—literature or informational text. The texts in this unit are informational. They all present factual information, but they are in differing sub-genres.

With the class, list the features of informative speeches and explanatory texts. Have students identify the characteristics these types of texts share, such as presenting information in an interesting way, and ways in which they would expect them to be different.

Focus Question

Have students read the Focus Question on Worktext page 157. Tell students that the texts they will read will help them answer the question.

Texts for Close Reading

Have students read to themselves the summaries about the texts in this unit.

There is no need to explain what students should expect to find in their close readings or to do any pre-teaching about the subject matter.

TEXT COMPLEXITY

Wind Farm
- Style: documentary
- Knowledge demands: medium
- Levels of meaning: literal

Problems Awaiting Solution

Quantitative: 1050L

Qualitative
- Structure: conventional
- Language: familiar
- Knowledge demands: medium
- Levels of meaning: literal/inferential

Wave of Discovery

Quantitative: 1110L

Qualitative
- Structure: conventional
- Language: academic
- Knowledge demands: high
- Levels of meaning: literal

Solar Basics

Quantitative: 1120L

Qualitative
- Structure: conventional
- Language: academic
- Knowledge demands: medium
- Levels of meaning: literal

Wind Farm

Set a Purpose

Explain to students that they will look at the image on page 158 to begin to gain a deeper understanding of sources of renewable energy.

Visual Text Analysis

Remind students that an image can be analyzed as a text by looking at its details and making inferences. Direct students' attention to the image on Student Worktext page 158.

1. Have students record their immediate impressions after they look at the image. Lead them to discuss as a whole class, in small groups, or with a partner, what they think is happening in the photograph.

2. Encourage students to make note of the details that support their observations in question 1. Have students explain as a whole class, in small groups, or with a partner, what details they noted and what those details suggest about renewable energy sources.

3. Tell students to record their thoughts and realizations about the image. Have them discuss how these reactions deepen their understanding of the Visual Text.

Provide any additional information you feel is appropriate to enhance the discussion:

- The San Gorgonio Wind Farm was developed during the 1980s in one of the windiest places in southern California.
- The farm includes more than 3,200 wind turbines, which range from 80 to 160 feet in height.

VISUAL TEXT

The San Gorgonio Wind Farm, Palm Springs, California, 2015

Look at the Visual Text to answer the following questions. Review the image or parts of the image as many times as necessary.

1. What is happening in this photograph?
   Sample answer: Wind turbines and power lines stand out against the desert as cars drive by on a road that cuts between sweeping hills.

2. What details support your first impression?
   Sample answer: Two cars drive on a desert road past power lines. The land is brown and mostly bare. Five white wind turbines stand along a ridge. We can't know if the blades of the turbines are turning, but I imagine them spinning in the wind.

3. What does the photograph make you think or realize?
   Sample answer: The area looks uninhabited, and the turbines look like huge white trees. The photograph highlights the connection between the turbines and the power lines. I wonder what impact the turbines might be having on the local environment.

158 • Unit 9

PROFESSIONAL DEVELOPMENT

Classroom Management: Peer Leadership in Small Group Activities

What Is It? Classroom management is the management of student behavior, interaction, and time management. Peer leadership involves placing students in leadership roles during brief small-group activities.

Why Is It Important? Leading an activity gives students practice in self- and peer-management, social interaction, and leadership and motivation. Having students lead group discussions and activities frees you up for close observation and formative assessment.

TEXT 1

✔ Self-Monitoring Strategies you used to help you check your understanding as you read.

☐ Visualize. ☐ Draw conclusions. ☐ Ask yourself questions. ☐ Reread to clarify.

Read the text to learn what a famous inventor told a 1917 graduating class about powering the future. Make annotations in the text and write your notes in the Annotation Notes column.

Sample annotations and notes appear throughout the text.

Some of the Problems Awaiting Solution

by Alexander Graham Bell

Bell delivered this speech to the graduating class of the McKinley Manual Training School in Washington, D.C., on February 1, 1917. It was later published in National Geographic Magazine.

1 What a glorious thing it is to be young and have a future before you. To the graduates, especially, of a scientific technical school like the McKinley Manual Training School, the outlook for the future looks bright and promising.

2 When I was a young man the institutions of learning, the ! high schools and colleges, paid a great deal more attention to the teaching of Latin and Greek than to the study of science. They made scholars rather than scientists.

3 The war has changed all that. And the man of science will be appreciated in the future as he never has been in the past. Knowledge is power. We now realize that the nation that fosters science becomes so powerful that other nations must, if only in self-defense, adopt the same plan. It is safe to say that scientific men and technical experts are destined in the future to occupy distinguished and honorable positions in all the countries of the world. Your future is assured.

We progress from candles to electricity in one lifetime

4 I said it was a glorious thing to be young; but it is also a glorious thing to be old and look back upon the progress of the world during one's own lifetime.

5 Now, I don't mean to insinuate that I am old, by any means! I had in mind an old lady, who is now living in Baltimore, at

ANNOTATION NOTES

1st Read:

Bell congratulates the graduates and then makes some pronouncements about the role of science in the world.

1917—World War I

2nd Read:

Bell uses "you" and "I."

Subheading signals a shift in topic.

3rd Read:

Bell has faith that science will lead people in the right direction. He considers scientific history "glorious."

How Do I Use It? Provide ample structure for student leaders. Assign specific leaders and, if necessary, other roles for students in each group. Assign an activity with a clear goal—for example, with the Visual Text, have small groups list details in the image and arrive at a statement about the image's meaning. Visit groups in turn. Observe student leadership, and provide one-on-one coaching with suggestions and encouragement. After the activity, allow peer leaders and other students in the group time for open-ended reflection to elicit what they enjoyed, what they may have found frustrating, and what they learned from the experience. Keep student reflections or take notes to help prepare for future peer-led activities.

Problems Awaiting Solution

Tell students that they will read to learn what a famous inventor told a 1917 graduating class about powering the future.

1st READ

Set a Purpose

Tell students they will be reading to find out what Bell's speech is about.

Have students read "Some of the Problems Awaiting Solution" independently, annotating as they read. Circulate and make notes of students' markings, questions, and confusions. Your notes can be used to inform instruction and as data for informal assessment.

Text-Dependent Questions

1. What is the main idea of Bell's speech? (Bell outlines advances in technology that created an ever-growing need for fuels.)

Scaffolded Support Use the following question and sentence frame as necessary to build comprehension.

What three sources of lighting does Bell point to in paragraphs 6–8?

Bell notes that most machinery runs on ________ or ________.

2. What sources of power does Bell mention in paragraphs 13–16? (He cites coal, oil, water, tidal, solar, wood, and alcohol as sources of power.)

3. How does Bell support his claim that alcohol is the fuel of the future? (He points out that alcohol is a renewable resource and that it is clean and efficient.)

Partner Talk Have students discuss Bell's thoughts about progress using evidence from the text.

Problems Awaiting Solution

2nd READ

Set a Purpose

Tell students they will read to analyze the author's use of language and the text structure.

Text-Dependent Questions

1. What is the tone of this speech? (The language is familiar and informal. Bell draws lessons from the past so the speech has the tone of an elder sharing his wisdom with the young.)

2. How are ideas in the text organized? (The main ideas are organized under subheadings. Bell summarizes the history of power sources, discusses the problem of nonrenewable fuels, and talks about alcohol as a fuel.)

Scaffolded Support Use the following sentence frame and question as necessary to build comprehension.

The text uses ________ to organize information.

What are the main topics Bell addresses in his speech?

3. What shift takes place from paragraphs 12 to 13? (Bell shifts from praising advancements to concern about fuels.)

4. Vocabulary: Word Parts Identify and discuss multisyllabic words that have roots, prefixes, and suffixes.

Paragraph 16: What do the parts of *indigestible* tell you about its meaning? (The word *digest* is the root. The prefix means "not" and the suffix means "able to," so the word describes alcohol that is "not able to be digested.")

Partner Talk Have students discuss the structure of the text as it relates to Bell's purpose.

ANNOTATION NOTES

1st Read:
A 107-year-old woman has witnessed "a whole century" of technical progress.

details the technological developments leading in steps to reliance on electricity

2nd Read:
stresses "electrical age"

figurative language—"threads of advance"

"Illuminant"— both literal (lighting) and figurative (knowledge)

3rd Read:
"the death rate was high"—Reread—is he implying that advancements in technology save lives?

the age of one hundred and seven—with mental faculties unimpaired. Possessed of a bright and active mind, she is able, from her own personal recollections, to look back upon a whole century of progress of the world.

This portrait of Bell was taken at about the same time as the speech he gave at the McKinley Manual Training School.

6 She was born in England and came over to America when quite young; and it is rather interesting to know what brought the family here. The father was a wholesale candlemaker in London and his business was ruined by the introduction of gas!

7 Gas as an illuminant is now being replaced by electric lighting; and there are many people in this room who saw the first electric lights.

8 I, myself, am not so very old yet, but I can remember the days when there were no telephones.

9 I remember, too, very distinctly when there were no automobiles here. There were thousands of horses, and Washington, in the summer-time, smelled like a stable. There were plenty of flies, and the death rate was high.

10 Now, it is very interesting and instructive to look back over the various changes that have occurred and trace the evolution of the present from the past. By projecting these lines of advance into the future, you can forecast the future, to a certain extent, and recognize some of the fields of usefulness that are opening up for you.

11 Here we have one line of advance from candles and oil lamps to gas, and from gas to electricity; We can recognize many other threads of advance all converging upon electricity. We produce heat and light by electricity. We transmit intelligence by the telegraph and telephone, and we use electricity as a motive power. In fact, we have fairly entered upon an electrical age, and it is obvious that the electrical engineer will be much in demand in the future. Those of you who devote yourselves to electrical subjects will certainly find a place and room to work.

PROFESSIONAL DEVELOPMENT

Annotations: Annotation Notes

What Is It? Annotations are markings readers make in a text to identify important ideas, confusions, connections, and other relevant information. Notes are words written in the margins for clarification.

Why Is It Important? While some annotation marks can stand alone, many benefit from added notes. Notes can identify exactly what a reader found confusing, the importance of a word or phrase, or which ideas are connected. They help prevent students from marking a text and then forgetting why upon rereading.

Many chances for the inventor

12 On every hand we see the substitution of machinery and artificial motive power for animal and man power. There will therefore be plenty of openings in the future for young, bright mechanical engineers working in this direction.

13 There is, however, one obstacle to further advance. It's in the increasing price of the fuel necessary to work machinery. Coal and oil are going up and are strictly limited in quantity. We can take coal out of a mine, but we can never put it back. We can draw oil from subterranean reservoirs, but we can never refill them again. We are spendthrifts in the matter of fuel and are using our capital for our running expenses.

14 In relation to coal and oil, the world's annual consumption has become so enormous that we are now actually within measurable distance of the end of the supply. What shall we do when we have no more coal or oil?

15 Apart from water power (which is strictly limited) and tidal and wave power (which we have not yet learned to utilize), and the employment of the sun's rays directly as a source of power, we have little left, excepting wood, and it takes at least twenty-five years to grow a crop of trees.

Possibilities of alcohol

16 There is, however, one other source of fuel supply which may perhaps solve this problem of the future. Alcohol makes a beautiful, clean, and efficient fuel, and, where not intended for consumption by human beings, can be manufactured very cheaply in an indigestible or even poisonous form. Alcohol can also be manufactured from corn stalks, and in fact from almost any vegetable matter capable of fermentation. Our growing crops and even weeds can be used. The waste products of our ! farms are available for this purpose and even the garbage from our cities. We need never fear the exhaustion of our present fuel supplies so long as we can produce an annual crop of alcohol to any extent desired.

17 Evolution in science has not always been accomplished by a series of gradual changes, each small in itself, but cumulative in effect. There have also been sudden "mutations" followed by advances of knowledge by leaps and bounds, and the establishment of new and useful arts never before even dreamed of by man.

ANNOTATION NOTES

1st Read:
Paragraphs 13 and 14—point to need for conservation of natural resources.

Coal and oil are limited in quantity; wood takes 25 years to be usable as fuel; alcohol is limitless.

2nd Read:
The speech moves from present to past, back to present, and then to future.

Reread paragraph 17—what does he mean by "mutations"?

3rd Read:
We're still faced with the energy production problem Bell outlines.

Science evolves in two ways: small steps and huge "leaps and bounds."

How Do I Use It? Have students jot down their ideas and use an arrow to visually emphasize a connection. When listening to group discussion, point out ideas that students could include as annotation notes. Encourage students to make annotation notes as their understanding increases, and to focus those notes near text that provides evidence for their understanding.

Problems Awaiting Solution

3rd READ

Set a Purpose

Tell students they will read to infer Bell's overall meaning and purpose.

Text-Dependent Questions

1. What is Bell's perspective on science? (He is a great proponent of science. He notes that a "nation that fosters science becomes . . . powerful," and he extols the "advances of knowledge.")

2. What is Bell's perspective regarding renewable energy sources? (Bell believes that finding renewable energy sources is essential because coal and oil "are strictly limited in quantity." He thinks alcohol made from corn will fill the need.)

3. What impact did Bell hope his speech would have on his audience? (Bell points to a "bright and promising" future to give the graduates confidence. Asking "What shall we do when we have no more coal or oil?," shows he wants them to pursue a solution to this problem.)

Think Aloud *I'm going to reread the text and look for points where Bell talks directly to the audience. In paragraph 1, he tells the students that their "outlook for the future looks bright and promising," and in paragraph 3, he says, "Your future is assured." In paragraph 14, he asks the graduates, "What shall we do when we have no more coal or oil?" I conclude that he wants them to feel good about their prospects, and he also wants to warn them about a problem they will have to face.*

Partner Talk Have students discuss Bell's view of the future.

Respond to Reading

You may want to check students' understanding by having them complete pages 162–163 in the Student Worktext.

1. Remind students to review their annotations and recall discussions they've had in order to complete the summary charts. Remind students that only evidence from the text should be included in the summary chart.

As students complete their summary charts, circulate and note which students struggle to identify the correct text evidence. Some students may benefit from small group instruction.

2. Remind students to include only the most important information in their summaries.

Have students work independently to complete page 162 of their Worktexts.

COLLABORATE When finished, have students exchange summaries with their partners and share their insights.

Return to the TEXT

Respond to Reading: Some of the Problems Awaiting Solution

Review your annotations and notes.
Think about how they can help you summarize the text.

1. Use this chart to help you summarize the text.

Summary Chart		
	Informational Text	
Who?	the people or subjects	Alexander Graham Bell speaking to an audience of graduates in the fields of science
What?	the topic or problem	technological progress and its effect on the future
Where?	the location or region events occur	speech given in Washington, D.C.
When?	the date, year, or time	intro says February 1, 1917
How?	the events, steps, or processes	Technological advances rely on electricity. Current fuels used to produce electricity aren't sustainable. Is alcohol the answer?

2. Write a 2–3 sentence summary of the speech by Alexander Graham Bell.

Sample summary: In this speech, Bell looks at how far science and technology have come, from horses to automobiles and from coal to natural gas. He calls these "threads of advance all converging upon electricity." He cautions against being spendthrifts of coal and oil and points to alcohol as a possible source of energy. He states that although sometimes science evolves gradually, some advancements happen suddenly "by leaps and bounds."

PROFESSIONAL DEVELOPMENT

Self-Monitoring Strategies: Drawing Conclusions

What Is It? A conclusion is a reasoned judgment. It differs from an observation, which is simply a recognition or restatement of an existing idea, and an inference, which is an assumption drawn from existing facts and/or background knowledge. A conclusion is a logical next thought or a rational interpretation, and can differ from reader to reader to some degree.

Why Is It Important? Drawing conclusions enables readers to extend the facts presented in a text in the directions suggested by the author, to predict possible outcomes of events in the text, to connect concepts in the text, to identify details that are missing from the text, and to analyze unspoken assumptions in the text.

Return to the TEXT

3. What was the effect of World War I on education in the United States? Cite textual evidence to support your answer.

Sample answer: In paragraph 2, Bell describes his own education as one that "paid a great deal more attention to the teaching of Latin and Greek than to the study of science." In paragraph 3, he states, "The war has changed all that." Science has become powerful and popular. Scientists and technical experts will "occupy distinguished and honorable positions," and their discoveries will establish advances that are "never before even dreamed of by man."

4. What examples of progress did Bell consider the most significant? Support your response with evidence from the speech.

Sample answer: Bell considered "Gas as an illuminant" a significant change, but in his day, it was being replaced by electric lighting. In paragraph 9, he cites automobiles as progress from a time when cities "smelled like a stable" and were full of flies. The inventions of the telephone and telegraph were significant, as were all substitutions of machinery for animal and man power. Finally, in paragraph 16, he suggests that finding ways to use alcohol as a fuel supply might be an answer to a problem that is "awaiting" solution.

5. What does Bell cite as the limitations or problems of coal and oil? Provide evidence to support your response.

Sample answer: In paragraphs 13 and 14, Bell admits that coal and oil prices are going up and that their supplies are strictly limited in quantity. He thinks that these factors constitute an "obstacle to further advance." He accuses humans of being "spendthrifts in the matter of fuel." He also cites that the "world's annual [coal] consumption has become so enormous" that the end of the supply is in sight.

REFLECT What words, phrases, or sections did you have to reread to make sure you understood the text?

Sample answer: I reread paragraph 17 because I was confused by the word "mutations." The author uses it to mean something I didn't understand: sudden scientific advancements that move knowledge forward "by leaps and bounds."

Return to the TEXT

Encourage students to refer back to the text and their annotations and notes to help them answer the questions.

3. You can support students by directing them to paragraph 2.

4. Suggest that students review the section "We progress from candles to electricity in one lifetime" and make notes on a timeline to answer this question.

5. Point out to students that they will need to find evidence that coal and oil supplies are problems that need solutions.

Have students work independently to complete page 163 of their Worktexts.

REFLECT Remind students that rereading is a **Self-Monitoring Strategy** and that they made annotations and notes about confusions they may have had. Suggest that they review their annotations and think about any words, phrases, or sections that they reread.

How Do I Use It? Consistently require students to provide evidence for their conclusions about a text. If they cannot find direct textual evidence, ask, *What words made you think that?* Have students pay special attention to predictions made in a text. If the verb is in the future tense, ask, *What is the evidence that it will happen?* or *What would have to happen before this could happen?* Have students identify any of their own assumptions or prejudices that may distort their interpretations of what the text says.

Return to the TEXT

Stop and Assess

Use the following rubrics to assess your students' understanding of the text.

Item 1 answers indicate:	
2	that Bell was concerned that fuels would run out in the future. The answer is supported by at least two pieces of text evidence.
1	an inference about Bell's view of the future supported by only one piece of text evidence.
0	no understanding about Bell's view of the future and no text evidence.

Item 2 answers indicate:	
2	Bell thought that inventors and scientists drive progress. The answer is supported by at least two pieces of text evidence.
1	a statement about Bell as an inventor with one piece of evidence from the text.
0	no understanding about Bell as an inventor and no text evidence.

Item 3 answers indicate:	
2	Bell believes that science is being recognized as supremely important in society. The answer is supported by at least two pieces of text evidence.
1	a reason that Bell says this to the class with only one piece of evidence from the text.
0	a lack of understanding of Bell's reason and no text evidence.

Option: If you choose not to work with Texts 2 and 3 and to conclude the unit here, use the Visual Text and "Some of the Problems Awaiting Solution" to answer the Focus Question: What are the challenges and rewards of renewable energy?

Return to the TEXT

Comprehension Check: Some of the Problems Awaiting Solution

Answer the questions to demonstrate an understanding of what the text means.

1. What can you infer about Bell's view of the future from his discussion about coal, oil, and alcohol? Use the text to support your answer.
Sample answer: I can infer that Bell sees a future in which people will consume more and more energy. In paragraph 13, he points to "one obstacle" to the "advance" he imagines—the fact that coal and oil will run out. In paragraph 14, he says that the "world's annual consumption has become so enormous" that these resources will soon run out, which suggests that he doesn't see the demand declining.

2. What do you learn about Bell as an inventor from this speech? Support your answer with evidence from the text.
Sample answer: Bell was an optimist who believed that science has the potential to improve people's lives. He attributed progress to the work of scientists and "technical experts." He pointed out how one technology is replaced with a better one, which is replaced with one that is even better, and so on (such as candles to gas lights to electric lights). In paragraph 10, he states that by "projecting these lines of advance into the future," we can forecast even more advancements and solutions. Bell thinks that there will be plenty of openings in the future for scientists and engineers, especially those working in the field of fuel and power.

3. Why does Bell tell the class, "Your future is assured"? Cite text evidence in your answer.
Sample answer: Bell tells the class that their futures are assured because he claims that after the war, society appreciated the scientist "as he never has been in the past." He considers nations that foster science as "powerful" and claims that "scientific men and technical experts" will occupy "distinguished and honorable positions in all the countries of the world" in the future. For Bell, these graduates are assured both jobs and respect.

PROFESSIONAL DEVELOPMENT

Annotations: Avoiding Over-Annotating

What Is It? As students read, they may circle, underline, or highlight so many words that the sense of the text disappears and they lose track of why they made the annotations. Over-annotating defeats the purpose of annotations.

Why Is It Important? Over-annotating can be a sign that a student is not sufficiently distinguishing main ideas from supporting details. It could also be evidence that a student is encountering many new key words and phrases. If a student is reading and annotating word by word, he or she might need help with reading and comprehending whole phrases.

TEXT 2

Read the text to learn about a new source of energy. If you need to read any sections more than once, note the reason in the Annotation Notes column.

Sample annotations and notes appear throughout the text.

Wave of Discovery

by Miles O'Brien

1 Capturing the power of ocean waves could become an important part of the world's renewable energy portfolio. But capturing that clean energy is not just the vision of 21st century scientists.

2 "There have been ebbs and swells of interest," says Ted Brekken, assistant professor of energy systems at Oregon State. "But a lot of people would agree that we have passed a turning point, and I think the interest level now is here to stay."

3 There is support now from federal and state governments, as well as some power companies. But that has not always been the case. "In 1998 when I was writing research proposals, people were saying 'she's crazy—we're not going to be able to harness energy from the ocean. It's too harsh of an environment.' It took a lot of persistence," says Annette von Jouanne, a world leader in wave energy research.

These mechanical arms are part of a pilot wave energy project in Brazil. The constant movement of the ocean keeps turbines spinning.

Engineering challenge

4 The same constant motion of waves that provides the energy is also continuously battering the hardware that is capturing it. So the engineering challenge is to make hardware strong and ? simple. "When you look at reliability and maintainability, you want devices out there that won't need regular maintenance. Otherwise, you would require people to go out there in vessels," adds von Jouanne.

5 In September 2008, Oregon State, working with Columbia Power Technologies and the U.S. Navy, deployed its eleventh

ANNOTATION NOTES

1st Read:
Support for wave energy from the ocean grows as scientists overcome engineering challenges.

2nd Read:
Quotations by two experts create both credibility and variety.

"maintainability"?

prototype = the first working model of something

3rd Read:
university, private business, government all working together: good way to solve problems

Author names solution: persistence. Solutions to complex problems take many years of research.

How Do I Use It? When you notice that students are over-annotating, ask them to pause for self-monitoring. Suggest that they sort out the information they have marked into categories and enter their notes on separate sheets of paper. For example, they might list all the new vocabulary words they have circled or list the subheads in order. Discuss how sorting the words and ideas in the text clarified their thinking and helped them recall important facts. Have them make note of any annotations that do not fall into their categories or that did not help clarify their thinking.

Wave of Discovery

Tell students that they will read to learn about another energy source.

1st READ

Set a Purpose

Tell students they will be reading to find out about a particular source of energy.

Have students read "Wave of Discovery" independently, annotating the text as they read. Circulate and note students' markings, especially questions and confusions.

Text-Dependent Questions

1. What is this article about? (The article is about wave power technology.)

2. What are two ways that wave energy engineers try to protect wildlife? (They use "acoustic deterrents" to keep animals away. They work to develop cables that "prevent entanglements" with sea creatures.)

Scaffolded Support Use the following scaffolded sentence frame and question as necessary to build comprehension.

Wave energy engineers are concerned about ________.

What keeps marine animals away from wave energy installations?

3. Vocabulary: Domain Specific Language Discuss any vocabulary related to renewable energy with which students may not be familiar.

Paragraphs 13 and 15: What does "onto the grid" mean? (The "grid" is the power system that flows electricity from a source to individual homes and businesses. Wave energy installations add energy to the grid.)

Partner Talk Have students discuss how waves produce energy.

Wave of Discovery

2nd READ

Set a Purpose

Tell students they will read to understand how word choices influence meaning and to examine the text's structure.

Text-Dependent Questions

1. What does the phrase "renewable energy portfolio" suggest in paragraph 1? (A portfolio is a collection of things. The world's energy needs won't be met through a single source: energy must come from many sources, one of which is wave power.)

2. In paragraph 15, why do proponents of wave energy describe it as "forecastable"? (*Forecastable* means "predictable." The forecastable nature of wave power is an advantage it has over solar or wind power. *Forecastable* suggests stability and is reassuring.)

Think Aloud *I'm not sure about the idea that wave energy is forecastable, so I'll reread paragraph 15. NOAA's buoys collect data that can tell us "how much energy the waves would be putting onto the grid." So, if we can know how much wave action is going on at any time, we can say how much energy the waves will produce.*

3. Vocabulary: Figurative Language Discuss figures of speech in the text.

Paragraph 2: Why is "ebbs and swells" a fitting way to describe wave power research trends? (This phrase reflects the motion of ocean waves and suggests that interest in the research has gone up and down.)

Partner Talk Have students discuss how the author's use of vocabulary contributes to the text's meaning.

TEXT 2

ANNOTATION NOTES

1st Read:
explanation of how it all works

2nd Read:
Subheadings introduce new topics.

lots of technical language in paragraphs 6 and 7

array = an ordered arrangement of objects

3rd Read:
Developers of the technology have learned from the past—protecting wildlife is built into the plan from the beginning.

wave energy prototype, a permanent magnet linear generator that creates power with few moving parts.

6 "A float heaves up and down with the waves. Underneath the float is a magnet assembly, and as that magnet assembly heaves up and down, it creates a changing magnetic field," explains von Jouanne. "That changing magnetic field induces voltage, and creates electricity."

7 The concept for a wave energy installation would be an array of these buoys. They would have a power takeoff cable going down to the sea floor, coming together at a central junction box. From that central junction box would be a subsea cable back to shore and onto the electrical grid.

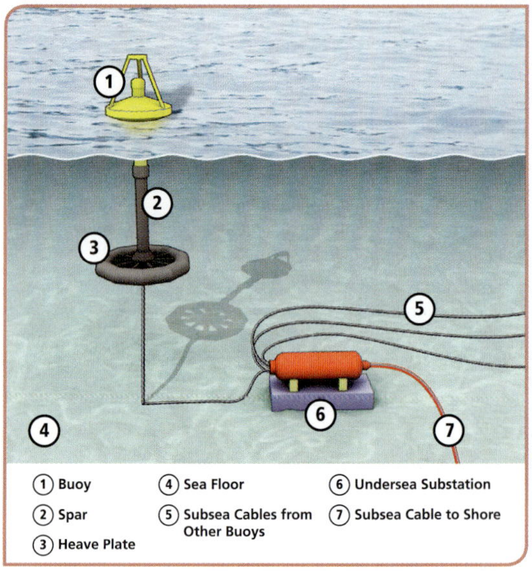

An array of buoys sends power from a generator back to shore and onto the grid.

Protecting wildlife

8 While there is great promise with this technology, there is also concern for the wildlife that will share the ocean

166 • Unit 9

PROFESSIONAL DEVELOPMENT

Productive Conversation: Examples

What Is It? Students provide specific examples to support an idea. A student may give an example from the text to support his or her own generality or inference. You may also ask students to find an example to support another student's idea during group or partner talk.

Why Is It Important? Specific examples can provide support for a student's argument. The lack of a relevant example can also reveal weakness in a student argument. Examples used in Think Aloud modeling provide concrete demonstrations of concepts.

How Do I Use It? When students generalize or make an inference, ask questions that elicit examples. For instance, with these energy devices. The teams putting together the wave energy plans have asked marine mammal specialists to be involved from the very beginning.

9 ! About 18,000 North Pacific gray whales migrate yearly between Alaska and Mexico, and often travel very close to shore. Their journey will take them near wave energy devices, which are expected to be anchored about two and a half miles off the Oregon coast.

10 "We're trying to be ready if issues develop. What we're looking at is testing a potential acoustic deterrent, if it becomes necessary to keep whales away," says Bruce Mate, director of the Marine Mammal Institute at Oregon State.

11 The cabling that will bring the energy from the buoys to the grid has to be designed to prevent entanglements. Thousands of whales, dolphins, turtles and other sea creatures are killed each year because they are caught in fishing gear.

12 "These animals weigh about 30 tons and are traveling at up to 4.6 miles per hour. Hitting something solid could constitute a problem," notes Mate.

Testing and deployment

13 So how close is wave energy to actually putting electricity onto the grid? Worldwide, the western sides of large land masses are optimal for capturing wave energy, because of the prevailing west to east winds.

14 While research in wave energy is 15–20 years behind renewables such as wind power, waves are far more reliable as an energy source. While solar power is only available about 50 percent of the time; and winds are not constant, waves are. Experts say wave energy might one day provide up to six percent of the electricity needs of the United States.

15 One of the positives of wave energy is that it is highly forecastable. The National Oceanic and Atmospheric Administration (NOAA) maintains a huge network of data collecting buoys. As a result, power companies could know with great accuracy how much energy the waves would be putting onto the grid.

16 Many are drawn to renewable energy research both by the engineering challenges and the desire to help solve the world's energy problems.

ANNOTATION NOTES

1st Read:
Equipment is also vulnerable to "hits" from huge animals.

wildlife challenge: "prevent entanglements"

potential for wave power to provide substantial amounts of energy

2nd Read:
"Hitting something solid could constitute a problem."—understatement

last paragraph—positive note

3rd Read:
An "acoustic deterrent" would keep whales away with sound?

"Constant" is the ideal. Waves are constant. Wind and solar are not.

students may give a general statement that wave power technology threatens marine life. If students cannot give any specific examples, you may have an opportunity to re-guide their conclusions. For instance, if students say they think whales die because of wave power technology, but cannot cite an example, redirect them to what the text says: "Thousands of whales, dolphins, turtles and other sea creatures are killed each year because they are caught in fishing gear." Fishing gear is not wave power technology. A more accurate conclusion would be that wave power engineers work hard to protect marine life from the kinds of entanglements that happen with fishing gear.

TEXT 2

Wave of Discovery

3rd READ

Set a Purpose

Tell students they will read to make inferences about wave power.

Text-Dependent Questions

1. Is wave power practical for the United States? What text evidence supports your answer? (The author says that wave power has "great promise" and quotes experts who say that it could eventually provide "six percent of the electricity needs of the United States." But it could prove to be impractical because of the cost, impacts, and upkeep of the offshore equipment; and it is certainly impractical for places that are not near one of the coasts.)

2. What qualities does Annette von Jouanne bring to her work involving wave energy? (Von Jouanne faced detractors who said harnessing the ocean to create power couldn't be done. But that didn't stop her. She believed in what she was doing, she was determined to continue, and she went about solving the problems that came up.)

3. What is the author's point of view toward wave power? What evidence in the text supports your answer? (The author presents a balance between challenges and advantages. He remains neutral about the topic but supportive of the research.)

Partner Talk Have students discuss how the inferences they made helped them understand the text.

Return to the TEXT

Stop and Assess

Use the following rubrics to assess your students' understanding of the text.

	Item 1 answers indicate:
2	engineering challenges because of the harsh ocean environment and protecting wildlife. At least two pieces of text evidence support the answer.
1	engineering challenges because of the harsh ocean environment or protecting wildlife. Supporting evidence may be insufficient.
0	no understanding of the big challenges in creating wave energy stations and no supporting text evidence.

	Item 2 answers indicate:
2	that wave energy is reliable and forecastable. At least two pieces of text evidence support the answer.
1	that wave energy is constant. Details and supporting text evidence may be insufficient.
0	a lack of understanding of why ocean waves are a good source of energy and no supporting text evidence.

	Item 3 answers indicate:
2	more investment in wave energy and wave energy as a regular part of America's "energy portfolio." At least two pieces of text evidence support the answer.
1	the general success of wave energy. Supporting text evidence may be insufficient.
0	a lack of understanding about how the author imagines the future of wave energy technology. No text evidence is given.

Return to the TEXT

Comprehension Check: Wave of Discovery

Answer the questions to demonstrate an understanding of what the text means.

1. What are the two biggest challenges in creating wave energy stations? Cite evidence from the text in your answer.
   Sample answer: The author claims that wave energy poses an engineering challenge because the hardware is constantly battered and often far from shore. The machinery needs to be rugged with "few moving parts." Also, protecting wildlife is a challenge because animals such as gray whales, dolphins, and turtles can get caught in underwater gear and lines.

2. Why are ocean waves a good source of energy? Support your answer with textual evidence.
   Sample answer: In paragraphs 13–16, the author lays out the advantages of wave energy. Because west-east winds make the western sides of land masses "optimal" for capturing wave energy, waves are a "far more reliable" energy source than even solar or wind. Another advantage is that wave energy "is highly forecastable." In addition, NOAA has a "huge network of data collecting buoys" that can show how much energy the waves could be putting out.

3. How does the author imagine the future of wave energy technology? Include examples from the text in your response.
   Sample answer: The author agrees with experts who predict that wave energy could provide up to "six percent of the electricity needs of the United States" and believes that, despite challenges, the field is opening up. He believes that scientists have "passed a turning point" and are now being funded by federal and state governments. In the last paragraph, he suggests that power companies will invest in wave energy research and meet its engineering challenges.

168 • Unit 9

PROFESSIONAL DEVELOPMENT

Productive Conversation: Reasoning

What Is It? Reasoning is the use of logic, inferences, and connections to draw conclusions. It is a critical thinking skill.

Why Is It Important? Reasoning is the process by which we find deeper meaning and connections between texts. It is also a metacognitive skill; when students can identify and analyze their own and others' reasoning, they are better able to apply it to new situations.

Read to find out about using sunlight to generate electricity. You may want to read some sections more than once and make different annotations and Annotation Notes each time.
Sample annotations and notes appear throughout the text.

Solar Basics

The U.S. Energy Information Administration publishes reports about U.S. consumption and outlooks.

Energy from the Sun

1 The sun has produced energy for billions of years. It is the ultimate source for all of the energy sources and fuels that we use today. People have used the sun's rays (solar radiation) for thousands of years for warmth and to dry meat, fruit, and grains. Over time, people developed devices (technologies) to collect solar energy for heat and to convert it into electricity.

Collecting and using solar thermal (heat) energy

2 An example of an early solar energy collection device is the solar oven (a box for collecting and absorbing sunlight). In the 1830's, British astronomer John Herschel used a solar oven to cook food during an expedition to Africa. People now use many different technologies for collecting and converting solar radiation into useful heat energy for a variety of purposes.

3 We use solar thermal energy systems to

- heat water for use in homes, buildings, or swimming pools
- heat the inside of homes, greenhouses, and other buildings
- heat fluids to high temperatures in solar thermal power plants

Solar photovoltaic systems convert sunlight into electricity

4 Solar photovoltaic (PV) devices, or solar cells, change sunlight directly into electricity. Small PV cells can power calculators, watches, and other small electronic devices. Arrangements of many solar cells in PV panels and arrangements of multiple PV panels in PV arrays can produce electricity for an entire house. Some PV power plants have large arrays that cover many acres to produce electricity for thousands of homes.

5 There are benefits to using solar energy. Solar energy systems do not produce air pollutants or carbon dioxide, and solar energy systems on buildings have minimal impact on the environment.

ANNOTATION NOTES

1st Read:
Sun is a source of energy on Earth. There are many devices for capturing the sun's energy.

description of PV devices in various sizes (tiny cells to enormous arrays)

2nd Read:
basics = essential facts or ideas

straightforward language

"we" in paragraphs 1 and 3—all Americans? all people?

3rd Read:
First paragraph describes history of use of sun's energy.

Anecdote about Herschel shows people have been thinking about harnessing solar energy for a long time.

Solar Basics

Tell students that they will read to find out about using sunlight to generate electricity.

1st READ

Set a Purpose

Tell students they will be reading to find out how people convert sunlight into usable energy.

Have students read "Solar Basics" independently, annotating the text as they read. Circulate and note students' markings, especially questions and confusions.

Text-Dependent Questions

1. What is the article about? (The article presents the history of solar devices, an explanation of how today's solar cells work, and important facts about solar radiation. These are some of the basics of solar power.)

2. Who was John Herschel and why is he mentioned in the text? (Herschel was a British astronomer in the 1830s. He invented an "early" solar collection device that he used to cook food during an expedition in Africa. He was a pioneer in this field.)

3. According to paragraph 4, what is a PV device? (A photovoltaic device changes sunlight into electricity. These solar cells are small enough to fit in a watch. They can also be arranged in large arrays to power homes.)

4. Vocabulary: Synonyms Discuss words that have similar meanings.

Paragraph 6: What word in this paragraph is a synonym of *variable*? (*Intermittent* is a synonym of *variable*.)

Partner Talk Have students discuss how solar energy works.

How Do I Use It? When asked, *Why do you think that?*, students are likely to volunteer their reasoning. Drawing students back to the text can allow you to help students untangle their reasoning by identifying what the student thought vs. what was stated in the text. *You say that solar power is most practical in arid areas. Why do you say that?* (Because arid areas get little rain, I conclude they are a practical place to collect solar power) *How did you draw the conclusion that the buoys make the energy source predictable?* (Since the buoys read wave action, scientists can predict the amount of power produced.) Conversations about reasoning can help students analyze both misconceptions and logical conclusions.

Solar Basics

2nd READ

Set a Purpose

Tell students they will read to observe how the author organizes ideas and details.

Text-Dependent Questions

1. What is the purpose of the bulleted list? (The list makes the information easy to understand.)

2. Why did the author end with the section "Where Solar is Found"? (The author wanted to end with the point that solar is everywhere and more abundant than any other energy source. It is the most compelling supporting evidence that developing and funding this technology should continue.)

Partner Talk Have students discuss the text structure as it relates to the author's purpose.

3rd READ

Set a Purpose

Tell students they will read to draw inferences about solar power.

Text-Dependent Questions

1. What conditions are best for solar technology? (Solar power is most practical in places that get a lot of sunshine.)

2. Reread the introductory sentence. Is the article more about energy consumption or outlooks? (It is about both topics equally. The first half describes solar energy collection and consumption; the second half focuses on practical issues around solar power affecting its development and adoption.)

Partner Talk Have students discuss and compare the energy sources presented in this unit.

TEXT 3

ANNOTATION NOTES

1st Read:
pros and cons of solar energy

2nd Read:
Bulleted lists and subheadings make topics easy to spot and understand.

intermittent = comes and goes

3rd Read:
sunlight: abundant but not constant, in contrast to waves in Text 1

Since solar radiation is intermittent and variable, finding ways to store solar energy is essential.

How Solar Works

(1) Solar panels convert sunlight into electricity.
(2) A control device converts the electricity so it can be used in the home.
(3) Electrical items in the home can use the energy for power.
(4) Any surplus energy is sold to the grid.

Where Solar is Found

6 ! Solar energy is sunshine. The amount of solar energy that the Earth receives each day is many times greater than the total amount of all energy that people consume. However, on the surface of the Earth, solar energy is a variable and intermittent energy source. The amount of sunlight and the intensity of sunlight varies by time of day and location. Weather and climate conditions affect the availability of sunlight on a daily and seasonal basis. The amount of sunlight reaching a square foot of the Earth's surface is relatively small. Therefore, the type and size of a solar energy collection and conversion system determines how much of the available solar energy we can convert into useful energy.

170 • Unit 9

PROFESSIONAL DEVELOPMENT

Intertextual Analysis: Comparing and Contrasting Big Ideas

What Is It? Some concepts are complex enough to engage a wide range of different texts. When students compare and contrast the texts' treatments of these ideas, they may do so in terms of nuance rather than simple alike-different comparisons.

Why Is It Important? Literature and informational texts approach complex ideas in different ways. The classroom gives students practice in grappling with these ideas. Understanding that texts can also present shades of meaning, rather than simple pros and cons, is a vital one.

Return to the TEXT

Comprehension Check: Solar Basics

Answer the questions to demonstrate an understanding of what the text means.

1. How have humans used solar power throughout history? Cite evidence from the text in your answer.
   Sample answer: Humans "have used the sun's rays (solar radiation) for thousands of years" to create warmth and to dry or cook food. In the last two hundred years, they have also figured out how to "collect solar energy for heat and to convert it into electricity." Most recently, scientists have created large "thermal energy systems" to heat buildings and water and to "heat fluids to high temperatures in solar thermal power plants."

2. What are the two biggest challenges of being dependent on solar energy? Provide text evidence to support your answer.
   Sample answer: The author describes the challenges in paragraph 6. First, "solar energy is a variable and intermittent energy source." The amount and intensity of sunlight produced depends on location, weather, and season. Second, "the amount of sunlight reaching a square foot of the Earth's surface is relatively small," so the amount of energy we can collect and convert is dependent on the size of the solar energy collection and conversion system.

3. What inference can you draw from the text about the development of solar energy systems going forward? Support your answer with evidence from the text.
   Sample answer: I can infer that the development will continue because solar energy systems "do not produce air pollutants or carbon dioxide," and putting solar panels on buildings results in "minimal impact on the environment." Those are huge advantages for energy production. Also, the author claims that the amount of solar energy the Earth receives is "many times greater" than what people consume, so it is a virtually limitless source of energy. Because sunlight is not constant, I can infer that finding ways to store energy generated by solar systems will be an important part of their development.

How Do I Use It? Rather than directly contrasting or comparing two texts that deal with related ideas, ask or use a sentence frame to guide students to return to and rephrase the text:

What does this text say about ________?

This text relates to the idea of ________ by ________.

In this unit, all three texts discuss how renewable energy sources may be more prevalent in the future, but they handle very different aspects of this idea. Have students identify the role the authors imagine alcohol, wave power, and solar power will play in the world's "energy portfolio." Guide students back to the texts by asking scaffolded questions about each energy source's challenges and advantages.

Return to the TEXT

Stop and Assess

Use the following rubrics to assess your students' understanding of the text.

	Item 1 answers indicate:
2	that humans have used solar power for heat and cooking and more recently they have begun to collect it in solar energy systems. At least two pieces of text evidence support the answer.
1	that humans have used solar power throughout history. Supporting text evidence may be insufficient.
0	a lack of understanding of how humans have used solar power throughout history with no evidence.

	Item 2 answers indicate:
2	that sunlight is not constant and that the amount of sunlight collected depends on the size of the collection system. At least two pieces of text evidence support the answer.
1	that sunlight is not constant and that the amount collected is not a sure thing. Supporting text evidence may be insufficient.
0	no understanding of the challenges of solar energy dependence.

	Item 3 answers indicate:
2	use of solar energy systems will continue to grow and finding ways to store solar energy will be a key part of the development. At least two pieces of text evidence support the answer.
1	that solar power will be popular. Supporting text evidence may be insufficient.
0	no understanding about the future of solar energy dependence and no evidence from the text.

ANALYZE and SYNTHESIZE ACROSS TEXTS

Return to the Focus Question

Explain to students that they will fill out a graphic organizer that helps them answer the Focus Question: What are the challenges and rewards of renewable energy?

CONNECT TEXTS Have small groups of students discuss how each text they read helps them answer the Focus Question.

Scaffolded Support You may provide the following sentence frames to support students in their use of academic language:

> In the text ________, the author/photographer makes the point that ________.
> He/she does this by ________.

Remind students to use their annotations and summaries to support their answers. They can also reread portions of the texts, if necessary.

Have students complete their graphic organizers individually.

REFLECT Remind students that each text provides different information about the challenges and rewards of renewable energy. Ask, *How did reading all four texts give you a greater understanding of these challenges and rewards?*

ANALYZE and SYNTHESIZE ACROSS TEXTS

Return to the Focus Question: What are the challenges and rewards of renewable energy?

Review your answers to questions about the texts as well as your annotations and Annotation Notes, and think about the discussions you've had about the texts. How does that information help you answer the Focus Question?

Use the graphic organizer to organize information about the texts.

1. In the appropriate box, record the details that help you answer the Focus Question.
2. Make connections between those details to answer the Focus Question. Write your answer in the box provided.

Wind Farm (Visual Text)
Sample answer: Wind power relies on large turbines, which are found in rural areas.

Wave of Discovery
Sample answer: Main challenge: Wave power is hard to engineer. Reward: forecastable

Problems Awaiting Solution
Sample answer: Challenge: depleting coal and oil supply; Solution: scientific research, alcohol as an alternative

Solar Basics
Sample answer: Challenge: amount of sunlight is not constant; Reward: minimal environmental impact

What are the challenges and rewards of renewable energy?
Sample answer: Challenges: reliability, safeguarding wildlife, engineering issues; Rewards: clean, efficient energy that won't run out

REFLECT How did making connections between the four texts enable you to answer the Focus Question?

Sample answer: The texts let me compare and contrast different power sources and identify the advantages and disadvantages of each. The written texts all remind me that science can solve many problems and improve our environment and lives.

PROFESSIONAL DEVELOPMENT

Intertextual Analysis: Citing Evidence from Multiple Texts

What Is It? When analyzing across texts, students must cite text evidence from each text in order to adequately support conclusions.

Why Is It Important? Continually citing text evidence gives students practice returning to the text and providing support for claims and arguments. Citing every text ensures that students do not draw conclusions that are only supported by one or a few texts. Additional text evidence can also introduce nuances and variations of conclusions or ideas.

WRITE

Writing About the Focus Question

Now that you have answered the Focus Question using all four texts, expand on your thinking and communicate your ideas through your writing.

USE EVIDENCE

- Explain what you have learned about the challenges and rewards of renewable energy sources. Use at least one piece of evidence from the Visual Text and at least two pieces of evidence from Texts 1, 2, and 3 to support your answer.
- If you need more room, use additional paper.

MONITOR

- Use the Writing Checklist as you write to make sure your writing meets all the necessary criteria.
- Use the rubric on page 174 when you have completed a first draft of your writing to help you evaluate, revise, and edit your work.

WRITING CHECKLIST ✓

Does my writing . . .

- ☐ answer the Focus Question?
- ☐ have a clear organizational structure?
- ☐ cite the correct amount of text evidence?
- ☐ correctly use language, spelling, and conventions?

How Do I Use It? When giving feedback or asking for text evidence, use a checklist of all the texts under consideration. Continue asking for text evidence until every text has been checked off. Citing text evidence can also be a collaborative effort. Partners or small groups can divide texts among individuals. Combining the contributions into one argument or conclusion ensures that all texts will be considered. It will also provide for multiple perspectives on the analysis.

Writing About the Focus Question

USE EVIDENCE Remind students that they should use their graphic organizers as well as their annotations in the texts to write their responses.

Allow students to revisit the texts as frequently as they need to in order to support comprehension and to respond to the Focus Question.

MONITOR After students have completed their responses, have them review the Writing Checklist and revise their writing response.

DIFFERENTIATE AND EXTEND

In addition to or instead of the writing response, consider having students complete one of the following assignments:

Write Beyond Have students imagine they are interns on a renewable energy research project. Have them write an article for a company newsletter convincing readers that the research will help their communities.

Read Beyond Have students find and read articles dealing with renewable energy and report on them to the class.

Research Have students research hydroelectric power or geothermal energy to round out the list of major renewable energy sources. Have them develop lists of challenges and rewards for one of these energy sources.

Debate an Issue Have students debate which will be the next major energy source.

SELF-ASSESS and REFLECT

SELF-ASSESS Have students use the Writing Rubric on page 174 to self-assess their writing response and write a final version. Tell them to assign themselves a score from 1–4 (with "4" being the highest) for each category in the first column.

Use the Writing Rubric on Student Worktext page 174 to assess each student's writing. Record points for each category in the first column of the rubric. Have students remove the page from their Student Worktexts and place it in their writing portfolios, along with the drafts and final versions of their responses.

SELF-ASSESS and REFLECT

Focus Question: What are the challenges and rewards of renewable energy?

This is the rubric that your teacher will use to assess your writing. Refer to it as you revise your work. After you have finished the final version of your response, assess your response and record your points for each category on the "Student" line in the first column.

	Accomplished (4 points)	Competent (3 points)	Developing (2 points)	Beginning (1 point)
RESPONSE Score: Student ____ Teacher ____	The response answers the question effectively and with insight.	The response answers the question effectively.	The response partially responds to the question but does not adequately address it.	The response addresses the texts but does not address the question.
ORGANIZATION Score: Student ____ Teacher ____	The main idea is convincingly stated. Ideas are organized in cohesive paragraphs that support the main idea.	The main idea is clearly stated. Ideas are organized in logical paragraphs.	The main idea is weak. Ideas are organized in a somewhat logical and cohesive way.	The main idea is missing. The organization of the paragraphs is not logical.
TEXT EVIDENCE Score: Student ____ Teacher ____	Response includes more than one piece of appropriate text evidence from each text. Evidence supports the main idea in a thorough way.	Response includes one piece of text evidence from each text. Evidence supports the main idea clearly.	Response does not include at least one piece of text evidence from each text. Text evidence does not adequately support the main idea.	Response does not contain relevant evidence.
LANGUAGE Score: Student ____ Teacher ____	Writing includes precise and sophisticated vocabulary related to the topic.	Writing includes appropriate vocabulary related to the topic.	Writing includes imprecise and inaccurate vocabulary.	Writing does not include vocabulary that appropriately reflects the topic of the response.
SPELLING AND CONVENTIONS Score: Student ____ Teacher ____	Response includes correct spelling, grammar, and punctuation consistently.	Response includes mostly correct spelling, grammar, and punctuation.	Response has many errors in spelling, grammar, and punctuation.	Response's errors in spelling, grammar, and punctuation make it extremely difficult to understand the response.

INTRODUCE THE UNIT

UNIT 10

Focus Question What impact do humans have on the environment?

Texts for Close Reading

GENRE STUDY

Discuss with students the genres of "Rachel Carson Biography," "The Buzz on Native Bees" and *Man and the Earth*.

Remind students that *genre* refers to the format and features of a text and typically falls into one of two categories—literature or informational text.

The texts in this unit are informational texts of varying subgenres and styles. A biography is a life story, and is often told using literature-like narrative prose. Web articles are informal, while explanatory texts tend to be formal.

With the class, list the features of biographies and explanatory texts. Have students identify the shared characteristics of biographies and explanatory texts.

Focus Question

Have students read the Focus Question on Worktext page 175. Tell students that the texts they will read will help them answer the question.

Texts for Close Reading

Have students read to themselves the summaries about the texts in this unit.

There is no need to explain what students should expect to find in their close readings or to do any pre-teaching about the subject matter.

TEXT COMPLEXITY

Trash Pile in a Creek
- Style: documentary
- Knowledge demands: low
- Levels of meaning: literal

Rachel Carson Biography

Quantitative: 1250L

Qualitative
- Structure: conventional
- Language: familiar
- Knowledge demands: medium
- Levels of meaning: literal

The Buzz on Native Bees

Quantitative: 1190L

Qualitative
- Structure: conventional
- Language: academic
- Knowledge demands: medium
- Levels of meaning: literal

Man and the Earth

Quantitative: 1170L

Qualitative
- Structure: conventional
- Language: academic/archaic
- Knowledge demands: high
- Levels of meaning: literal

Trash Pile in a Creek

Set a Purpose

Explain to students that they will look at the image on page 176 to learn about humans' impact on the environment.

Visual Text Analysis

Remind students that an image can be analyzed as a text by looking at its details and making inferences. Direct students' attention to the image on Student Worktext page 176.

1. Have students identify both the subject and setting of the photo.

2. Have students try to identify individual objects in the creek.

3. Ask students to speculate about where the objects they listed in their answers to question 2 came from.

Provide any additional information you feel is appropriate to enhance the discussion:

- Many manufactured materials such as plastics and foams do not biodegrade, or decay, and can pile up in the environment.
- Solid waste is just one form of water pollution. Substances not visible in photographs, such as pesticides, fertilizers, petroleum products, and industrial chemicals can also pollute water.

VISUAL TEXT

A giant trash pile floats in a small creek surrounded by thick forest by David Hanson

Look at the Visual Text to answer the following questions. Review the image or parts of the image as many times as necessary.

1. What is happening in this image?
   Sample answer: A bunch of trash is floating in a creek.

2. What details helped you answer the previous question?
   Sample answer: I see lots of plastic, bags, cups, tires, and other debris on top of the water. The creek seems remote. It is surrounded by beautiful trees, and the only sign of humans is the trash caught up in floating logs.

3. When you look at the image again, what are you thinking and feeling?
   Sample answer: I feel disgusted that the water is so dirty and angry that so many people threw their trash in the creek. I also feel sorry for the animals that live there.

176 • Unit 10

PROFESSIONAL DEVELOPMENT

Visual Text: ELL

What Is It? Visual text analysis requires identifying an image's structural components, subject, details, meaning, and purpose.

Why Is It Important? Visual texts allow ELL students to apply close-reading techniques and analytical thinking without a language barrier. However, visual text analysis will present challenges to ELL students, as they will be expected to express and support ideas about the images in English.

TEXT 1

✔ Self-Monitoring Strategies you used to help you check your understanding as you read.

☐ Visualize. ☐ Draw conclusions. ☐ Ask yourself questions. ☐ Reread to clarify.

Read the text to learn about one person's impact on the environment. Make annotations in the text and write your notes in the Annotation Notes column.

Sample annotations and notes appear throughout the text.

Rachel Carson Biography

1 (1907–1964)

2 Rachel Carson was born in a small rural Pennsylvania community near the Allegheny River, where she explored the forests and streams around her 65-acre farm. As a young child, Carson's consuming passions were the nature surrounding her hillside home and her writing. She was first "published" at the ! age of 10 in a children's magazine dedicated to the work of young writers.

3 In 1925 Carson entered Pennsylvania College for Women as an English major determined to become a writer. Midway into her studies, however, she switched to biology. Her first experience with the ocean came during a summer fellowship at the U.S. Marine Laboratory in Woods Hole, Massachusetts. Upon graduation from Pennsylvania College, Carson was awarded a scholarship to complete her graduate work in biology at Johns Hopkins University in Baltimore, an enormous accomplishment for a woman in 1929.

4 Carson's distinction in writing and biology won her a part-time position with the U.S. Bureau of Fisheries in 1935 where she wrote a series of short radio programs on marine life. She also continued to write on conservation and nature for newspapers and magazines. She urged the need to regulate the "forces of destruction" and consider the welfare of the "fish as well as that of the fisherman." Her articles were published regularly by a number of newspapers.

5 In 1936, Carson was appointed a junior aquatic biologist with the Bureau of Fisheries. She became one of only two women ! then employed with the Bureau at a professional level. Her work allowed her to visit the Chesapeake Bay region, where she

ANNOTATION NOTES

1st Read:

biography—this is Carson's life story

Carson was interested in both nature and writing from an early age.

2nd Read:

Biographies are told in time order.

emphasis on studies and interaction with the environment

3rd Read:

Combination of writing and science knowledge led her career.

How Do I Use It? The accessibility of a visual text may allow ELL students greater confidence. Elicit responses that allow ELL students to "translate" visual impressions into the English expression with which they are most comfortable. Pair ELL students with native English speakers to encourage ELL students to express complex thoughts using basic English. Use the Visual Text as an opportunity to model and reinforce the academic language of text analysis. Provide ample models or sentence frames to give students practice with terms like *details, composition, style, purpose,* and *audience*.

Rachel Carson Biography

Tell students that they will read to learn about one person's impact on the environment.

1st READ

Set a Purpose

Tell students they will be reading to find out what this text is about.

Have students read "Rachel Carson Biography" independently, annotating as they read. Circulate and make notes of students' markings, questions, and confusions. Your notes can be used to inform instruction and as data for informal assessment.

Text-Dependent Questions

1. What is this text about? (It is about the life and work of biologist and writer Rachel Carson.)

2. What was Carson's career? (She worked at the Bureau of Fisheries and Fish and Wildlife Service as a spokesperson, and later she became a full-time writer.)

Scaffolded Support Use the following scaffolded question and sentence frame as necessary to build comprehension.

What organizations did Carson work for?

Carson's projects at her job included ________.

Partner Talk Have students discuss key moments in Carson's career.

Rachel Carson Biography

2nd READ

Set a Purpose

Tell students they will read to identify the structure the author uses and how it affects their understanding of the text.

Text-Dependent Questions

1. How is the text organized? (The text is organized in chronological order and uses important dates in Carson's career as a scientist and writer.)

Scaffolded Support Use the following scaffolded question as necessary to build comprehension.

Look for dates in the text. What events do they describe?

2. What clue does the text organization give you to the text's purpose? (The organization emphasizes Carson's career and writing. The author is focusing on Carson's public achievements.)

3. Vocabulary: Multiple Meaning Words Discuss identifying homographs in context.

Paragraph 8: What is the meaning and pronunciation of *minute* in the phrase "documented in minute biological detail"? (I thought of the unit of time, but *minute*— pronounced my-NOOT—means very small.)

Think Aloud *After reading paragraph 8, I felt the text was about to talk about something important. As I reread, I see the second-to-last sentence starts with* but *which signals a shift in focus. It emphasizes* Silent Spring *and shows it is important.*

Partner Talk Have students discuss the text structure in respect to genre and author's purpose.

TEXT 1

ANNOTATION NOTES

1st Read:
Carson wrote a couple of books about what she learned about the ocean.

2nd Read:
Author follows Carson's careers in science and in writing.

pique = awaken or stimulate

3rd Read:
Carson had the unique talents needed to make science interesting to non-experts.

spoke with watermen and toured commercial plants and conservation facilities in an effort to understand the economics and culture of the area.

Before Carson's work, pesticides were showered on crops and waterways with little regulation.

6 Carson's first book, *Under the Sea-Wind*, published in 1941, highlighted her unique ability to present deeply intricate scientific material in clear poetic language that could captivate her readers and pique their interest in the natural world. In 1943, Carson was promoted to the position of aquatic biologist in the newly created U.S. Fish and Wildlife Service. There she authored many papers directed at the public. One series, known as "Conservation in Action," was devoted to exploring wildlife and ecology on national wildlife refuges in layman's terms. Another series was entitled "Food from the Sea" and offered information on the proper preparation as well as the advantages of a diet including fish and shellfish to a public unused to eating freshwater fish.

7 Carson became editor-in-chief of all Fish and Wildlife Service publications, congressional testimony, and speeches.

8 In 1951 Carson's second book, *The Sea Around Us*, was published and eventually translated into 32 languages. It was on *The New York Times'* best-seller list for 81 weeks. The success of her second book prompted Carson to resign her position in the Service in 1952 to devote her time to writing. *The Sea Around Us*, along with *The Edge of the Sea*, a third book published in 1956,

178 • Unit 10

PROFESSIONAL DEVELOPMENT

Productive Conversation: Extending

What Is It? Productive Conversation moves are ways to guide students to clarify comprehension and arrive at the next level of understanding. Extending takes existing statements and uses them to make a connection, draw a conclusion, or expand an idea.

Why Is It Important? Extending generates a model for synthesis, connecting, and drawing conclusions. The technique of extending can help students practice collaborating, brainstorming, and contributing to classroom conversation.

opened a new perspective to concerned environmentalists on the term "ecology," the study of "our living place." But it was her last book, *Silent Spring*, published in 1962, that awakened society to a responsibility to other forms of life. In it, Carson documented in minute biological detail the true menace to the ecosystem caused by harmful pesticides.

9 Carson had become interested in the danger of pesticides while still associated with the Fish and Wildlife Service. Her concern was accelerated with the introduction of DDT in 1945. Her marine studies at the Service had provided her with early documentation on the effects of DDT on marine life. Since abnormalities always show up first in fish and wildlife, biologists were the first to see the effects of impending danger to the overall environment.

10 Carson had long been aware of the dangers of chemical pesticides but was also aware of the controversy within the agricultural community, which needed such pesticides to increase crop production. She had long hoped someone else would publish an exposé on DDT but realized finally that only she had the background to do it.

11 ? As expected, her book provoked a firestorm of controversy as well as personal attacks on her professional integrity. The pesticide industry mounted a massive campaign to discredit Carson even though she did not urge the complete banning of pesticides. Rather she advised that research be conducted to ensure pesticides were used safely and alternatives to dangerous chemicals such as DDT be found. The federal government, however, ordered a complete review of its pesticide policy and Carson was asked to testify before a Congressional committee along with other witnesses. As a direct result of this study, DDT was banned. With the publication of *Silent Spring*, Carson is credited with launching the contemporary environmental movement and awakening concern by thinking Americans about the environment

12 In a television interview, Carson once stated that "man's endeavors to control nature by his powers to alter and to destroy would inevitably evolve into a war against himself, a war he would lose unless he came to terms with nature." The Fish and Wildlife Service named one of its refuges near Carson's summer home on the coast of Maine as the Rachel Carson National Wildlife Refuge in 1969 to honor the memory of this extraordinary woman.

ANNOTATION NOTES

1st Read:
Silent Spring told of the dangers of pesticides.

inspired the environmental movement

2nd Read:
lots of text devoted to *Silent Spring* and its effects—important

3rd Read:
Carson was an activist, but she was a scientist first—her background in science led her to call for more studies on DDT.

How Do I Use It? When modeling extending, begin by restating the ideas you will connect or extend. For example, say, *The text explains that Carson loved writing and studied English but then switched to science.* To challenge students to extend, continue to restate the ideas and use a sentence frame or scaffolded question to guide responses. *We can conclude that Carson used both her writing and science training in her career. Her career used each of these by ________.*

Rachel Carson Biography

3rd READ

Set a Purpose

Tell students they will read to understand the results of Carson's work.

Text-Dependent Questions

1. In paragraph 11, what point is the author making about Carson's work and *Silent Spring*? (The book and Carson's testimony helped bring about the ban on DDT use.)

2. What conclusion can you draw about the pesticide industry's reaction to Carson's work? (I can draw the conclusion that the pesticide industry thought Carson was a credible threat to their products and sales.)

Scaffolded Support Use the following scaffolded question and sentence frame as necessary to build comprehension.

What did the pesticide industry do to Carson?

Their goal was to ________.

3. What inference can you make about the longer-term effects of Carson's work? (Carson inspired others who were concerned about human impacts on the environment to confront environmental issues in an organized way. She is credited with launching the contemporary environmental movement.)

Partner Talk Have students discuss their connections and conclusions about Carson's work.

Return to the TEXT

Respond to Reading

You may want to check students' understanding by having them complete pages 180–181 in the Student Worktext.

1. Remind students to review their annotations and recall discussions they've had in order to complete the summary charts. Remind students that only evidence from the text should be included in the summary chart.

As students complete their summary charts, circulate and note which students struggle to identify the correct text evidence. Some students may benefit from small group instruction.

2. Remind students to include only the most important information in their summaries.

Have students work independently to complete page 180 of their Worktexts.

COLLABORATE When finished, have students exchange summaries with their partners and share their insights.

Return to the TEXT

Respond to Reading: Rachel Carson Biography

Review your annotations and notes.
Think about how they can help you summarize the text.

1. Use this chart to help you summarize the text.

Summary Chart		
	Informational Text	
Who?	the people or subjects	Rachel Carson, biologist and environmental writer
What?	the topic or problem	Carson's life and career
Where?	the location or region events occur	various locations in the eastern United States
When?	the date, year, or time	lived from 1907 to 1964; main career from late 1930s to early 1960s
How?	the events, steps or processes	After studying science, Carson wrote books including *Silent Spring*, which warned against the dangers of pesticides.

2. Write a 2–3 sentence summary of "Rachel Carson Biography."

Sample summary: Rachel Carson grew up loving both nature and writing. After studying biology and working with the U.S. Fish and Wildlife Service, she published a series of books about nature. Her book *Silent Spring* warned of the dangers of DDT and is credited with sparking the environmental movement.

PROFESSIONAL DEVELOPMENT

Think Aloud Modeling: Conversation

What Is It? In think aloud modeling, the teacher assumes the role of a student reader and models a thinking process or skill. To model a conversation, the teacher might play two or more roles, acting out a dialogue to focus students' attention, or asking one or more students to help start the conversation.

Why Is It Important? When they are given a topic to discuss, many students need help in sharing ideas with others and listening to and learning from others. Acting out a conversation shows students how to use key ideas from the text in their comments and discussions. A conversational model also reminds students to get their answers and support their opinions from the text.

Return to the TEXT

3. What were Carson's most significant accomplishments, and why were they significant? Include details from the text in your answer.

Sample answer: In 1929, Carson was awarded a scholarship to attend graduate school at Johns Hopkins University, an "enormous accomplishment for a woman" at that time. She was an accomplished scientist, becoming "one of only two women then employed with the Bureau [of Fisheries] at a professional level." She published several best-selling books before writing *Silent Spring*. Her book *Silent Spring* "is credited with launching the contemporary environmental movement."

4. How is the text organized, and why? Use evidence from the text to support your answer.

Sample answer: The text is organized in time order. The author introduces many facts by stating the date, as in, "in 1936, Carson was appointed a junior aquatic biologist" and "Carson's first book, *Under the Sea-Wind*, published in 1941 . . ." The text is in time order because it tells the story of Carson's life.

5. What information about Carson's life did the author choose to include in the biography, and why?

Sample answer: The author included mostly information about Carson's education, careers, and writings. The early paragraphs talk about her "passions" for nature and writing, and her college majors of English and biology. Paragraphs 4 through 8 detail the jobs she had and the books, articles, and programs she wrote. The last part of the biography deals in detail with the content and impact of *Silent Spring*. The author chose to focus on Carson's career achievements to emphasize their impact and importance.

REFLECT What words, phrases, or sections did you visualize to make sure you understood the text?

Sample answer: I visualized Carson working closely with fishermen in Chesapeake Bay because it helped me understand how thoroughly she studied her subjects.

How Do I Use It? Model the Collaborate assignment in which students share summaries by modeling how to compare different summaries, noting similarities and differences. Emphasize asking partners to explain or support facts that each understood differently, such as, *You emphasized Carson's congressional testimony. Why do you think that's important? How does that connect to the idea of how humans impact the environment?*

Return to the TEXT

Encourage students to refer back to the text and their annotations and notes to help them answer the questions.

3. Have students refer to their summaries and graphic organizers on page 180.

4. Have students scan each paragraph for dates and time-signal words.

5. Have students consider the characteristics of Carson's personality that are inferred in the text through the author's information on Carson's career, accomplishments, and her work.

Have students work independently to complete page 181 of their Worktexts.

REFLECT Remind students that visualization is a **Self-Monitoring Strategy** that can help them imagine concrete details, such as Carson's work in the Chesapeake Bay, as well as abstract relationships, such as the interaction between Carson's study of science and writing to check their comprehension of the text.

Return to the TEXT

Stop and Assess

Use the following rubrics to assess your students' understanding of the text.

	Item 1 answers indicate:
2	the publication of *Silent Spring,* with at least two pieces of text evidence.
1	her book publications, with some text evidence.
0	no relevant evidence from the text.

	Item 2 answers indicate:
2	Carson's passionate and determined character, with two or more text details.
1	Carson's determined character, with inadequate text support.
0	no inference about Carson's character, with no text examples.

	Item 3 answers indicate:
2	Carson raised awareness of environmental problems, supported by two text details.
1	Carson inspired environmentalism, with one text detail.
0	no understanding of Carson's work, with no text support.

Option: If you choose not to work with Texts 2 and 3 and to conclude the unit here, use the Visual Text and "Rachel Carson Biography" to answer the Focus Question: What impact do humans have on the environment?

Return to the TEXT

Comprehension Check: Rachel Carson Biography

Answer the questions to demonstrate an understanding of what the text means.

1. What aspect of Carson's work had the most far-reaching effects? Support your answer with details from the text.

Sample answer: The event in Carson's life that had the greatest impact was the publication of *Silent Spring*. The author says that this book "awakened society to a responsibility to other forms of life." The book also made enough of an impact that it "provoked a firestorm of controversy," led her to "testify before a Congressional committee," and resulted in the banning of DDT.

2. What can you infer about Carson's character from the text? Support your inference with details from the text.

Sample answer: I can infer that Carson was dedicated to studying and protecting the environment despite adversity. The text notes that she was given a scholarship to Johns Hopkins, "an enormous accomplishment for a woman in 1929," and then became "one of only two women" at the Bureau of Fisheries at the time. I can infer that she must have overcome discrimination to do what was considered a man's job. Carson also "realized finally that only she had the background" to write *Silent Spring* after hoping someone else would do it.

3. How did Carson help change the relationship between Americans and the environment? Support your answer with examples from the text.

Sample answers: Carson made Americans think more carefully about their effect on the environment and helped inspire new rules protecting the natural world. Carson's writing "could captivate her readers and pique their interest in the natural world." *Silent Spring* "awakened society to a responsibility to other forms of life" and began "the contemporary environmental movement." Her work eventually led to a ban on DDT.

PROFESSIONAL DEVELOPMENT

Annotations: Confusions

What Is It? Annotations record a reader's thoughts, ideas, and understandings while reading. Confusing areas of the text can be indicated with a question mark, an underline, or a written question in the margin.

Why Is It Important? Making annotations is a metacognitive strategy for self-monitoring comprehension. Emphasizing the use of confusion-related annotations can encourage persistence with difficult passages.

TEXT 2

Read to find out about native bees. If you need to read any sections more than once, note the reason in the Annotation Notes column.

Sample annotations and notes appear throughout the text.

The Buzz on Native Bees

by Hannah Hamilton and Catherine Puckett

1 It's National Pollinator Week, and ecosystems—whether agricultural, urban, or natural—depend on pollinators, great and small. Pollinators in the form of bees, birds, butterflies, bats and beetles provide vital, but often invisible, services. These range from supporting terrestrial wildlife and plant communities to supporting healthy watersheds. USGS and federal partners are studying native bees and their behaviors at selected sites across the country.

Bevy of Bees

2 Bees are nearly ubiquitous, occurring on every continent except Antarctica. Wherever there are insect-pollinated flowering plants—forest, farms, cities and wildlands—there are bees. And just because you don't see plants blooming, this does not mean that there are no bees around. There are nearly 20,000 known bee species in the world, and 4,000 of them are native to the United States. From the tiny and solitary *Perdita minima*, known as the world's smallest bee, to the large carpenter bee, to the brilliant blue of the mason bee, native bees come in a variety of shapes, sizes and colors. And all these bees have jobs as pollinators.

Native bees come in many shapes, sizes, and colors beyond the familiar black and yellow stripes.

Providing Ecosystem Services

3 Native bees pollinate native plants like cherries, blueberries and cranberries. They were here long before European honeybees were brought to the country by settlers. Honeybees, of course, are well known for pollinating almond and lemon trees, okra, papaya and watermelon plants. But native bees are estimated to pollinate 80 percent of flowering plants around the world. And very few of them sting. Really!

ANNOTATION NOTES

1st Read:
There are lots of kinds of bees besides honeybees.

Native bees pollinate native plants.

2nd Read:
"pollinator" repeated often

Headings introduce facts.

3rd Read:
Honeybees are just one species, but there are many native bee species.

How Do I Use It? Encourage students to mark any difficult or confusing passages on first read with a question mark and to include questions to come back to in annotation notes. Model annotating a confusion: *In paragraph 1, I'm not sure what the words "terrestrial wildlife and plant communities" or "healthy watersheds" refer to. I'll mark these phrases so I remember to look up some of the confusing words when I read again.*

The Buzz on Native Bees

Tell students that they will read to find out about native bees.

1st READ

Set a Purpose

Tell students they will be reading to find out what this text is about.

Have students read "The Buzz on Native Bees" independently, annotating the text as they read. Circulate and note students' markings, especially questions and confusions.

Text-Dependent Questions

1. What is this text about?
(It is about native bees and how they benefit people and the environment.)

2. What is the relationship between native bees and plants?
(Native bees pollinate native plants.)

3. Which bees are NOT native bees?
(honeybees)

Scaffolded Support Use the following scaffolded question and sentence frame as necessary to build comprehension.

What is compared to native bees in paragraph 3?

The text identifies bees as either native or ________.

Partner Talk Have students discuss the bees found in the United States and what they do.

The Buzz on Native Bees

2nd READ

Set a Purpose

Tell students they will read to examine how the text is organized.

Text-Dependent Questions

1. How is the text organized and how does that contribute to your understanding? (Subheadings organize the text. Each heading tells me what topic will be addressed in the text that follows.)

Think Aloud *I will reread and make a quick outline as I go to help me summarize the text. I'll use the headings as bullet points. I looked up the word* bevy *and found that it means a large group. The paragraph under* Bevy of Bees *describes lots of native bees. The paragraph under* Home Sweet Home *describes bee nests.*

2. Vocabulary: Words in Context Discuss the domain-specific meanings of words in context.

Paragraph 7: What does *fragmentation* mean in the phrase "habitat loss and fragmentation"? (It means habitats that have been broken up into areas that are too small to sustain the organisms that were living there.)

Partner Talk Have students discuss how the subheads contribute to the organization of the text.

TEXT 2

ANNOTATION NOTES

1st Read:
Pollinators are economically important.

2nd Read:
Some facts do not have separate headings.

3rd Read:
Cuckoo birds must lay their eggs in other birds' nests.

Native bees play more roles in ecosystems in addition to their economic importance.

4 According to the USDA, bees of all sorts pollinate approximately 75 percent of the fruits, nuts and vegetables grown in the United States. One out of every four bites of ! food people take is courtesy of bee pollination. In sum, bee pollination is responsible for more than $15 billion in increased crop value each year.

5 Bees are vegetarians who descended from wasps about 125 million years ago when the first flowering plants evolved. Some wasps switched from hunting prey to gathering pollen, evolving to become bees. Bees feed on both nectar and pollen—the nectar is for energy, and the pollen provides protein and other nutrients. Most pollen is used by bees as larvae food, but bees also transfer it from plant-to-plant, providing the pollination services needed by plants and nature as a whole.

Home Sweet Home

6 Most native bees build nests and provide food for their offspring, but about 20–25 percent have gone the way of the cuckoo birds, ? laying their eggs in the nests of others. Aside from the "cuckoo" bees, all bees build nests. They stock them with pollen and nectar before laying their eggs. Some, like the sweat bee, build nests underground. Others, like the leafcutter bee, choose hollow stem or holes in trees.

Native bees build many types of nests, from hives in hollow trees to holes in the ground.

Population Declines: Beyond Honeybees

7 Colony collapse disorder, the cause of which is unknown, affects only European honeybees and has been recorded across the country. The primary symptom of the disorder is having no or low numbers of adult honeybees present in a hive; no dead ? honeybees are present, but a queen is. Immature bees will be

PROFESSIONAL DEVELOPMENT

Productive Conversation: Clear Up Confusions

What Is It? In any classroom conversation, students will inevitably give incorrect or incomplete responses. In productive conversation, we don't punish or simply correct the student, but recognize that a wrong answer is an opportunity to examine and redirect the student's understanding.

Why Is It Important? To arrive at independent conclusions, students learn best when they are guided to examine direct evidence and their own thinking.

TEXT 2

present and honey will still be in the hive. Fortunately, colony collapse disorder does not affect native bees, though some native bees and other pollinators are also experiencing population declines and range reductions. Native bee species are being affected by at least some of the same factors affecting honeybees such as habitat loss and fragmentation as well as the use of pesticides.

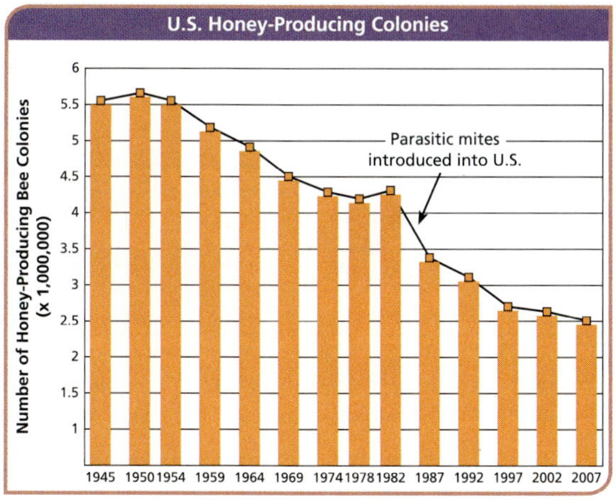

Colony collapse disorder has high economic costs for both beekeepers and farmers who depend on bees to pollinate crops.

What can you do for native bees?

8 To increase or improve habitat for native bees, plant a diversity of pollen and nectar sources native to your area that bloom at various times during the year. Native plants and native pollinators have mutually adapted over the millennia. Many native bee species are pollen specialists and need to provide their young with pollen from native plants, so providing native plants will increase the diverse community of native bee species. If possible, avoid use of pesticides and provide a source of pesticide-free water, and mud, which is used as a nesting material by some bee species. You can also provide nesting habitat for native bees by rototilling a bare spot in the lawn or garden, leaving standing dead trees, or building a bee house. This will provide housing for native bees.

ANNOTATION NOTES

1st Read:
Bee populations are declining.

tips for supporting native bees and their habitats

2nd Read:
shifts from explanatory text to "how to"

3rd Read:
Since native bees rely on native ecosystems, natural areas help them.

How Do I Use It? The rule of thumb when clearing up confusion is to return to the text. If a student reaches an incorrect conclusion, or has a misconception about what the text says, ask for evidence to support the idea. Wait time is critical in this situation. The student must have enough time to do a thorough search of the text. If the student does not find the text evidence, ask, *What does the text say about your idea?* If a student offers text that is irrelevant or misunderstood, ask, *What is that sentence saying, in your own words?* Then, ask again for specific words or phrases within the chosen sentence that support the student's thinking. Give wait time. Allow the student to get a full sense of the evidence. Only then turn to peers or Think Alouds to offer alternative interpretations.

The Buzz on Native Bees

3rd READ

Set a Purpose

Tell students they will read to understand the authors' point of view.

Text-Dependent Questions

1. Why do the authors contrast native bees and honeybees? (The authors hope to inform readers about less-familiar native bees by contrasting them with more common non-native honeybees.)

2. The authors say that native bees do not suffer from colony collapse disorder. Why did the authors discuss CCD in the article? (The article emphasizes the importance of all pollinators, which includes honeybees.)

3. Overall, do the authors seem to favor one kind of bee over another? (The authors seem to think that both types of bees are important but want the reader to learn more about the importance of native bees to the ecosystem.)

Scaffolded Support Use the following scaffolded question and sentence frame as necessary to build comprehension.

What information do the authors include about native bees, and about honeybees?

The authors devote more paragraphs to ________.

4. What conclusions can you draw about the authors' point of view? (The authors think that native bees are important and their populations should be supported and encouraged to increase.)

Partner Talk Have students discuss conclusions they can draw about how native bees affect the ecosystem.

Stop and Assess

Use the following to assess your students' understanding of the text.

Item 1 answers indicate:	
2	identification of the two types of bees and their importance as pollinators, with text evidence for each box.
1	general understanding of the two types of bees and their importance, with insufficient text support.
0	no relevant information or text support in any part of the organizer.

Item 2 answers indicate:	
2	habitat loss and possible connection to colony collapse, with strong text evidence.
1	habitat loss and colony collapse, with one piece of text evidence.
0	no understanding of humans' impact, and missing text support.

Item 3 answers indicate:	
2	native bees support native plants and ecosystems, with at least two supporting details.
1	native bees support native plants, with one supporting detail.
0	no understanding of the role of native bees, with no text support.

Return to the TEXT

Comprehension Check: The Buzz on Native Bees

Answer the questions to demonstrate an understanding of what the text means.

1. Compare and contrast how the authors describe native bees and how they describe honeybees, and draw a conclusion about why both are important.

Native Bees	Honeybees
Sample answer: pollinate native plants; pollinate "cherries, blueberries, and cranberries;" support diversity	Sample answer: pollinate "almond and lemon trees, okra, papaya and watermelon plants"

Importance of Both
Sample answer: pollinate and support crops as well as native plants; economically important; in danger because of human activity

2. How have humans affected bee populations? Provide text evidence to support your answer.

Sample answer: Human actions have caused the bee population to fall. No one is sure what causes colony collapse disorder. However, the text says that native bee populations suffer from "habitat loss and fragmentation" and "the use of pesticides." People are encouraged to avoid pesticides when providing homes for bees.

3. What does the text tell you about the importance of preserving native bee populations? Provide text evidence to support your answer.

Sample answer: It is important to help native bees because many native plants depend on those bees for pollination. Paragraph 1 says that native bees are vital to "supporting terrestrial wildlife and plant communities." In paragraph 3, the authors say that native bees pollinate 80 percent of flowering plants. The guide to supporting native bees says that bees and plants have "mutually adapted." From this, I can infer that specific plants might rely on specific kinds of bees, so saving the bees means saving plants, too.

PROFESSIONAL DEVELOPMENT

Intertextual Analysis: Comparing and Contrasting Themes

What Is It? When analyzing more than one text, the deepest level of analysis is to compare themes, or overarching messages, and how each text treats them.

Why Is It Important? While topics, opinions, and techniques may be shared by multiple texts, each text's treatment of a theme is different. Since the theme constitutes some of the deepest meaning of a text, comparing and contrasting themes allows students to understand a text's meaning on multiple levels and from multiple perspectives.

TEXT 3

Read the text to learn one scientist's opinion about humans' impact on Earth. You may want to read some sections more than once and make different annotations and Annotation Notes each time.

Sample annotations and notes appear throughout the text.

Man and the Earth

by Nathaniel Shaler

This is an excerpt from Shaler's full-length book of the same name, which was published in 1905.

1 Ever in increasing measure as he mounts toward civilization, man becomes a spoiler.

2 As soon as stone implements begin to be replaced by those of metal, man begins to draw upon the limited stores of the under-earth. With each advance in his arts, the demand becomes the greater. At the present time, in the United States, iron requisition is at the average rate of about five hundred pounds per annum for every man, woman, and child in the land. It seems eminently probable that before the end of the ! present century it will require a ton of iron each year to meet the progressive desires of this insatiable man.

3 Even two centuries ago, the energy available for man's work was mainly limited to that obtained from domesticated animals. The wind served in a small measure through the sails of ships and of windmills, and there were water-wheels. The average amount of energy at his service was certainly less than one horse-power per capita. At the present time it may safely be reckoned that in the United States, the average amount is at least ten times as great. The use of falling water as a source of power does not keep pace with that of coal, which is obtained from a store which is in process of rapid exhaustion. It cannot be relied on for more than a few hundred years to come. If the world keeps the rate of consumption with which it enters the twentieth century it will be exhausted before the twenty-third.

4 As soon as agriculture begins, the ancient order of the soils is subverted. In order to give his domesticated plants a chance to grow, the soil-tiller has to break up the ancient protective mantle of plants and to expose the ground to the destructive action of the rain. How great this is may be judged by inspecting any newly ploughed field after a heavy rain. A single heavy rainstorm may lower the surface of a tilled field to the amount

ANNOTATION NOTES

1st Read:
Humans are using up mineral resources too fast.

2nd Read:
Each paragraph moves from the past to the present and the future.

"ancient order of the soils," "protective mantle" = exposing bare soil

3rd Read:
I wonder how much iron Americans actually use per year today.

Author seems to blame industry and civilization for resource use.

How Do I Use It? Thematic comparison should take place after students have completed their analysis of individual texts. After students finish each text, have them summarize the theme. When they have completed their analysis of each individual text, have them use compare/contrast and connection graphic organizers (Venn diagrams, T-charts, webs) to visualize the connections between themes. Writing is often a helpful tool for analyzing the deeper connections between texts. To help students tackle the cognitive load, encourage the use of a standardized essay form, such as the five-paragraph essay. Provide multiple writing scaffolds, including frames, outline forms, and model paragraphs using a main-idea/supporting-detail structure.

Man and the Earth

Tell students that they will read to learn one scientist's opinion about humans' impact on Earth.

1st READ

Set a Purpose

Tell students they will be reading to find out what the text is about.

Have students read the excerpt from *Man and the Earth* independently, annotating the text as they read. Circulate and note students' markings, especially questions and confusions.

Text-Dependent Questions

1. What three resources are discussed in this text? (metals, energy resources, and soil)

Scaffolded Support Use the following scaffolded question and sentence frame as necessary to build comprehension.

What resource is paragraph 2 about?

Paragraph 3 describes ________.

2. What concern about the resources is expressed in the text? (Shaler says that these resources are being depleted faster than they can be replaced.)

Partner Talk Have students discuss the scientist's view of humans' impact on Earth.

Man and the Earth

2nd READ

Set a Purpose

Tell students they will read to analyze how the author reveals meaning.

Text-Dependent Questions

1. How do the photo and caption on this page contribute to your understanding of paragraph 4? (The paragraph describes the effects of poor agriculture and predicts that soil and fertility loss will get worse. The photo and caption show that prediction coming true during the Dust Bowl.)

2. Vocabulary: Multiple-Meaning Words Discuss words with multiple layers of meaning.

Paragraph 4: What meanings of the word *subverted* are used in the phrase, "the ancient order of the soils is subverted"? (In one meaning, soil is "subverted" because topsoil is physically plowed under. In another meaning, the original purpose of the soil to support native plants is destroyed.)

Partner Talk Have students discuss the effect of the author's word choice.

3rd READ

Set a Purpose

Tell students they will read to understand the author's purpose.

Text-Dependent Questions

1. What is the author's message to readers? (The author's message is that if humans keep using resources at the same rate, we will run out.)

Partner Talk Have students discuss how the author uses factual support for his argument.

TEXT 3

ANNOTATION NOTES

1st Read:
Farming causes soil loss and loss of nutrients from what soil is left.

2nd Read:
reread last paragraph—still don't understand last sentence

3rd Read:
Author's predictions are dire. I wonder if he presents solutions in the rest of the book.

! of an inch. This is a greater waste than would, on the average, be brought about in natural conditions in four or five centuries. Nearly all parts of the arable lands which have been long subjected to the plough are thinned so that they retain only a part of their original food-yielding capacity. Moreover, the process of cropping takes away the soluble minerals more ? rapidly than they are prepared. There is a double waste in body and in the chemical materials needed by the food-giving plants.

Soil erosion caused by plowing contributed to the Dust Bowl, years of drought and massive dust storms in the 1930s.

PROFESSIONAL DEVELOPMENT

Text Complexity: How to Manage Challenges

What Is It? Occasionally, complex texts may be inaccessible to students because of high knowledge demands and lack of background information. Students without sufficient background information will have difficulty comprehending a text, no matter how deeply they analyze it.

Why Is It Important? Building background information allows all students an equal opportunity to comprehend the complex texts.

Return to the TEXT

Comprehension Check: Man and the Earth

Answer the questions to demonstrate an understanding of what the text means.

1. What cause-and-effect relationship does the author establish in this text? Cite evidence from the text to support your answer.
   Sample answer: The author says that civilization and industrialization have led to the destruction of resources. The author directly says that as humanity "mounts toward civilization" people spoil things. In paragraph 2, he offers the example of ever-increasing use of iron from the stone age to the modern age.

2. What is the structure of the text, and how does it help the text fulfill its purpose? Support your answer with examples from the text.
   Sample answer: The author uses several examples that start in the past, move to the present, and then predict the future in order to warn people about what might happen if we continue to use resources. Paragraph 2 starts in the stone age, and predicts that we will need a ton of iron per person by the end of the twentieth century. The third paragraph starts "two centuries ago" and predicts that coal will run out before the end of the twenty-third century.

3. What is the mood and tone of the text, and what does it communicate about the author's view of humans' relationship with the environment? Cite specific text examples in your answer.
   Sample answer: The tone is very serious and dire, which makes it seem like humans are doomed to destroy the environment. The very first sentence calls man a "spoiler." He describes humans as "insatiable" and describes resources as being "exhausted," "subverted," and a "waste." In each case, the tone reinforces the text's predictions that humans will use up their natural resources soon.

How Do I Use It? Before providing background information, have students return to the unit texts with questions. Use frames and questions to have students use context, inference, and other strategies to predict what an unfamiliar concept might be. Encourage student-led investigation and have students conduct their own research with provided materials so they can practice using text features and making intertextual connections. Use group and partner work if peers have additional background knowledge. Peer explanations help both the learner and the more knowledgeable student connect the knowledge to the text.

Return to the TEXT

Stop and Assess

Use the following to assess your students' understanding of the text.

Item 1 answers indicate:	
2	civilization leads to resource overuse, with at least two specific text examples.
1	humans overuse resources, with one specific text example.
0	no understanding of causes and effects in the text.

Item 2 answers indicate:	
2	repeating chronological structures about different topics, with two or three specific examples.
1	organization by different topics, with one or two text examples.
0	no understanding of the text's organization, and no examples.

Item 3 answers indicate:	
2	a serious, scientific, but pessimistic tone, with at least two specific text examples.
1	a pessimistic tone, with one specific text example.
0	no analysis of tone, and no text support.

ANALYZE and SYNTHESIZE ACROSS TEXTS

Return to the Focus Question

Explain to students that they will fill out a graphic organizer that helps them answer the Focus Question: What impact do humans have on the environment?

CONNECT TEXTS Have small groups of students discuss how each text they read helps them answer the Focus Question.

Scaffolded Support You may provide the following sentence frames to support students in their use of academic language:

> In the text ________,
> the author/artist makes
> the point that ________.
> He/she does this by ________.

Remind students to use their annotations and summaries to support their answers. They can also reread portions of the texts, if necessary.

Have students complete their graphic organizers individually.

REFLECT Remind students that each text provides different information about environmental impacts. Ask, *How did reading all four texts give you a greater understanding of humans' environmental impact?*

ANALYZE and SYNTHESIZE ACROSS TEXTS

Return to the Focus Question: What impact do humans have on the environment?

Review your answers to questions about the texts as well as your annotations and Annotation Notes, and think about the discussions you've had about the texts. How does that information help you answer the Focus Question?

Use the graphic organizer to organize information about the texts.

1. In the appropriate box, record the details that help you answer the Focus Question.
2. Make connections between those details to answer the Focus Question. Write your answer in the box provided.

Trash Pile in a Creek (Visual Text)
Sample answer: Human pollution damages waterways.

The Buzz on Native Bees
Sample answer: Native bees sustain ecosystems, but their populations are shrinking.

Rachel Carson Biography
Sample answer: Pesticides harm wildlife; regulations can help.

Man and the Earth
Sample answer: Humans are using up Earth's resources too quickly.

What impact do humans have on the environment?
Sample answer: Humans damage the environment through trash pollution, pesticide pollution, "habitat loss" for bees, and the "consumption" of natural resources. We can help by using chemicals carefully and making space for living things.

REFLECT How did making connections between the four texts enable you to answer the Focus Question?

Sample answer: Each text describes different aspects of humans' impact on the environment. The Visual Text and Text 3 show how "man becomes a spoiler." Texts 1 and 2 show how people can help the environment through action.

PROFESSIONAL DEVELOPMENT

Differentiation: Visual Learners

What is It? The Differentiate and Extend activities at the end of each unit in this text are designed to reinforce and extend what students have already learned through close reading and to provide learning experiences other than classroom discussion, which may not be the preferred or best way of learning for some of your students. For example, the Create a Visual Text activity provides an opportunity for visual learners to explore and expand upon what they've learned in a creative, personalized way.

Why Is It Important? Visual learners learn and express their thoughts best when using pictorial images and writing. The Create a Visual Text activity allows visual learners to

Writing About the Focus Question

Now that you have answered the Focus Question using all four texts, expand on your thinking and communicate your ideas through your writing.

USE EVIDENCE

- Explain the impact humans have on the environment according to the texts. Use at least one piece of evidence from the Visual Text and at least two pieces of evidence from Texts 1, 2, and 3 to support your answer.
- If you need more room, use additional paper.

MONITOR

- Use the Writing Checklist as you write to make sure your writing meets all the necessary criteria.
- Use the rubric on page 192 when you have completed a first draft of your writing to help you evaluate, revise, and edit your work.

WRITING CHECKLIST ✓

Does my writing . . .

- ☐ answer the Focus Question?
- ☐ have a clear organizational structure?
- ☐ cite the correct amount of text evidence?
- ☐ correctly use language, spelling, and conventions?

explore and express their understanding in a way that is most comfortable for them. In addition, this assignment strengthens computer literacy.

How Do I Use It? Encourage students to be creative in how they express their ideas visually while fulfilling their purpose of answering the unit Focus Question. Approaches might include making a collage, selecting a set of images to caption, or creating a visual timeline.

Writing About the Focus Question

USE EVIDENCE Remind students that they should use their graphic organizers as well as their annotations in the texts to write their responses.

Allow students to revisit the texts as frequently as they need to in order to support comprehension and to respond to the Focus Question.

MONITOR After students have completed their responses, have them review the Writing Checklist and revise their writing response.

DIFFERENTIATE AND EXTEND

In addition to or instead of the writing response, consider having students complete one of the following assignments:

Write Beyond Have students analyze the human impact on a small natural area near their school or neighborhood and present their findings in a written report.

Read Beyond Have students read *Silent Spring* in full. Allow class time for whole class or small group discussion about the concerns and arguments expressed in the book. Are Carson's concerns still relevant?

Research Have students research the origins, history, and contemporary celebrations of Earth Day.

Create a Visual Text In the medium of their choice, have students illustrate an impact that humans have on the environment.

SELF-ASSESS and REFLECT

SELF-ASSESS Have students use the Writing Rubric on page 192 to self-assess their writing response and write a final version. Tell them to assign themselves a score from 1–4 (with "4" being the highest) for each category in the first column.

Use the Writing Rubric on Student Worktext page 192 to assess each student's writing. Record points for each category in the first column of the rubric. Have students remove the page from their Student Worktexts and place it in their writing portfolios, along with the drafts and final versions of their responses.

SELF-ASSESS and REFLECT

Focus Question: What impact do humans have on the environment?

This is the rubric that your teacher will use to assess your writing. Refer to it as you revise your work. After you have finished the final version of your response, assess your response and record your points for each category on the "Student" line in the first column.

	Accomplished (4 points)	Competent (3 points)	Developing (2 points)	Beginning (1 point)
RESPONSE Score: Student ____ Teacher ____	The response answers the question effectively and with insight.	The response answers the question effectively.	The response partially responds to the question but does not adequately address it.	The response addresses the texts but does not address the question.
ORGANIZATION Score: Student ____ Teacher ____	The main idea is convincingly stated. Ideas are organized in cohesive paragraphs that support the main idea.	The main idea is clearly stated. Ideas are organized in logical paragraphs.	The main idea is weak. Ideas are organized in a somewhat logical and cohesive way.	The main idea is missing. The organization of the paragraphs is not logical.
TEXT EVIDENCE Score: Student ____ Teacher ____	Response includes more than one piece of appropriate text evidence from each text. Evidence supports the main idea in a thorough way.	Response includes one piece of text evidence from each text. Evidence supports the main idea clearly.	Response does not include at least one piece of text evidence from each text. Text evidence does not adequately support the main idea.	Response does not contain relevant evidence.
LANGUAGE Score: Student ____ Teacher ____	Writing includes precise and sophisticated vocabulary related to the topic.	Writing includes appropriate vocabulary related to the topic.	Writing includes imprecise and inaccurate vocabulary.	Writing does not include vocabulary that appropriately reflects the topic of the response.
SPELLING AND CONVENTIONS Score: Student ____ Teacher ____	Response includes correct spelling, grammar, and punctuation consistently.	Response includes mostly correct spelling, grammar, and punctuation.	Response has many errors in spelling, grammar, and punctuation.	Response's errors in spelling, grammar, and punctuation make it extremely difficult to understand the response.